THE BASS PLAYER

Stephen Travers was a founding director and the first editor of *The Irish World* newspaper in the UK. He is also an author, composer, arranger and record producer. Stephen was a special observer with the international charity Children in Crossfire in East Africa and has addressed victim support and radicalisation awareness network conferences and universities across Europe and the USA on numerous occasions. In 2019, Stephen received the Chicago iBAM Person of The Year Award. Stephen Travers is a survivor of the Miami Showband massacre. He has lived in Cork City since 1997.

THE BASS PLAYER

SURVIVING THE MIAMI SHOWBAND MASSACRE

STEPHEN TRAVERS

WITH YVONNE WATTERSON FOREWORD BY ALEXANDRA ORTON

THE BASS PLAYER
First published in 2025 in Ireland by
New Island Books
Glenshesk House
10 Richview Office Park
Clonskeagh
Dublin D14 V8C4
Republic of Ireland

newisland.ie

First published in 2025 in Britain by
Birlinn Ltd
West Newington House
10 Newington Road
Edinburgh EH9 1QS

birlinn.co.uk

Copyright © Stephen Travers, Alexandra Orton and Yvonne Watterson, 2025

The right of Stephen Travers, Alexandra Orton and Yvonne Watterson to be identified as the authors of this work has been asserted in accordance with the provisions of the Irish Copyright and Related Rights Act, 2000 and the British Copyright, Designs and Patents Act, 1988.

Print ISBN: 978-1-84840-833-3
eBook ISBN: 978-1-78885-782-6

All rights reserved. The material in this publication is protected by copyright law. Except as may be permitted by law, no part of the material may be reproduced (including by storage in a retrieval system) or transmitted in any form or by any means; adapted; rented or lent without the written permission of the copyright owners.

British Library Cataloguing in Publication Data: a CIP catalogue record for this book is available from the British Library.

Permission to reproduce lyrics of 'There Were Roses' on pp. 215–218 given by Tommy Sands, songwriter.

Product safety queries can be addressed to New Island Books at the above postal address or at info@newisland.ie.

Set in 11.50 on 17 pt in Calluna
Typeset by Compuscript Limited, compuscript.com
Cover design by Stuart Polson, stuartpolsondesign.com
Printed by L&C Printing Group, Poland, lcprinting.eu

New Island Books is a member of Publishing Ireland.

Birlinn is a member of Publishing Scotland.

10 9 8 7 6 5 4 3 2 1

Contents

Foreword — ix

1. When the Wall Fell — 1
2. The Pigeon — 5
3. The Piano Player — 9
4. The Bass Player — 15
5. The Sinner — 23
6. The Miami — 27
7. The Last Waltz — 33
8. The Killing Field — 36
9. Albert — 44
10. The Alternative Tour 2007 — 47
11. Forgotten — 51
12. Rubber Bullets — 54
13. The Savage Watch — 63
14. Truth and Reconciliation Platform — 69
15. The King and I — 81
16. Survival — 87
17. Rock Royalty — 101
18. The Jigsaw — 116
19. The Long and Winding Road to Justice — 127
20. Demons — 143
21. Heroes — 146
22. Diversion — 150
23. The Fox in Charge of the Hen House — 153

24. Netflix	163
25. Sharing the Pain	175
26. Do You Know Who I Am?	179
27. Electric Wood and Carbon Graphite	184
28. 'America, America'	191
29. 'You were right all along'	195
30. Learning Curve	197
31. Every Dirty Trick in the Book	205
32. Victim Impact Statement	210
33. Setting the Record Straight	212
34. Finale	214
Epilogue	219
Afterword	221
Endnotes	223
Index	229

For my wife, Anne, and our daughter, Dr Sean Josephine Ettie Travers

When the screaming subsides and the blood dries on the ground only to be carried away by the winds of change and you are asked if you spoke out for the innocent, what will your answer be?

Foreword

When Stephen Travers asked me to write the foreword to *The Bass Player*, I was both flattered and instantly nervous. Stephen and I have known each other since 2017 when we filmed the Netflix documentary *ReMastered: The Miami Showband Massacre*. However, whereas Stephen is a world-class musician, and a peace advocate through his organisation, Truth and Reconciliation Platform (TaRP), and therefore perhaps a little more used to telling his story, I am a documentary filmmaker and documentary filmmaking is a communal activity. Many people, from the crew to the subjects themselves, work together to tell a story. It is strange to be asked to contribute my perspective alone, and plainly in my own words, when I have spent the past sixteen years of my life being a name in the credits of other people's lives. Nevertheless, after the year we (and many others) spent making the film, I have both a profound respect and deep loyalty to Stephen. I have developed fulfilling working relationships with many of the subjects in the documentaries I've filmed, but Stephen is rare among them. To know Stephen Travers is to know someone who is somehow eternally youthful in his passion and dedication to music and also someone who is a shrewd, wise and committed political activist. It's as if he is almost two separate people in one body: the innocent bass player of his youth and the relentless activist who emerged from the fiery wreckage of 31 July 1975. That duality is evident in *The Bass Player*.

In the spring of 2017 I received an email from a documentary production company called All Rise. Netflix was financing an eight-film documentary series investigating unknown political dramas in the music industry. The tagline was 'The music you know; the stories you don't.' The production was staffing up in Burbank, California, just down the road from the iconic Warner Brothers Studios. They were curious if I wanted to produce. It was a tantalising offer and I signed on immediately.

The *ReMastered* documentary series examined how, buried under the glitz and glamour of spectacle, some of our favourite entertainers have stumbled into injustice or scandal. While I had some familiarity with a few of the narratives – Bob Marley's alleged brush with the CIA, for instance, or the murder of Sam Cooke – there was one story that was utterly foreign to me. It was the story of an Irish 'showband' counterintuitively called the Miami. (I was unfamiliar with the term 'showband' but I loved the film *The Commitments* and figured it was something like that.) The members of the Miami Showband had been pulled over at an apparent military checkpoint in the summer of 1975 only to realise too late that it was an ambush by loyalist paramilitaries. After the loyalists' bomb prematurely detonated, the paramilitaries massacred half the band in an attempt to cover their tracks. Since then, the survivors had been trying to piece together the truth of what happened to them and their quest was led by their dogged bass player, Stephen Travers.

I read Stephen Travers' first memoir, *The Miami Showband Massacre: A Survivor's Search for the Truth*, annotating along the way and, when I finished, I flipped right back to the front and began studying it again. The book had all the elements of my favourite stories: an international setting, government intrigue, rich history and, at the core, relatable, regular human beings who pushed through loss and disillusionment to better understand the world and perhaps change it for the better.

When I read Stephen Travers' book, I leapt at the chance to learn more. I first spoke with Stephen during the summer of 2017. We arranged Skype calls so we could discuss his memories of the attack and his subsequent investigations. From the beginning, I noticed that Stephen had a few pronounced characteristics. The first was that he was very careful about security. He insisted on secure platforms and encrypted emails and text messages. His awareness of data protection was the first clue that he had become much savvier than the bass player I met in his book and that the massacre continued to profoundly shape his daily life.

The second thing I noticed was that he was a very accomplished storyteller. He would freely answer any question I asked. Ever since Stephen reported hearing a British officer's voice on the night of the attack, certain people have questioned its credibility. He told me his story again and again over many months and the details never changed. Sometimes people alter the details every time they tell a story – it's night instead of day, or events happened in a slightly different order, or someone's parting line is different. Stephen's story stayed the same. It was helpful on two fronts: it made it easier to check facts, and it also made it easier to anticipate what he would say during his on-camera interview. Stephen had a natural way of turning the corners of his story; you had to keep listening to find out what was going to happen next and, even more importantly, you didn't just want to know what was going to happen, you wanted to know how it would affect *him*. That's when you know you've got a protagonist.

When I eventually met Stephen, I realised that he was far more than just a good documentary interview or a celebrity in the music world or a survivor of the Irish conflict. He was a man of deep integrity and compassion whose commitment to telling his story was fuelled by his intense desire to ensure that the violence of those years is never, ever repeated.

Those of us who live outside Ireland can't appreciate the real, life-altering experiences of the Troubles. The survivors carry the trauma with them every day as invisible and present as a second soul. With all of that weight on their shoulders, even simply defining the Troubles – saying out loud what happened to them, what they lived through – becomes both an act of courage and a political high-wire act. Our crew learned this first-hand when we were filming an interview with Stephen and we asked him to explain, in one sentence, what the Irish Troubles were about. For the purposes of the documentary, international audiences needed a definition of the conflict that was simple to absorb and Irish and British audiences needed to feel the explanation was accurate. Of course, the reality is that you cannot explain the complicated conflict in a single sentence. It took an entire crew from America, Ireland and Northern Ireland, plus Stephen Travers and a couple of hotel visitors who wandered onto the set, a good couple of hours to debate all the different sentences Stephen could construct to explain the conflict and, in the end, no one felt confident they got it right.

Later, I wondered what Stephen thought of that request. Perhaps he found it silly or frustrating, but you would have never known. I realised that his many years of emotional TaRP events and heated political debates have uniquely prepared him to field every question and comment with equanimity and patience. Perhaps the best example of Stephen's preternatural calm is his continued willingness to sit down with members of the paramilitary organisation responsible for the Miami attack. Despite losing his friends and bandmates, Brian McCoy, Fran O'Toole and Tony Geraghty, Stephen has repeatedly engaged with high-ranking members of the Ulster Volunteer Force. While he originally met with 'the Craftsman' because he was looking for answers to why the Miami was targeted and who specifically was colluding with an illegal paramilitary organisation, he largely seems to have moved past that. When we were filming the documentary, his primary interest seemed to be to bring the UVF into a public conversation where they would commit, on the record, to maintaining the peace despite rising tensions as a result of

Brexit. It struck me that Stephen's personal narrative fits the classic hero's journey. Though he began his investigation to find answers for himself and his family, his journey soon broadened his mission. Now, he was working not for himself, but for a wider peace.

To do that, he was willing to break bread with the very people who had caused him, and so many others, immeasurable pain. It is not a choice everyone would make. As he writes in *The Bass Player*, many people have criticised him for it. Stephen's approach is distinctly different from blatantly refusing to engage with the other side – any other side – in order to maintain moral and rhetorical purity. Instead, Stephen is uncommonly willing to extend compassion to everyone even when people in his own camp dislike it. As this memoir makes evident, Stephen throws himself on the proverbial tracks again and again for the democratic ideal that dialogue, no matter how painful or tedious, is the surest method of peace-making.

The reality is that human nature is chillingly alien to us. The primatologist Jane Goodall said that the question isn't whether behaviour is 'natural' to a species. If it is possible, it is natural. The useful question is what circumstances and environments push a species toward pro-social behaviour instead of anti-social behaviour, toward community instead of conflict. I wonder about the changes in environment that push some people towards violence and others, like Stephen, towards an almost compulsive push for reconciliation and peace.

Stephen has met with several former and current members of the UVF in his activism. Whatever those men have done in the past, they too have met with Stephen to attempt peace. Whether or not they had ulterior motives, they gathered over coffee and tea – a radically different approach than planting a bomb in a band's bus. In the documentary, we interviewed Reverend Chris Hudson who preached that most people find it unsettling to accept the reality that the peacemakers aren't just the people who never raised a weapon.

There can be no peace until the people who picked up their weapons lay them down. When they do, they too are peacemakers. It unnerved me, and it still makes me uncomfortable to cede them the title when others have never taken up arms in the first place – never taken anyone's son or wife. Others like Stephen Travers.

When reading *The Bass Player*, I see that the risks Stephen takes can border on recklessness. If Stephen thinks something can illuminate corruption or secure peace, he moves toward it without a second thought. I've often wondered what it must be like to be his wife, who almost lost him fifty years ago and must continually wrestle with the worry she could lose him again because he so consistently puts himself in danger for the sake of others. The Stephen we know now is perhaps a braver and bolder man than the bass player she married. This new Stephen was born of fire at the hands of the UVF and their colluders. In a way, everyone in the Miami died that night in 1975. Neither Des McAlea nor Stephen could survive it, not as their old selves.

Over the last seven years, Stephen and I have had many long conversations about that field where he unwillingly bid goodbye to the bass player. He's told me about the pull that field still has on him. How he'll sometimes drive there as one might visit the cemetery where their parents lay. His life is tethered to that field, which has already claimed his old self and still beckons to his present self. I can understand why he keeps returning. It's the scene of the crime, the scene of this new Stephen's birth, and possibly, if he only returned at the right moment, with a little luck, he might find the bass player there. Might pull him up off the grass, into his arms, and they could walk together into his life, reconciled at last. I've seen that nostalgia in him so often. When he's gushing animatedly about a bass he's repairing or recording with fellow musicians or telling me that his family ordered him out of a night watching movies on the couch because he whipped out his bass to play along with the film score,

I see flashes of that young man I never really got to meet, that boy who wanted to tour the world in a rock or blues group instead of travelling from country to country talking about civil conflict and survivor's guilt. In some ways, I think this book is both his love letter and his eulogy to that young man. But it is also a prayer for hope.

I'm not sure how many hours Stephen and I have spent talking about the field, the bass player and the trauma of life and death, but inevitably we will circle back to wondering what happens after we die. Both of us hope there's something more. Both of us hope that we all emerge from the field, suddenly in the bloom of youth again, with all our hard-earned wisdom intact. I can never really know what Stephen has gone through. I can never truly understand what all of the survivors of the Irish conflict have gone through. The whole beautiful island, Ireland and Northern Ireland alike, all of its people, they were all in the field. In *The Bass Player*, Stephen winds through many of their stories. Look at it from one end, and he's trapped in his trauma. Look at it from the other end, and he's spending every day of his second life pushing to pull as many people out of that field as possible, to pull whole countries out of that field, to give everyone a life after death.

At the tail end of our documentary-filming in Northern Ireland, we wrapped our last day in Belfast and one of our talented local crew members asked if we had any plans for the evening. He explained that we happened to be in town during an annual music festival. At night, bands played in the pubs and restaurants and poured onto the streets. The city closed the roads to vehicle traffic and Belfast citizens filled the lanes in merry abandon. He observed that even then, in 2017, it was one of the few times of the year when people forgot their divisions and, for one weekend, Catholics and Protestants and nationalists and unionists celebrated side by side without a care for religion or politics. It was simply about enjoying the music, just like the days of the Miami. The director, Stuart Sender, and I took him up on his offer and we spent the night sharing lager and laughter with total strangers. No one mentioned religion (unless your religion is *Game of Thrones*, which *everyone* mentioned). Every person we met was proud of their city – boastful, even. And they were right. Belfast was magical, lively, interesting, exciting, complex and fully, endearingly human. It was a reminder of why we were making the documentary. Not just for the enduring safety of these people, though of course that was critical, but a lasting peace that should vouchsafe far more than security. It should vouchsafe joy. This was why Stephen spent his life campaigning on the mantra that no side has a monopoly on suffering. Because no side can ever have a monopoly on joy. It is shared or it is forever elusive.

Alexandra Orton
October 2025

1
When the Wall Fell

A long-delayed response to grief and trauma unexpectedly overwhelms me and takes me back in time.

It was a glorious spring morning in 2013 when I landed at Liverpool John Lennon Airport. I soon spotted Jo Dover in the arrivals area. We hugged, happy to see each other. Jo is an expert on the long-term impact of terrorism on victims. We were well acquainted, having spoken on peace and reconciliation issues at numerous conferences throughout Europe. Jo had finally convinced me to attend her 'dialogue residential' – an opportunity for victims to convene and commiserate, share their unique experiences and to learn from one another. She was confident that I could inspire other victims by sharing how I managed to successfully overcome trauma in my own life. I was confident too, but I had accepted the invitation only on condition that my participation would be as a survivor, not as a victim. At that stage of my life, I rejected the 'victim' label, which I felt signified weakness or, worse still, an admission of defeat.

Soon, together with a dozen other attendees, we were on our way to the Peace Centre in Warrington – a town still associated with an atrocity that occurred there on the day before Mothering Sunday in 1993 when, without warning, the Provisional IRA detonated two bombs in a busy shopping area. The blast injured fifty-four people and took the lives of two children. Johnathan Ball, aged 3, died at the scene as a result of shrapnel-inflicted injuries and, five days later,

12-year-old Tim Parry succumbed to fatal head injuries. Nobody was ever prosecuted for their murders. Inspired by young people they met in Northern Ireland who were living in the midst of what was seen as a never-ending conflict, Tim Parry's parents, Colin and Wendy, established a charitable foundation to work for peace. Their exchange programmes for young people from Belfast, Dublin and Warrington were so successful that Wendy Parry proposed a Peace Centre, not only to commemorate the victims of the bombing, but also to afford a unique and valuable east–west dimension to the protracted and complex peace process across both islands.

On entering the Peace Centre building, I paused to look at the pictures on the wall of the long hallway. The innocent faces of the two murdered children stared back at me. At that moment, the Warrington Peace Centre came alive to me and, for the first time, I was overwhelmed by a 'Troubles'-related incident. I put it down to tiredness but something in me had fundamentally changed: the two children had breached the protective firewall that had stood me in good stead for decades.

Jo made us all comfortable in a room strewn with soft couches and gentle lighting, and I was optimistic that the event would be a great success. The warm and welcoming space held the promise of an evening of calm, if not easy, conversation, and I was ready to dispense words of comfort and assure everyone that it was possible to confront and overcome traumatic experiences, just as I had done. The twelve attendees had been split into two groups of six in separate rooms and, one by one, the six participants in our group introduced ourselves. As instructed, we had each brought a personal object that connected us with our life-changing experience, which we would place on a low table in front of us when it was our turn to speak. I brought a used guitar string, an artefact I'd almost forgotten to bring, a last-minute choice hastily pocketed as the taxi pulled up to take me to Cork Airport. 'That'll fit nicely,' I thought when I spotted it on my bookshelf. Still in its original grease-proof pouch, my friend and Miami Showband bandmate Tony Geraghty had left it at our house just a few days before he was murdered, forty years earlier.

Six relics of grief would cover the low table, representing decades of tangible, distressing remembrances and haunting spectral echoes, before the evening was done: the faded photograph of a proud father holding his newborn son for the first time; a lock of golden hair carefully preserved in a tiny glass frame; a pair of leather driving gloves, well-worn by a loving father murdered when his daughter was just a little girl; and a toy fire engine. As the heartbreaking stories behind each precious object unfolded, some eyes welled up while others steeled themselves against the threat of telltale tears. With each recounting I grew more determined to help the narrators overcome the grief and trauma that clearly haunted them.

Some stories were laced with such harrowing detail that they tested even my composure. The story of the toy fire engine, relayed by a man who grew increasingly distraught as he explained its significance, was particularly disturbing. The owner, a former British soldier, had been exposed to terrible atrocities throughout the Radfan Campaign during the Aden Emergency of 1964. His story began with childhood abuse and, with each consecutive phase of his life, his problems were compounded. All he ever wanted to be was a fireman but, with that ambition unfulfilled, he had turned to drugs and alcohol for comfort. Substance abuse had taken its toll and, consequently, his life story was narrated as one of crushing failure.

I was convinced that, when it was my turn to speak, I would find the right words to soothe his pain and inspire him to get on with living, as I had managed to do for the past thirty-five years. I reflected for a moment on how wise Jo had been to give me an opportunity to offer hope to someone like this sad, broken soldier. I was sure that my personal 'success' story would change the trajectories of the lives around me that evening. However, my confidence was misplaced and, as I carelessly allowed myself to slide into a false sense of security, I failed to notice the precarious cliff-edge I was approaching.

Expecting the usual motivational words that she had heard from me so many times before, Jo invited me to speak. We had discussed and prepared for such events when we met in Madrid, at the Hague, and prior to my speech at the Spanish University of Extremadura. Keen to help the participants around me, I stood up and approached the table. Confidently reaching into the inside pocket of my jacket for Tony's guitar string, I began to speak. 'My name is Stephen Travers and the object I've brought with me today is ...' but the words stopped coming. I was struck dumb and blinded by an outpouring of tears such as I had never shed before. As I wept uncontrollably, I felt the arm of the tormented British soldier around my shoulder, consoling me, *comforting the comforter,* but to no avail. I was in the grip of terror and paralysed by it. Although I could hear the jumbled reassurances of the others, I was unable to respond. Just as a psychiatrist had predicted in 1976, 'the wall' had fallen on me. A delayed response to grief and trauma swallowed me. The voices around me faded away and I was no longer in Warrington.

2
The Pigeon

A loss of innocence, the enormous weight of guilt and
an omen of things to come.

I wanted an air rifle or 'a slug gun' as we called it in 1966. My next-door neighbour, Noel, had one and I hoped to convince my father to buy me one, but he felt that, at 15, I wasn't mature enough. Looking out a back window at the stone outhouse where he kept his work tools, he asked, 'If you saw a rat running across that roof, what would you do?'

'I'd fire,' I replied instantly.

'And if you missed, where would the bullet go? Don't you think it would carry on and possibly hit someone? You're not ready for a gun yet, son.'

That was the end of the discussion. There was no wheedling or arguing back. I idolised my dad, a quiet man who wouldn't say two words if one would do, so I reasoned that maybe because, like tens of thousands of other Irishmen who joined the British army at the outbreak of the Second World War in 1939, he'd had more than enough of guns and wasn't keen to see one in his son's hands.

It seemed unlikely that I would get my own gun, but Noel let me borrow his now and then to shoot at tin cans in the town landfill. I quickly acquired a reputation for being a good shot. I'm not left- or right-handed or ambidextrous, I'm cross-dependent, sometimes called mixed-handed: I do some things with my left hand and others with my right. I throw with my right hand and catch with my left. I play guitar right-handed and I play pool left-handed. For me, firing a rifle was a left-handed affair, and one I had a talent for – as my friends would say, 'He'd knock a berry off a bush.'

At that time, many of the lads from our area were in the local reserve army, the FCA, or Fórsa Cosanta Áitiúil to give it its official Irish name. I knew they were training with rifles but, at 15, I was too young to join. While the awful, heavy wool uniforms didn't appeal to me, I was envious when my friend Billy Byrne, who was just a year older than me, would return from the FCA summer camp with enough money to buy Fanta Orange fizzy drinks and Club Milk chocolate bars and Tayto Crisps to last him a month.

Once a week, Sergeant Hackett of the regular Irish army at Kickham Barracks in Clonmel would come down to Carrick to teach the fledgling defenders of the state the mundane protocols of properly shouldering arms. Even then, I wasn't much of a team player and regimentation didn't work for me, but, in light of my ability to hit a target, Billy told me about an annual shooting competition where the local FCA could compete against the regular Irish army. As luck would have it, Sergeant Hackett was keen to give the regular army shooting team a run for their money and, on hearing from Billy about the promising youngster, he decided to give me a try.

The thought of chocolate and fizzy drinks and crisps excited me and so I announced to my family that I was 'joining up'. My father was convinced that I wouldn't make a good soldier: 'You'll have to cut your hair and keep your brass buttons gleaming and shine your boots so you can see your own reflection in them,' he said. My mother who, as a young woman, had witnessed the German army march into Paris, was appalled that I would even consider taking up arms.

Undeterred by my parents' reservations, I sought out Sergeant Hackett at the town hall in Carrick where Billy was training. However, because of my age, the sergeant would have to bend the rules a little so I could take part in the contest the following week – and bend them he did. Not yet 16, I was sworn into the FCA, and off I went to compete in the shooting contest in Clonmel, where I was given a Lee-Enfield rifle that was specially modified to take .22 calibre bullets for target practice.

The contest began with 'grouping' – one of the most important skills in shooting, which demonstrates both the accuracy of a rifle and its average point of impact. I had only seen grouping in war films where an intrepid soldier would lie down with his rifle resting on a sand bag and fire a succession of shots at the same target without moving from his position. Although I didn't yet have a uniform, as an official competitor in the grouping contest, I was living out a scene straight from the movies, firing alongside 'other soldiers' and confidently awaiting the sergeant's assessment of my performance. However, when he inspected my target, he laughed. 'Well, young man, you only hit the target once.' Joining in the laughter was a talented competitor from Carrick, a lad who was irritated by my attendance at such a young age. He was ready and waiting to criticise me, delighted to get an opportunity so early on. However, the sergeant spoke up again – but this time his tone was different. 'No, wait, hold on,' he said. 'This is remarkable. This young lad put all his bullets in the *same hole*.' Soon I was firing other exciting weapons that I never dreamed I'd get my hands on. I was in my element.

One day, as the summer was coming to a close, I borrowed Noel's familiar air rifle again – now a common exercise – and went off with a few friends for target practice. Alerted by a sudden movement in a bush, I reflexively fired. Approaching the undergrowth, I parted the brambles to find that I'd hit a pigeon. It was terminally wounded and I watched in horror as each diminishing, futile flap of its wings failed to propel it into the sky where it belonged. I was distraught. Tormented by guilt, I couldn't sleep. I couldn't function. I was, and still remain, profoundly sorry.

For many years, that beautiful bird circled and swooped over my head in my dreams, soaring and flapping its angelic wings, assuring me that it survived the shooting, having fulfilled its mission. Perhaps it was an omen of things to come. I never fired a gun again.

3
The Piano Player

The building blocks of my musical formative years and how music enhanced my friendships and intensified my loyalty to those who played a special part in my life.

My friend and neighbour Noel Kelly played rhythm guitar with the Webb, a popular local beat group, and, when their bass player quit in 1966, Noel asked me to play bass with them. I'd been playing guitar for about three years, but I'd never played bass. Nevertheless, from the very first rehearsal, I was hooked for life. I was fascinated by the power and influence the instrument had on the character and overall sound of the band, underpinning, connecting, fusing, steering and supporting the melody, harmony and rhythm – the core elements of the music.

Throughout my career, I've been influenced by many of the great bassists including Jack Bruce, Carol Kaye, Joe Osborn, James Jamerson, Jaco Pastorius, Francis Rocco Prestia and Cranston King, a wonderful, inspirational bass player from Cork city but Paul McCartney is, in my opinion, the greatest electric bassist of all time. Paul is the genius who plays the perfect note(s) in the right place every time and that, for me, is what bass playing is all about.

We played songs by the Rolling Stones, the Kinks, the Animals and other popular bands of the day. The Webb taught me the role of the bass player and how the instrument should function within a band. Playing bass also taught me important life lessons that have stayed with me, not least the importance of getting to the root of things. The Webb was like driving school: I was allowed to get it wrong until I got it right.

When the penny dropped and I eventually saw the light, I was invited to join Sheamie O'Brien and the Crystals. Based in Bunmahon, a lovely seaside village in County Waterford, the band leader, Sheamie, whose enthusiasm was infectious, was a terrific vocalist and an excellent rhythm guitarist. Our lead guitarist, John Trehy, played a Burns guitar just like his hero, Hank Marvin of the Shadows, before Hank switched to a Fender Stratocaster. Our drummer, Pat 'Tiny' Maher, despite his nickname, was a gentle giant. It was a very happy band at a very happy time in my life.

The Crystals had just added a young electric piano and organ virtuoso named Liam Sherlock. Visually, keyboard players found it difficult to compete with guitarists whose instruments were comparatively small and light and allowed them to move around the stage interacting with the rest of the band and with the audience. Keyboard players were often seen as the 'professors' of the band, many of whom never dreamed they'd be in pop or rock bands but, quite often, because their parents had sent them for piano lessons when they were children, found themselves teaching the self-taught guitarists how to make the most of their natural, if unschooled, musical ability. Liam Sherlock had talent in abundance and an image to match. He was a groovy guy, always laughing and always fun to be with. He lived in Piltown, County Kilkenny, just four miles from Carrick-on-Suir and, as cool as any Irish teenager could be at the time, he rode a little Honda 50 motorbike. However, with his feet barely under the table, Liam suggested that the band would do well to recruit a 16-year-old bass player he'd heard with a beat group called the Webb. So Sheamie knocked on our door and I became a Crystal.

When news got out that I could play an instrument – a really cool instrument – I became the new kid in town and, suddenly,

I was popular. After sixteen years of obscurity, I was now part of the Swinging Sixties, the new Renaissance and Beatlemania. There was no going back: the bass guitar changed my life and offered me the future I was impatient for.

The Crystals introduced me to a carefully crafted pop music that, quite often, involved more complicated musical arrangements, chords and chord sequences than I had encountered up to then. It was different to the British, blues-based material I'd played in the Webb. Of course, the Beatles were massively popular but they weren't 'pop' anymore; the release of their brilliant, ground-breaking album *Rubber Soul* in 1965 and the phenomenal *Revolver* in 1966 changed everything, but you had to *be* the Beatles to play Beatles music. For me, no one else could write like them or sound like them and they remain my favourite band of all time. I loved the Rolling Stones too and, while they retained their rhythm and blues edge, by 1967 they were also experimenting with psychedelia on *Between the Buttons* and *Their Satanic Majesties Request*. There was an edge to British music that I still love, a sense of danger to bands like the Animals and the Spencer Davis Band and the Yardbirds that I didn't find in American music until Woodstock – as evidenced by the fact that my all-time guitar hero, Jimi Hendrix, had to go to London to be recognised and appreciated.

The only American music I'd been listening to was blues, soul and Tamla Motown. Thanks mainly to the Rolling Stones, I was introduced to the music of B. B. King, Albert King, Freddie King, Howlin' Wolf, John Lee Hooker, Muddy Waters, Robert Johnson, Buddy Guy, Otis Redding and Ike and Tina Turner. I was hugely influenced by the great Motown bassist James Jamerson, but, in general, I had bypassed American pop music until Liam Sherlock introduced me to the sophisticated arrangements of bands like the Beach Boys, the Association and the Turtles. He loved the Southern California sound – the multi-layered harmonies that Brian Wilson produced on *Pet Sounds* and the amazing playing of their recording-studio musicians. Very soon he had me listening to music I had previously ignored, because I felt it didn't have the edge of bands like John Mayall's Bluesbreakers.

My growing admiration and respect for American bands was copper-fastened in 1968 with the release of a CBS sampler album called *The Rock Machine Turns You On* that introduced me to some of the best bands and the best music I'd ever heard. In fact, I got to play with one of my favourite artists from that mind-blowing album in 1982, when, following his concert at the National Stadium in Dublin, Taj Mahal asked his driver, Victor 'Smith' McCoy, to take him and his band to hear 'a good, original, Irish band'. I was playing with the Crack at the time and we were also signed to CBS Records. When I saw Taj Mahal and his band take their seats at a table right in front of us at the Country Club in Portmarnock, I thought I was hallucinating, and, to make it even more surreal, after about ten minutes, Victor told us that Taj Mahal would like to join us on stage. Our vocalist, Tommy Lundy, was playing a Gibson Les Paul, but he also had his Fender Stratocaster with him, which the great man put on, plugged in and played with us for the best part of an hour. It was pure magic. We loved it and he loved it and his band loved it and the audience loved it, and we all hung out together that night and most of the following day, and we saw them off at Dublin Airport. To this day, I still get an enormous buzz when I recall playing 'Statesboro Blues' and 'Six Days on the Road' and 'Crosscut Saw' with Taj Mahal.

Liam Sherlock and I just 'got' each other, and we grew together musically just as I would connect with gifted guitarist Tony Geraghty almost a decade later. We loved exploring the magical musical labyrinth and its inexhaustible avenues of wonder and possibilities. I still recall Liam and I trying to convince the other lads to play songs we'd heard on the pirate stations Radio Luxembourg and Radio Caroline, or on AFN, but they'd point out that the pattern changes in

'Good Vibrations' or 'God Only Knows' ruled them out for dancing. We didn't appreciate that it was necessary to keep the dancers happy if we were to stay on the road, but we were young and naive and it was all part of our valuable musical apprenticeship. Nevertheless, we did convince Sheamie to add the Beach Boys' 'Then I Kissed Her' and 'California Girls' to the set. I loved playing with Liam and being in his company. We were both eagerly setting out on our respective magical mystery tours, but, even though we would take different routes, little did we know that we were both on our own separate, customised Highway to Hell.

I finished secondary school in the summer of 1968 and left the Crystals to go to London the following February, ostensibly to get a 'real' job – but my secret plan was to get as much musical experience as possible in what was then the centre of the musical universe. My parents were relieved when I got a 'real' job with a prestigious insurance firm in the City, but I quit that after just six months to play music. At one point I was playing in five different bands simultaneously, rushing from one gig to another, and I loved every minute of it. I was learning and soaking it all in, pop, country, jazz, soul and Latin and anything else that excited me. I even composed bass lines in my head to the sound of the city traffic and to the rhythm of footsteps scampering up and down the stairs of the big red double-decker buses and to the clickety-clack of the underground trains, which, on many occasions, caused me to miss my stop. I stayed in London for a year before returning home in January 1970 to be part of the booming country music scene in Ireland.

One day in the summer of 1972 I spotted my old friend Liam Sherlock outside a supermarket on Main Street in Carrick-on-Suir. He was loading groceries into the back of a car with his father. I stopped to say hello, but he just stared at me. He said nothing, got into the car and they drove off. I was baffled and I was annoyed but, most of all, I was hurt. *Maybe he doesn't recognise me*, I told myself.

Maybe he's angry because I left the band or because I didn't stay in touch. I never got an opportunity to ask him. I never saw him again, but the hurt I felt that afternoon stayed with me for many years, because a beautiful chapter had been ripped out of the wonderful, happy-ever-after book of life I was writing.

As the years went by, bewilderment gave way to curiosity. What became of Liam? How did his life turn out? Perhaps he married the pretty girl he used to walk hand-in-hand with on the beach in Bunmahon and had a family and settled into 'normal' life, or maybe he left Ireland to pursue a successful classical musical career abroad. He was certainly good enough.

Then, some years ago, a small religious Christmas card was forwarded to my home in Cork city by my family in Carrick-on-Suir, which simply read, 'To Steve, Happy Christmas, Liam'. Inside the card was a neatly folded €5 note. I know dozens of Liams, but there was no indication as to who this particular Liam was. Year after year, for almost a decade, I continued to receive a similar small Christmas card. As I had no idea who the sender was, it became a Christmas tradition to put the neatly folded €5 into 'the poor box' in our local church and say a quiet prayer for the mystery sender. Unbeknown to me, for all those years, our quiet Christmas prayer was for my old Crystals band mate.

In 1972 Liam Sherlock was diagnosed with schizophrenia and, subsequently, spent most of his adult life in a mental institution. The lovely little Christmas cards stopped when, at 64 years of age, Liam took his own life. I realise now that they were his way of telling me how much our friendship meant to him too. I am so very sorry that I ever doubted you, my beautiful, gentle, talented friend.

4
The Bass Player

I am thrown in at the deep end.

All roads led to the Arcadia that balmy Wednesday evening. Located in the historic market town of Cahir, County Tipperary, the ballroom was ready to welcome Brendan Bowyer and the Big 8 Showband. Freshly returned from their annual six-month residency at the Stardust Hotel in Las Vegas, the band was guaranteed yet another full house – a foregone conclusion amid the fever pitch of Ireland's dancehall obsession. Showbands had been packing ballrooms, dancehalls, marquees and parochial halls for over a decade, changing the country and liberating a people who had long succumbed to an oppressive Ireland that exemplified the 'high-banked clouds of resignation' as noted in Seamus Heaney's 'From the Canton of Expectation'. Unique to Ireland, Irish showbands were part of the modern world ushered in by the Irish prime minister, Taoiseach Seán Lemass, helping to transform the country from a dark place without electricity to an industrial, forward-looking nation. The little island where musicians once powered their public address systems with car batteries was now pulsing with the sound of amplified guitars and the ecstatic cheering of young fans. Even in the middle of nowhere, there was *always* a venue large enough to host a showband.

With the Irish economy rapidly opening up and with access to more transit options, young people were no longer limited to the range of their pedal-powered bicycles. The world beyond the parish hall awaited them and the restrictions that once kept them from new places of entertainment and new music and new friends were gone. A growing number of young folk criss-crossed the border to dance – from Armagh to Monaghan and Donegal to Derry. Even as tensions in Northern Ireland began to surface in the 1960s, dancehalls stayed full and offered respite and refuge. Never sectarian, never prying into political affiliation or religious background, showband music provided a sanctuary and, indeed, an alternative world. Within the welcoming walls of a dancehall, who knew or cared about the religion or politics of the giddy strangers dancing, cheering and singing along beside them?

A showband typically consisted of a charismatic lead singer plus a rhythm and a brass section. Playing covers of the most popular songs in the charts along with classic hits, they gave the people what they wanted to hear and dance to. The *Father Ted* actor Ardal O'Hanlon once described showbands as 'versatile, hardworking mobile jukeboxes in shiny suits', and, as such, over 650 fully professional showbands performed the soundtrack to Ireland's adolescence. It was a golden age for Irish musicians because never before, nor since, were so many of them in full-time work. Young people were tuning into the 'sponsored' programmes on Radio Éireann and listening on their transistor radios, under the bedcovers, to late-night Radio Luxembourg and Radio Caroline, longing to hear that music performed live. Fans knew they could rely on the showbands to deliver and they made their way, in their thousands, to wherever they were playing.

The public demanded 'instantly recognisable music' and the showbands were happy to oblige. They played virtually every song on the pop charts, covering the entire musical spectrum from the multi-layered harmonised music of the Beach Boys to the heavier rock sound of Blood Sweat and Tears, Chicago and Tower of Power. As Les McKeown of the Bay City Rollers proclaimed at the Grand Opera House in Belfast: 'All you needed to get a job with a top-flight

Irish showband like the Miami was the ability to play everything.' Not only were showbands influencing the musical, social and economic life of twentieth-century Ireland, but they were also playing their part in shaping the global musical future by training and producing a host of game-changing artists that included Van Morrison, Rory Gallagher and Henry McCullough. The Irish showband roll of honour is endless and the apprenticeship they offered priceless.

The Royal Showband, one of the most popular in Ireland, had been guided to international stardom by their manager, T. J. Byrne. The best in the business in his day, T. J. was a giant of the Irish music industry. With frontman Brendan Bowyer, the Royal Showband played in such storied venues as New York's Carnegie Hall and London's Royal Albert Hall; in 1962 the Beatles, then a relatively unknown local band, opened for them at the Liverpool Empire. The Royal was also among the first of the showbands to record and, because there were very few commercial studios in Ireland at the time, they recorded at Abbey Road in London before the Fab Four made it the most famous recording studio in the world. The Royal had an annual six-month residency at the Stardust Hotel in Las Vegas where even 'the King' himself, Elvis Presley, was a fan. In 1965, their cover of 'The Hucklebuck', which had been recorded previously by Frank Sinatra and Chubby Checker – the biggest of their six number one hits – went platinum.

After a decade at the top of Ireland's lucrative showband scene, the Royal's frontmen, Brendan Bowyer and Tom Dunphy, quit and, with T. J. Byrne at the helm, reinvented themselves by recruiting six of the best musicians in the country to create a newer, revitalised sound. Now called 'the Big 8', they soared to new heights on both sides of the Atlantic. On the Las Vegas strip, where they were known as 'the Irish Showband', they were on first-name terms with some of the biggest entertainers in the world including Frank Sinatra, Roy Rogers, Sammy Davis Jr and Liberace. Nevertheless, for them, the thrill and trappings of international fame paled in comparison to their love of touring Ireland every summer where they invariably sold out every major ballroom and festival.

That Wednesday evening at the Arcadia Ballroom was to be no different. Fans travelled from far and wide to see the Big 8, their excitement unaffected by distance. Along with the adoring fans, music industry chiefs took time out of their hectic summer schedules to check out what the band had brought back from the most competitive entertainment strip on the planet.

Despite T. J. Byrne having led the Royal Showband to international stardom, as he stepped out of his Mercedes in Cahir just hours before the gig, he couldn't shake an uneasy feeling. He was facing an unexpected hitch, something even he had no control over: Tom Dunphy, their legendary bass player, was down with flu and the band needed a suitable stand-in as quickly as possible. Clearly concerned, T. J. asked the road manager if the relief band's bass player would be up to the task. In those days every dancehall hired 'relief' or support bands to warm up the crowd and get them dancing before the main act appeared on stage. Employing a top-class relief band guaranteed the venue over three hours of music and a warmed-up audience by the time the headliners came on.

Within minutes of T. J. sharing the urgent need for a substitute bassist, the relief band arrived. Impressed by the state-of-the-art equipment on stage, their bass player made a beeline for Tom Dunphy's amp, obviously thrilled at the opportunity to play through it. 'Maybe you'd like to play it all night,' the road manager suggested, but the bass player shook his head. He wasn't interested. 'Ah, if you gave me a million, I wouldn't chance it. Every bass player in the country will be here tonight and I know my limitations.' Who would they suggest? As a busy, popular relief band, they knew every musician on the circuit and the road manager was met with one name in response, a resounding and unanimous 'Stephen Travers, he's your man.' The die was cast. T. J. Byrne quickly assembled a posse to find me and get me to Cahir without delay.

Although the rest of the world was headed up the road to see the Big 8, I was in the Regal Cinema in Clonmel where the British comedy *Carry On Henry* was showing. Having played ten nights straight with Gerry Walsh and the Cowboys, I wanted a break from dancehalls. There was hardly a dozen people in the cinema as I settled in with a big bag of popcorn about halfway down the aisle on the right-hand side – the perfect seat. No sooner had the lights gone down than I was chuckling away at the on-screen antics of Sid James and the *Carry On* gang. However, I was surprised when someone tapped me on the shoulder and, as I instinctively stood up, I wondered why anyone would choose my row when practically every seat in the theatre was empty. Turning around, I recognised the popular local guitarist Martin Hennessy. 'Lucky I spotted your car outside the cinema,' he said breathlessly. 'T. J. Byrne wants you up in Cahir this minute. You're to play bass with the Big 8 because Tom Dunphy has the flu.'

I certainly knew who Tom Dunphy was; everyone did. I spotted him in Sinnott's record shop in Waterford when I was 16 and I took advantage of the opportunity to introduce myself as a 'fellow bass player'. Full of confidence, I even asked the great man to let me know if any gigs came up. Bemused by the cocky teenager, he said he would. As I listened, it began to dawn on me that Martin might actually be serious, but I told him that my bass guitar was at home in Carrick, fourteen miles in the opposite direction. 'No problem,' Martin said. 'You can use Tom's bass.' I wondered if it was an elaborate joke. Was I being set up by my bandmates in the Cowboys or was fate continuing a series of events that began with a chance encounter between a superstar and a hopeful teenager, all those years ago, which would end in tragedy for both of us in the final three days of July 1975?

I had played with Brendan Bowyer when he did a short, impromptu guest spot at an event I was playing at in London in 1969. It didn't daunt me then, but this would be different. I must admit I felt a rush of excitement at the thought of playing with 'the King of the Showbands' and his elite band of musicians in front of a huge audience in my home county, so I got into my white Fiat 124, put my foot on the accelerator and sprinted every inch of the ten-mile drive from Clonmel to Cahir. Rolling up to the Arcadia, I could hear the muffled sound of the band inside. The show was already underway. Driving as close as I could to the entrance, I was immediately approached by the unmistakable T. J. Byrne who, without any introduction, pointed at one of the doormen and said, 'Give him your car keys,' before swiftly whisking me through the heaving crowd up to the bandstand. Although the band was in full flight, T. J. signalled to the bandleader, Paddy Cole, to come to the side of the stage. 'This is Stephen,' he said. 'He'll play the bass.' Before I knew it, I had strapped on Tom Dunphy's Fender Jazz Bass, plugged the lead into his amplifier and hit the standby switch just in time to join the Big 8 as their powerhouse drummer, Mickey O'Neill, counted in their next number. Head down, fingers wrapped around the mic still on its shiny chrome stand, right fist punching the air in time, Brendan Bowyer glanced left, acknowledged me with a wink and then, like a pouncing tiger, the big man launched into a sensational medley of Elvis Presley's rock and roll hits, kicking off with 'Jailhouse Rock'. The huge crowd went wild. The Big 8 – Brendan, Twink, Dave, Michael, Jimmy, Paddy and Mickey – insisted that I stood out front with them, making me feel like I was one of the band, and when Brendan introduced me as a Tipperary native, the massive audience roared their approval. It was a night I'll never forget and one that would lead to a lot of job offers. And yet, despite becoming a target for some of the music industry's head-hunters, I was determined that if I were to leave the Cowboys, who had their own following of devoted fans, it would be for one band only.

The Mick Delahunty Jr Big Band boasted the cream of 'serious musicians' and featured a collection of jazz giants that included the brilliant saxophonist Harry Doherty and legendary trumpeter Paddy Byrne, who would light up Monday night jazz sessions throughout the county and across the southeast. One night they invited me and my guitarist friend Gay Brazel to play at a jazz session in Clonmel. Unlike these veteran musicians, Gay and I played everything by ear. We hadn't learned to read music so Gay, a fabulous guitarist who prepares meticulously for every gig, was clearly concerned when the band leader handed us a music chart covered in what Gay said looked like 'bunches of grapes', but, since there was no way out, I just shrugged my shoulders. Moreover, when Harry called an up-tempo bebop number that I'd never even heard of, I knew I'd entered what was, for me, unknown territory. When I asked Paddy Byrne, 'How does it go?' he just laughed and replied, 'Don't think about it, son, just feel it,' and that's exactly what I did. At one point, following a succession of scorching trumpet, alto sax, tenor sax, baritone sax, clarinet, trombone, piano and drum solos, Harry gave me a nod that signalled 'take a solo'. Stunned, but too terrified to refuse, I went for it, blindly improvising over the melody that I'd just picked up rather than the chord sequence. After the gig I expected to face a *different* kind of music and braced myself for some stinging criticism, but, to my surprise, when an enthusiastic jazz fan asked Paddy where he found the inspiration for his amazing solos, Paddy replied, 'Ah, sure I just go with it,' and pointing at me, added, 'This young fella knows what I mean.' In that moment I thought, *Yeah, I managed to get through it because I just went with it and the freedom was truly awesome and liberating.*

The day after my unrehearsed appearance with the Big 8 at the Arcadia, Mick Delahunty Jr called to my parents' house and, without any preamble, announced that he wanted me to join his band. Still not convinced that I was worthy of being in the company of such amazing musicians, I gingerly admitted that I didn't read music. Unfazed, Del Jr persisted, 'I don't care. If you can do for me what you did for Brendan Bowyer last night, I'll be very happy.' It was an offer I couldn't refuse and, while I was having great fun in the Cowboys, I knew it was time to move on. The transition to the Mick Delahunty Jr Big Band was a big step forward in both my career and my musical journey. I learned something new at every rehearsal and every night that I played with them. It was a very humbling experience. And the band was also conveniently based in Clonmel, close to Carrick-on-Suir where my fiancée, Anne, and I were building a house and making wedding plans.

5
The Sinner

Throwing caution to the wind, I break all the rules.

It was impossible to grow up in Carrick-on-Suir without being aware of Liam Dwyer. Liam had toured with his friends and neighbours, the world-famous Clancy Brothers and Tommy Makem on their farewell tour of Ireland. Musically, Liam and I were worlds apart. I was a disciple of the 1960s cultural revolution. I had cut my professional teeth playing rhythm and blues, pop, rock, jazz, blues and soul music in smoky London pubs and clubs and at American air bases across the UK in 1969. Liam, on the other hand, was popular with older audiences. Handsome and charismatic, he was always in demand for weddings, corporate and social functions. He was a superstar in our hometown and across its hinterlands because, whatever the X factor is, Liam Dwyer had it in spades.

My first direct interaction with him was late on Christmas Eve 1972. Shortly after leaving the Cottage Restaurant on Main Street with my friend, the phenomenal vocalist Bill Doherty, we came across a man lying on the pavement in the pouring rain. Recognising Liam, we hoisted his arms around our shoulders and carried him home. Having helped the intoxicated but good-humoured reveller to his bed, we left him to sleep it off. Some weeks later, a very contrite Liam Dwyer apologised for being so drunk on Christmas Eve and expressed his gratitude for helping him home.

That following summer, I was surprised to hear from my first cousin John Finn that his friend Liam Dwyer was eager to talk to me. I was curious. As we strolled along the riverbank, Liam revealed his grand plan: 'There's room for a good, versatile group in the southeast,' he said. He went on to say that venues throughout South Tipperary, Waterford and Kilkenny were 'crying out for something new and exciting', and then he asked the burning question: 'Would you consider putting a band together with me to play that circuit?'

I was hesitant. I knew Liam was popular but, although he was only 27, just five years older than me, I wasn't convinced that he could connect with a new, young audience. I was willing to be proven wrong on that, but I had a more pressing concern. 'You're a bit fond of the drink, Liam,' I replied frankly, 'and there's more to being a successful band than talent; professionalism and reliability are essential too.' At that, Liam stopped in his tracks, looked me in the eye and said, 'If you form this band with me, you'll never see a drop of alcohol cross my lips as long as we're playing together.' Impressed by Liam's resolve, I agreed to give it a go.

Although I wouldn't fully realise it until many years later, Liam Dwyer was a central figure in my personal and musical life. As a bandleader, he had an uncanny ability to anticipate popular taste. Early in 1975, on hearing the first few bars of 'Jive Talkin'', Liam predicted a massive second career for the Bee Gees. 'Mark my words,' he assured me, 'they'll be huge again, bigger than ever.' Of course he was right. He could pick a winner and predict the hits. Confident and persuasive, Liam had no doubt that this new band would be a success. He would front the band on lead vocals, I'd play bass, and, for guitar, he suggested Andy Burrows, a barman at the Comeragh Lounge on Main Street.

When I met Andy, I was immediately struck by his engaging personality. He was also hilariously funny, although he seemed entirely unaware of how entertaining he was. He told me he played a bit of acoustic guitar. Liam asked him if he'd ever considered 'taking up the electric'. 'I'm thinking about it,' Andy replied sheepishly.

'I tell you what, Andy,' Liam continued, 'if you get an electric guitar, you can join our band.'

Although I had never heard him play, I was learning to trust Liam's intuition. As the conversation went on, I was also mulling over a prospective drummer. By far the best drummer I knew from the locality was Paul O'Keefe, who I'd played with in the Cowboys. Apart from being rock-steady, Paul was also a tasty 'musical' drummer whose understanding of light and shade made him one of the most dynamic on the circuit.

Paul agreed to play drums, saying that if I was in the band, he was in too. While I knew that Liam could hold a mature crowd in the palm of his hand, I still wondered if he could captivate a younger audience, but any reservations I had would soon disappear.

Paul was on holiday in South Africa for a few weeks but Liam, Andy and I rehearsed every day. Without a drummer, I adopted a distinctive, percussive, rhythmic style of bass playing that I based on the energy and push of Ireland's phenomenal bodhrán players and which I continued to develop throughout my career. There is nothing as exciting, or funky, as a top-class bodhrán player in full flight. Andy concentrated on playing a solid rhythm on his shiny new electric guitar and Liam kept saying, 'This is great, they're gonna love this.' We were breaking every rule I had ever learned as a musician, but I began to wonder if it was crazy enough to work. Liam was full of surprises too: covering stomping hits by popular artists like Slade, Mud, Suzie Quatro, the Sweet and Ireland's very own superstar, Joe Dolan, he constructed a set that would drive any audience wild.

Andy was not an experienced lead guitarist, but, by the time Paul returned, I'd got them through rehearsals by using a wah-wah pedal, a distortion unit and an octave divider. I have always used a pick (plectrum) between my thumb and forefinger and, simultaneously, with the other three fingers of my right hand, I'd play double and triple stops to fatten out the sound. While Andy was coming to grips with his new role, I was, in as far as possible, playing bass and lead at the same time for rehearsals, but Liam insisted that was how we should always sound.

We decided on the Kickham Inn for our first gig, mainly because it was unlikely to have a crowd. At that time, the Kickham was not an overly popular venue and we assumed that nobody would show up to criticise us while we were finding our feet, but we couldn't have been more wrong. The place was packed to the rafters and so the only thing to do was to go for it. Throwing all caution to the wind, we brought as much equipment as we could to create as big a sound as possible. Although it was clear that we went down a storm with the crowd, I secretly hoped that there were no musicians in the audience to hear me hammering out a bass line and Eric Bell's iconic 'Whiskey in the Jar' guitar riff at the same time. Nevertheless, I had a strange feeling that the Sinners had something special. The sound was certainly different, but it was powerful and we had Liam Dwyer. He was magic, and soon we were packing every place we played. By the beginning of 1974 we were popular enough to consider augmenting the band and becoming a fully-fledged showband, but Liam resisted the idea of going professional. He was passionate about local politics and, in May 1974, he was first elected to Carrick-on-Suir Urban District Council. I realised then that there was no professional future with the band and I began to look further afield for new opportunities.

I continued to hone my craft, constantly learning and changing and seeking out new musical challenges playing with various rock, blues and progressive rock bands, but with very little consideration for financial returns. However, as with any major life event, my indifference to our financial situation was no longer sustainable after Anne and I married on 27 July 1974, and I soon realised that I had to earn a living. I now had a mortgage and bills to pay so I put the word out that I was in the market for a well-paid gig.

6
The Miami

Just another step up the ladder on my way to the stars.

In September 1974 Anne and I had just moved into our new house in Carrick-on-Suir when a letter arrived from Topline Promotions in Dublin, inviting me to audition for the Miami which, by that time, had dropped the word 'Showband' from its name to reflect their more modern image and style. I called the office and we agreed a date. By then, the Miami was fronted by the dynamic young vocalist and keyboard player Fran O'Toole and they performed innovative arrangements of classic and contemporary hits, as well as their own original material. I showed up for the audition at the West County Hotel in Ennis, County Clare, where the band was booked to play that night. The audition went well, and a few days later Topline contacted me to say they'd like me to join the band – but not as their bass player. Instead, they asked me to play lead guitar because their guitarist, Dave Monks, wanted to play bass. I had no interest in playing lead guitar. I'm a bass player; I don't think like a guitarist. It was like asking a plumber to fix your electrics and so I declined their offer and continued to play the local circuit. In a way I was relieved because, apart from a steady wage, I didn't see any future for me in a pop group. I was pleased with myself for passing the test and for being invited to join one of the most successful bands in the country, and that was more than enough to move me up another level on my musical journey. Nevertheless, Dave Monks did switch over to bass guitar, making way for the brilliant Tony Geraghty to become their lead guitarist.

In May 1975 Topline approached me once more to play bass with the Miami but, to my surprise, I had to audition again and this time there would be tough competition from some of the best bass players in the country. Along with the Topline executives and my competitors, most of whom I frequently saw and admired on television, I carefully watched each individual audition. I soon realised that, although they were all very impressive, they played the bass parts exactly as recorded. When it was my turn, Fran O'Toole, recognising me from the previous audition, gave me an encouraging thumbs-up. Showing me the band set list he said, 'Okay, Steve, what do you want to do?' Since the other bassists had all played the recorded parts perfectly, leaving little room for improvement, I suggested that we might jam and loosen up first. I was, in fact, turning the tables and throwing out a challenge to the band. Fran grinned at the opportunity to improvise and signalled to the others to follow me. I made up an up-tempo soul riff on the spot and the rest of the band quickly joined in. We were jamming for about five minutes when Fran stopped the band and, turning to the Topline directors, said, 'This is the bass player I want, this is the man.' The other band members – Brian, Tony, Ray and Des – nodded in agreement and it was soon announced on the radio and in the newspapers that I was the new bass player with the Miami, 'Ireland's top pop band'. The die was cast. My fate was sealed.

Although he knew it would end any chance of the Sinners re-forming, Liam appeared genuinely happy when I broke the news to him. Effusive and always exuberant in music and politics, he was a performer through and through, and I wondered if his reaction was a performance. I wondered how Liam could possibly be so happy for me, but it wouldn't be until December 2022 – many decades later – that I would fully realise how important Liam Dwyer was in my life.

A few days after the audition I returned to Dublin for an official photo shoot at St Anne's Park in Raheny. Just two months later the pictures taken that sunny day were destined to be embedded in Irish history forever. One particular image, a casual shot, has become the iconic 'last official photograph' of the band. It features Tony Geraghty in a jacket that Fran retrieved from the boot of his purple Ford Capri to help give the photographer the additional contrast he needed. An exceptional guitarist, revered among his peers, 25-year-old Tony was the only Dubliner in the band at the time, having recently quit the much heavier rock circuit to earn a steady wage, build a house and get married. Standing next to him, hands on his hips, is the outrageously charismatic Fran O'Toole from Bray in County Wicklow, who, despite his reputation as a world-class soul singer and keyboard player, was humble and down to earth, with a razor-sharp wit. Beside Fran, smiling broadly in a check shirt, is Ray Miller from County Antrim, whose powerhouse drumming drove the band like a freight train. Ray also drove fast cars and was always seen in the latest high-performance sports models. Des Lee is standing next to Ray with his arms folded, but it would be weeks before I realised that Des, who played saxophone and was also an excellent vocalist, was the band leader since Fran was the musical director and, undoubtedly, the star of the show. Brian McCoy is on my right in a white jacket. With a calm air of confidence he seemed older than his 32 years, and it was soon clear to me that he had the respect of the whole band. Along with Fran and Des, Brian had joined the Miami Showband on trumpet and vocals in 1967 after the band, which was originally formed in 1962, had a major split in its ranks. Tony and Ray joined later. I instantly connected with Tony and, before long, we were inseparable.

After the St Anne's Park photo shoot, Fran gave me a reel-to-reel tape with a live recording of the band's most recent gig and asked me to learn all the songs so that I'd be ready to play when they returned from their annual two-week holiday. Nonchalant, I threw the tape on the back seat of my car and went on holiday with Anne. I had no intention of learning the material. Years later I admitted to myself that I didn't really care about the job, I only cared about the challenge. I had beaten off stiff competition for the Miami gig, but I fully intended to leave the band when a more exciting challenge presented itself.

My first gig with the Miami was at the Pavilion Ballroom in Blackrock, just outside Dundalk. In those days, when Dublin-based bands travelled north, they typically met at the Crofton Airport Hotel. I arrived there in good time to transfer my bass amp and tall four-by-twelve Marshall bass cab to our roadie's gear van. Brian Maguire was one of the most experienced road managers in the business and was always on the road hours ahead of the musicians. The band had its own VW personnel minibus, but that evening I had arranged to travel with the road manager rather than wait around for the personnel minibus. Nearing the Pavilion, I was unprepared for the sight of hundreds of young people heading towards the venue. For a fleeting moment, I began to regret not listening to the tape that Fran gave me before the holidays, but I've always loved living on the edge; it's what excites me and keeps me interested. Where's the thrill in knowing exactly what's going to happen? I've taken musical risks all my life, waiting for the surprise, the buzz that comes with every performance. Can I pull something out of the air when it matters most? Just count it in and we'll see where it goes.

Smiling through their Mediterranean tans, my new bandmates were in great form when they arrived. The DJ had already warmed up the audience and when he announced 'the Miami!' the excited crowd surged forward.

As we walked on stage to the screams of the fans, I witnessed an amazing transformation in the friendly, relaxed guys I remembered from the audition and the photo shoot. They radiated charisma, especially Fran. The band's young front man was in a league of his own and, although Brian and Des shared some of the vocals, Fran had that intangible magic that defies description.

When we opened with a stomping version of the Four Tops classic 'Reach Out I'll Be There', I knew instantly that I was in the most exciting pop band in the country. I was mesmerised by the tone that Tony coaxed from his cherry-red Gibson 335 guitar. His dynamic rhythm and confident melodic lines interacted telepathically with Fran's keyboard. Brian's trumpet and Des's saxophone brass arrangements were punchy and powerful and Ray's drumming rock-solid. Although I hadn't rehearsed with the band or practised the material, I improvised, and when we finished the last song, Fran hugged me and I exited the stage on a high. The first gig was a major boost to my confidence and I felt genuinely proud to be part of such an exciting outfit.

The Miami hit the ground running and, night after hot summer night, life with my new bandmates got even better as the musical interplay became tighter. Our hectic schedule meant playing six nights a week and included some hotel stay-overs. Anne and I were now sharing a house in Dublin with my lifelong friend Billy Byrne, his wife, Maria, and their little daughter Ruth, so I felt some consolation in knowing that Anne was in the best of company while I was away. With so much time spent travelling in the minibus, I got to know the lads very well. On the way to every gig I sat in the middle seat between Fran and Tony, and on the way home I sat up front with Brian McCoy at the wheel while the others slept. I was now in the premier league and arriving at gigs as a bona fide pop star with my picture in all the newspapers and music magazines and a full diary of engagements in the biggest and best venues in the country. I was living the dream.

I had only been in the band about two weeks when Fran presented me with a tantalising offer. One evening, with time to spare before our gig at Caproni's ballroom in Bangor, County Down, Fran asked me to go with him to the local shop where a star-struck shop assistant filled a brown paper bag with his favourite Liquorice Allsorts. It was soon clear that he had an ulterior motive for getting me away from the others that sunny afternoon. As we made our way back to the ballroom he told me that the management had big plans for him – a solo career in the US. 'If my singer/songwriter showcase in Las Vegas works out, I'll be forming my own band and I want you to be my bass player.' It was a huge compliment, but Fran didn't know that I was already mulling over Tony's offer to form a progressive rock band the following spring. Ironically, since other plans for the Miami – which were destined to change history – had already been set in motion, I never got to make that decision.

7
The Last Waltz

The best-laid plans of mice and men.

Wednesday 30 July was bright by the time we got back to Dublin. The annual Galway Races brought thousands of sun-seekers to the nearby popular seaside resort of Salthill and we had just played two consecutive nights to huge crowds at the Seapoint Leisure Complex. I was glad to catch a few hours' sleep before setting off again to Banbridge in County Down, which, at that time, was about half an hour's drive north of the Dundalk/Newry border. One by one, we arrived and parked our cars at the Crofton Airport Hotel to rendezvous with our blue and white minibus. Our trumpet player Brian McCoy, who kept the bus at his home in Raheny, was already there and chatting with a group of musicians who also used the hotel as their 'band call' when travelling north. Tony was the last to arrive – he'd just seen his brother Carl off at the airport on his journey to South Africa where he and his group, the Bubble Band, intended to start new lives. Tony had considered joining them, but, having discussed it with his fiancée, Linda, decided to buy a house in Dublin instead. Dave Monks, who I'd replaced in the Miami, was in the new band winging its way to the southern hemisphere.

It wasn't long before we were on our way too and heading north towards the border. The mood in the bus was somewhat subdued because of the untimely death of our friend, Tom Dunphy, who had been killed in a car crash just three days before. At 39, Tom was a legend in the showband world; bass guitarist with the Royal Showband and then with the Big 8, which had continued the Royal's six-month winter residency at the Stardust Hotel in Las Vegas, he famously made the British charts with his first record. But we were young and we didn't dwell on life-and-death matters for long, and soon a cassette of Edgar Winter's album *Roadwork* was blasting through our VW speakers and all was well with the world again.

As usual, we finished the gig with the audience-participation number 'Clap Your Hands, Stamp Your Feet', a recent hit for the band, and, after the customary autograph signings, we changed our clothes and chatted with the catering staff over a cup of tea. Oddly enough, we were offered Irish stew, which some of us accepted, before Brian, Fran, Tony, Des and I climbed into our minibus for the relatively short journey back to Dublin. Since we were due to have the following day off, our drummer, Ray, who had driven directly to Banbridge in his own car, continued on to Antrim to stay with his parents and spend some time with his girlfriend, Anne.

It was unusual, too, that Brian Maguire, our road manager, had the equipment packed and loaded into his gear van and had left the venue a few minutes before us, but we were enjoying the rare opportunity to take our time after a midweek gig. A security system in operation in Banbridge town centre required us to wait about five minutes until the police arrived to raise a metal barrier and allow us access onto the main road heading south towards Newry and the border, but we were soon on our way back to Dublin. At first, I sat up front beside Brian, but when I realised that the others had no intention of sleeping, I climbed back through the bus to chat with Tony while Fran and Des played cards. The banter between all five of us, and especially between Fran and Brian, who were just as quick-witted as each other, was hilarious.

As we approached the junction of the main Belfast–Newry road and Buskhill Road – about six miles north of Newry – Brian alerted us to a uniformed figure waving a red light in the middle of the road. He knew the drill; turning off the headlights but keeping the sidelights and the interior lights on, he drove slowly towards the soldier. As usual, he opened his window expecting to show his driving licence and be waved on our way (quite often, the soldiers, especially the Ulster Defence Regiment (UDR) – the largest regiment in the British army, but who were mainly local part-timers – would recognise us and ask for autographs or even a free record), but this time we were told to 'stand out of the bus'. Brian, almost apologetically, relayed the surprise order to us, saying, 'Lads, we've got to get out while these gentlemen do a check on the bus.' First, however, he asked the soldier if he could move the bus off the road onto the hard shoulder because there was a car fast approaching from behind. The soldier beckoned us in and we duly began to exit the minibus. I was the last to step out but I had no inkling that I was stepping into a terrible new world where I would never again be just 'the bass player'.

8
The Killing Field

One life ends and another begins.

In 1975 the conflict in the North was raging and, understandably, the British authorities wanted security tightened on the southern side of the border in order to curtail the movements of the IRA. However, local politicians in the Republic of Ireland were reluctant to stop and search every constituent who criss-crossed the border on a daily basis to buy cheaper petrol, cigarettes or groceries or, in some cases, to tend to their farms that straddled the border. So in order to force the Irish government to agree a more stringent security policy and to justify that policy to a watching world – especially to Irish America – a plan was hatched by British Military Intelligence Section 5 (MI5).

Locally, MI5 was controlled by the Northern Ireland Office (NIO), which was staffed by people from Britain's Ministry of Defence, the Home Office and some from the Foreign Office, and the key figures were military and civilian intelligence officers. In 1975 the dominant faction was a high-powered cabal from MI5, a department of the Home Office.

MI5's writ gave them responsibility for security and intelligence operations in the UK and – more importantly – in Britain's colonies. They were well used to working with local police Special Branch departments and the British army. By 1975 the tactics they deployed in Aden, Africa and elsewhere had been deployed in Northern Ireland for a number of years. MI5 had developed a policy of using undercover forces to masquerade as indigenous forces in places such as Aden. They had also recruited local terrorists by 'fair means and foul' to carry out their dirty work. In Northern Ireland the tactics were adapted. One of the gangs they manipulated was the notorious loyalist terrorist organisation, the Ulster Volunteer Force (UVF). They also controlled Royal Ulster Constabulary (RUC) Special Branch agents and members of the Ulster Defence Regiment (UDR), the largest regiment of the British army at that time.

As we stepped out of the van in the early hours of 31 July 1975, we were ordered to line up at the side of the road and to face towards the ditch with our hands on our heads. I was in the centre with Brian McCoy on my right, Tony Geraghty on my left, and Fran O'Toole was on Tony's left. Our saxophone player, Des (McAlea) Lee, was on Brian's right and within touching distance of the back of our minibus. Despite having submachine guns pointed directly at us, the atmosphere was relaxed and there was friendly banter between us and some of the five soldiers that were initially visible to us.

For me, the new bass guitarist, it was just part of a great new adventure. Nevertheless, when I heard the opening click of a guitar case clasp, I instinctively dropped my hands from my head, stepped back from the line-up, walked the two or three paces to the back of the bus and asked the soldiers who were searching the bus to be careful with my bass guitar. My beloved Dan Armstrong plexiglass bass was an unusual instrument that I didn't want some awkward soldier manhandling. Tony's guitar, a cherry-red Gibson 335, and my bass were usually the only musical instruments we carried in our personnel bus but, sometimes, as was the case that morning, Des brought his saxophone too. Neither Tony nor I would ever leave our precious instruments in the gear van with Brian Maguire. Our guitars were always stored on the back shelf of our minibus, which was accessible by lifting the small rear window directly over the engine. The soldiers seemed unconcerned when I stepped out of line. Nevertheless, one of them questioned me about the contents of a small brown case beside the guitars. He asked me if there were 'any valuables in it'. When I assured him that it only contained my bass guitar effects pedals, one of the other soldiers spun me around by the shoulder and punched me in the lower back, winding me and knocking me back into line between Brian and Des.

For the first time, I felt that something wasn't right.

The soldier who had at first appeared to be in charge ordered another to take our names and addresses, which he proceeded to do by writing them in a small notebook. He began with Fran, but he had barely moved on to Tony when another soldier made his presence felt. I hadn't noticed this man until then. Perhaps he arrived in the fast car that Brian was concerned about earlier and which hadn't driven past when Brian moved the minibus onto the hard shoulder. Upon this particular soldier's arrival, there was a palpable change; all banter stopped and the casual atmosphere immediately dissipated. He stood within three feet of me but spoke only to the soldier who, until then, had appeared to be in charge. He asked what orders had been given to the man with the notebook and, on being told that it was names and addresses, replied, 'I want names and dates of birth.' Then, more aggressively, he snapped, 'Names and dates of birth.'

I immediately recognised his educated, upper-class English accent from my trainee insurance broker days in the City of London. It reminded me of some of my former bosses and colleagues. I was fascinated by this officer's style. He wore a fawn-coloured beret, his fatigues were a lighter colour than the other soldiers' uniforms. Clearly, a very senior officer was now in charge. Brian McCoy nudged the tip of my elbow with his and said, 'Don't worry, Steve, this is British army.' Des turned to me and said, 'The British army are usually careful with the instruments.' Born and reared in Northern Ireland, both Brian and Des could easily distinguish between British soldiers and local UDR men, and so I was content that this officer would conduct the check quickly and professionally and that we'd be on our way home without undue delay.

However, while we were being questioned, two men were secretly planting a bomb under the driver's seat of our minibus. Their plan was to send us on our way with a hidden bomb on board. According to forensic reports, we would all have been blown to pieces within ten to fifteen minutes while passing through Newry, and subsequent examinations would have shown that the Miami had been carrying a large bomb. No one would ever have known about the checkpoint and we would have been framed as terrorists attempting to transport a bomb for the IRA. If the most trusted and beloved commuters in Ireland could have been successfully framed as terrorists, then nobody would have been exempt from their rigorous stop and search policy. While their false-flag operation would have hampered the activities and movements of the IRA – since the Irish government could no longer reasonably object to Britain's demand to stop and search everyone crossing the border – the consequences would have been catastrophic and everlasting for us and for our families and future generations. The Miami Showband would have gone down in history as terrorists and our families tarnished forever, but, fortunately, their plan failed.

Suddenly, there was a massive explosion and the whole world turned red. I would find out later that while setting the bomb in position, the two men inadvertently triggered the wristwatch timing mechanism and instantly detonated ten pounds of commercial explosives. It was so powerful that it blew the bombers to pieces, ripping off their heads, tearing both arms off one man and a leg off the other. The blast obliterated our bus. The enormous force of the explosion lifted me into the air. I tried to run, but my feet were off the ground. Stunned and furious, the terrorists opened fire, shooting wildly. As I twisted in mid-air, a dumdum bullet pierced my right side, exploding, inside me, into sixteen pieces. Part of the shattered bullet continued ripping through my chest, collapsing my left lung before exiting under my left arm.

At first, everything felt like slow motion and, as I began to descend through the hedge into the field that lay about three metres below the level of the road, I could feel every branch and twig and leaf that touched me, even through my clothes. Time appeared to be slowing to a standstill until I suddenly hit the ground with tremendous force. Two of my bandmates crashed down on top of me. They quickly got to their feet and one of them tried to pull me across the field, away from the carnage, but I couldn't walk, I was a dead weight. The gunmen jumped down into the field, roaring obscenities and emptying their weapons into my bandmates. Brian, whom they shot in the hands, arms, body and head, was the first to be murdered. They quickly caught Fran, and although I heard him beg for mercy, they shot him twenty-two times – thirteen times in the face. They shot Tony in the back and in the back of the head. We didn't stand a chance. They had guns and we had guitars.

The shooting and screaming eventually gave way to the sound of squelching footsteps making their way through the carnage. Screaming obscenities, one of the gunmen kicked the lifeless bodies, shooting them again. As he approached me he stopped to kick Brian, who was lying beside me. Again and again he kicked, roaring louder and louder each time. Finally, he stepped towards me. I held my breath. I kept my eyes closed and my face pressed against the ground. He stood over me for what seemed like an eternity. Should I kneel up and beg for mercy or should I remain perfectly still and pretend to be dead? My mind was racing. My only thought was of survival. I steeled myself in anticipation. I was determined not to cry out if I were shot again. I told myself it would be quick and painless, but then, miraculously, a voice from the road called out, 'Come on, those bastards are dead, I got them with dumdums.' As the gunman turned and began walking away, I counted every fading step, hoping and praying that, if he changed his mind and discharged his pistol one more time, his aim would be off. Another bullet would surely find its mark, but it might not be fatal. My concentration was totally focused on not making a sound. But that bullet never came.

Gradually, as a haunting silence descended upon the field, broken only by the crackling of the burning ditch, I realised that our attackers had left and I tried to make sense of what had just happened. I had never heard of dumdums, so I reasoned that, since I felt no pain, it meant that they were dummy or blank bullets. At that moment, the worst possible scenario I could envisage was that the band might be off the road for a few days and that we might have to reschedule our gigs for the coming weekend. I recalled that, after a recent gig in the north, Fran and I were talking to a girl who told us that she and her boyfriend were caught in crossfire during a street battle in Belfast. She said they were both hit by stray bullets and that her boyfriend was killed. Fran and I were in awe, fascinated to meet someone who had actually been shot and, when we asked her how it felt, she explained that, because she felt a gentle rain on her face as she lay wounded on the stone steps, she knew she was alive. As I lay in the field under the half-moon in the clear summer sky, I too longed for a gentle rain on my face. But it didn't come.

Drifting through different levels of consciousness, I heard a familiar voice: 'Fran ... Brian ... Tony ... Steve ... are you okay?' It was Des, calling out from the ditch close to where he landed after the explosion. I was the only one to answer but, not wanting to make a fuss, I replied, 'I'm grand.'

In a statement taken at Newry police station later that morning, Des said that he survived by hiding in the ditch. As the flames spread towards him he feared being burned alive, but the killers left just in time and he managed to get up onto the main road. Having first been refused by a frightened passing lorry driver, he was eventually taken to the police station by a young couple who slowed down to navigate their car through the burning wreckage on the road.

A smell of cooking flesh and burning blood hung in the warm early morning air as I rolled onto my back. Staring up at an indifferent half-moon, I slowly brought my hands across my chest to count my fingers: as a musician, it was of the utmost importance that my fingers were intact. I was relieved that they were all accounted for and undamaged and I thanked God when I heard my platform shoes click against each other. I still had both legs. I crawled around that blood-soaked field for almost an hour, sometimes on my hands and knees and sometimes dragging myself on my swollen stomach, assuring Brian and Fran and Tony that help would soon arrive and we would all go home.

'Brian? Are you okay? They're gone. Des is gone too. He'll knock at someone's door. You stay here. I'll get the lads and we'll go home ...

'Oh, there you are Fran ... I thought you might be gone with Des. Brian is out for the count. He got an awful fall ... It's a fair drop off the road. Are you alright? You scratched your hand a bit ... I'm not surprised though, that ditch is full of briars and brambles. No harm done. Not a bit of harm. I just have to get Tony and then we can go ...

Lads! Brian – Fran, I have Tony. He's here! Did you hurt yourself, Tony? I'm grand myself ... Only that soldier gave me a dig in the back and knocked the wind out of me. You wouldn't want to move Tony in case you hurt your back in the fall. How are the hands? We're alright as long as we don't break a finger, aren't we? Here, I'll check 'em for you. One – two – three – four – five, here, give me your other hand, one – two – three – four – five, all good, nothing broken! You'll be tearin' across the fretboard again tomorrow ... you might even bring the Telecaster. Tony, don't worry ... don't you worry about anything. Des'll be back soon ... I'll hold your hand 'til Des gets back ...'

When I heard the distant, nasal tones of walkie-talkies, I was convinced that the murderers had returned to finish me off. (I found out later that, fearful the bodies might be booby-trapped, neither the police nor the emergency services would enter the field until an army helicopter had surveyed the awful scene and declared it safe to do so.) Despite my injuries, I was determined not to let them shoot me on the ground like they had done with Fran. I would stand up and face them. But every time I pushed myself up on my knees and staggered to my feet, I fell down. Again and again, I repeated that macabre, liminal dance between life and death in the crackling light of the burning hedge that illuminated the bodies and body parts strewn around the killing field. The horrendous light show continued as I staggered to a tree by the ditch where I leaned against a low branch to get my breath. It was only when a torchlight was shone in my face and I heard a Northern accent say, 'It's okay, son, we're the police,' did my body give way and stumble forward.

The plan devised by the architects of the Miami Showband massacre was much more ambitious than to simply frame a pop group in order to tighten border security. The ultimate goal was to monitor and restrict the movement of an entire people. Had they succeeded in convincing the world that a much-loved Catholic and Protestant band from North and South were terrorists, then every Irish-passport holder would have been deemed a legitimate suspect and given 'special attention' at airports, ferry ports and border crossings. It was a brilliant strategy. We were not supposed to live, but we survived to tell the world what happened.

Nevertheless, it raises an important question. How many times did they actually succeed in framing innocent people?

9
Albert

I am made aware that my story might be an inconvenience for some who would go to extraordinary lengths to see it buried and forgotten.

There was a stiff breeze blowing through Donegal town that Sunday morning as I walked across the road from the hotel to try to get a signal on my mobile phone. It was late August 2007, and the book *The Miami Showband Massacre: A Survivor's Search for the Truth*, which I co-wrote with Neil Fetherstonhaugh, was due to be published in less than two weeks. Given the nature of the book, I wanted someone who bridged the gap between music and politics to launch it, and I felt that there was no one more suitable than the former Taoiseach, Albert Reynolds. Albert had been a ballroom owner and a music promoter before he entered politics.

'Morning, Albert, I hope I didn't wake you!'

'No, I just finished breakfast, how are things? You sound like you're on top of a mountain.'

'Close enough. I'm up in Donegal, so before I lose this connection, do you fancy launching our book? You're the perfect man for the job!'

'Just tell me when and where and I'll be there, but come up to the Four Seasons next week and we'll catch up.'

Although Neil was a journalist with the *Dublin People* newspaper and sometimes wrote for the *Sunday World* and I was a founding director of the *Irish World* newspaper in London and its first editor, it had taken us a year and a half to write the book. Now it was finally ready. My co-writer was as driven and personally invested in the project as I was. In fact, Neil's forensic research, independent auditing and unbiased scrutiny of every detail throughout our shared journey helped to exorcise the imposter syndrome that constantly haunted me.

I arranged to have lunch with Albert and our mutual friend, the journalist Ken Murray. Albert was in great form and immediately launched into stories about his ballroom days. Eventually, the conversation turned to the book: to my astonishment, he quoted passages and asked questions about characters and events with which he was clearly familiar. It was obvious that he still had a keen interest in the machinations of the so-called Troubles. Albert did, however, caution me that there were 'powerful individuals within our own media and beyond' who would prefer that our book would never see the light of day.

In the following days, our publisher's PR agent took me on a whistlestop promotion tour that included a prime-time interview on RTÉ's popular *The Marian Finucane Show*, which received a huge, positive response. The *RTÉ Guide*, one of Ireland's biggest-selling magazines at the time, gave our book an excellent review. We sent out lots of invitations and, while I didn't have contact details for many of my old musician friends, I mentioned, during my interviews, that they were all welcome to the launch at 7 p.m. on Tuesday 11 September. But I was still apprehensive. Would anyone turn up?

It was a balmy autumn evening as Anne and our daughter, Sean Josephine, walked the short distance from the Conrad Hotel to Eason Fred Hanna's bookshop at No. 1 Dawson Street. I knew I'd be expected to say a few words, but I didn't give it much thought since Fr Brian D'Arcy, 'the unofficial chaplain to the showbands', was also speaking at the event and I knew that Brian would have any audience enthralled with his anecdotes and recollections of the Miami. As we approached the venue, I was relieved to see a crowd gathered outside the large glass doors, but I wasn't prepared for what awaited us inside. The bookshop was packed to capacity. Copies of our book filled every shelf and posters of the cover adorned every wall. Microphones were set up for the speakers at the Trinity College end of the room and an RTÉ TV crew was already filming interviews with celebrities for the *9 O'Clock News*.

Musicians and sports personalities, together with families and friends and neighbours, interacted with politicians and academics in a strangely heightened atmosphere – the anticipation of a hitherto unspoken trauma, hiding in plain sight on every shelf and wall in the room.

Fr Brian spoke first, taking the audience through the whole gamut of emotions, conjuring up images of dancehalls and marquees and of being young and free; the thrill and pride of hearing Ireland's favourite showbands on the radio and seeing them on TV; the excitement of one-night-only appearances in towns and villages; and the bewildering heartbreak of losing one of the very best. Fr Brian contextualised the event perfectly.

Albert Reynolds alternated between music promoter and politician, interweaving fun, fear, dancing, danger, music, mayhem, laughter and loss. However, it was his generous acknowledgement of the invaluable contribution that the Miami Showband, along with all of the other showbands, made to society during those dark, despondent days that impacted me most. I felt enormously proud.

After Neil said his piece and I spoke, you could hear a pin drop, and then people smiled and people cried and everyone hugged each other and we signed copies of the book and the celebrities signed copies too and hundreds of photographs were taken and, as book launches go, it was a great success. Twelve years later, the book we were launching in Dublin on that balmy September evening would inspire the Emmy-nominated Netflix documentary *ReMastered: The Miami Showband Massacre*. I have no doubt that, were he still with us, my old friend Albert would be very proud.

10
The Alternative Tour 2007

The widening gap between those who transitioned from wartime leadership to political leadership and those who trusted and believed in them.

I've always loved driving. And as it's all motorway now – along with my Bonnie Raitt collection for company – I hardly noticed the 434 kilometres from Cork to Belfast. As I passed that lonely spot between Newry and Banbridge where my life changed forever, I thought how different the world is now compared to that of 1975.

I reflected, as I always do when passing Buskhill Road, on the senseless loss of five young lives in the small hours of a July morning beneath those mute, shell-shocked trees that, today, stare into a field once saturated with the blood of the innocent and the guilty. It was almost inconceivable that I was on my way to a reception at Stormont Castle, so long the imposing icon of prejudiced, sectarian rule in the province.

Tonight, two months after I launched my book, the Reverend Ian Paisley would launch the autobiography of Eurovision Song Contest winner and former Member of the European Parliament (MEP) Dana Rosemary Scallon, a Catholic from the Bogside in Derry. I looked forward to meeting old friends and colleagues as well as the inevitable celebrated associates of a lady whose career is as diverse as it is interesting. The mix of showbiz, politics and religion would surely make this event unique. Martin McGuinness would be there too and

I was intrigued to find out, at first hand, if the two men, having been sworn enemies for most of their lives, really deserved to be called the Chuckle Brothers. That Paisley and McGuinness were now leader and deputy leader of a power-sharing executive was almost too good to be true. As I zipped up the motorway towards Belfast, my phone's ringtone abruptly interrupted Ms Raitt in full flow. On the line was Ken Murray, journalist, broadcaster and co-author of Dana's autobiography, calling to ask me not to go directly to the reception at Stormont Castle but to meet him at the nearby Stormont Hotel instead. He wanted to take me on 'the alternative tour', as he put it, 'before we get caught up in the back-slapping glitzy event and lose the run of ourselves'.

We hardly spoke as Ken drove up the Falls Road, down the Shankill Road, along Sandy Row, across East Belfast and past housing estates with names forever burned into the memory of anyone who listened to or watched news bulletins during the Troubles. In stark contrast to the phoenix-like rejuvenation of Belfast city centre, privation and restlessness were evident in the appearance and demeanour of young people half-sitting against windows of closed-down shops and loitering outside late-hour mini-markets. Surprise and suspicion were manifest on the faces as our southern-registered vehicle threw shadows across the facades of their local haunts. Murals commemorating 'fallen idols of the conflict' stood guard over well-flagged protectorates and huge signs put us on notice that we were 'now entering' the fiefdom of some republican or loyalist faction. It could have been 1975 but, tragically, it was thirty-two years on.

When we eventually arrived at Stormont Castle, we were greeted by the usual razzmatazz that accompanies such events and before long I was, as Ken had predicted, shaking hands with dignitaries, hugging old friends, posing for pictures. Yes, Ken was right … it was all too easy to lose the run of ourselves.

Moving slowly like a colossus, Ian Paisley entered through a side door of the Great Hall to a deafening hush. All eyes were on him, yet the large gathering opened like the Red Sea before Moses as he carved his pilgrimage towards the foot of the grand staircase. I had mixed emotions. I couldn't but be impressed by his charisma, but now, more than ever, I wished he had employed that God-given allure to unite people rather than to sow so much hatred, suspicion and division all those years ago. *Better late than never*, I thought to myself. Some of the guests gingerly moved forward to shake his hand, but I stepped back. Why? After all I had no problem shaking hands with a leader of the terrorist organisation that murdered my friends and left me for dead! Before I could resolve my quandary, however, the unexpected happened: his wife, Eileen, left the procession and walked straight over to me. She took my hand and said, 'I'm delighted to see you here, you are very welcome.' That simple gesture settled my dilemma and I got on with enjoying the rest of the evening. I was bemused, if not surprised, at the pop-star reception given to Martin McGuinness. Everyone wanted to be photographed with him, and I still have a picture somewhere of Albert Reynolds, Martin McGuinness and me, doing exactly what Ken Murray had predicted earlier that afternoon.

About a week later, over lunch in the canteen in Leinster House, Ken asked for my thoughts on the day. I admitted I was concerned that the politicians appeared to have moved into a different world, leaving their constituents behind and bewildered. I worried that their people would find it difficult to understand how the gulf between them had widened so much and so quickly when so little had changed in their own lives. I was fearful that all the components and conditions still existed for violent expressions of disappointment, disillusionment, frustration and anger. I feared that the much proclaimed and celebrated 'peace' might be little more than a veneer to gloss over the deep cracks that still existed within society. Nevertheless, I trusted the pleasant, friendly people we mingled with that evening to provide the leadership necessary to eventually bring their people with them. I was sure the intelligentsia and the middle classes would embrace new opportunities. Commerce and pragmatism would surely hasten an expedient new order for the benefit of all, and I expected the working classes, and even their elders, many of whom were born into sectarianism, to put aside old hostilities for the sake of peace and prosperity. Ultimately, it fell to the great and the good to lead by example and I was convinced that they were eager to do so. Had I expected too much?

11
Forgotten

I find my voice.

For the majority of victims of the so-called Troubles, 'acknowledgement' is vitally important, but establishing those victims as 'real human beings' in the public consciousness is not always easy. Perhaps there's a natural self-preservation mechanism that disconnects the public from those whose experiences it feels it can't handle. Do we actually accept that people who have been physically or psychologically damaged or broken by grief are really 'the same as us' or do we semi-dehumanise them by labelling them 'abnormal', 'unfortunate', 'exceptional', 'unusual' or 'atypical', in order to save ourselves the inconvenience of having to empathise with them or to put ourselves in their shoes? How often are the names of horrific atrocities like 'Dublin and Monaghan', 'Bloody Sunday', 'Enniskillen' or 'Omagh' used as a general collective term for the names of real people? Do we know their names? How will the victims be remembered? Do their names matter to us? The Nobel Peace Prize-winner and Holocaust survivor Elie Wiesel wrote, 'To forget the dead would be akin to killing them a second time.'

I recall a lady on BBC Radio Ulster one morning speaking about her husband, who had been murdered forty years previously. It was a harrowing story to which a lot of listeners responded but, to my surprise, she called the radio station again the following morning to thank the presenter saying, 'Before I spoke on your programme yesterday, my late husband was nobody and I was nobody but now he is somebody and I am somebody.' I remember feeling guilty that she and her husband had been forgotten while my own story is firmly ingrained in the public consciousness.

However, I regularly have to remind myself at how shocked I was when I began to promote the Miami Showband 30th Anniversary Concert at Vicar Street in Dublin in 2005 only to find that the Miami Showband massacre had been all but forgotten too.

Although the biggest names of the showband era were confirmed for the concert scheduled for 1 August, I received a call from the manager, Bren Berry, to say that ticket sales were poor. Bren advised me to defer the concert to a later date. I was stunned, and embarrassed for all involved. The thought of going to the families of my murdered bandmates to tell them that there was 'very little public interest' in the thirtieth anniversary concert seemed almost unconscionable. I knew that I would have to relay the bad news to my fellow members of the steering group that we had set up to oversee the project. The other committee members were Mike Hanrahan, vocalist and guitarist with the celebrated Irish folk band Stockton's Wing, accountant John Matthias Murphy and the former Miami Showband bass player Paul Ashford.

I decided to call John Murphy first, as I felt he would be the most sympathetic to our predicament. John is an exceptionally kind and measured man and one of my closest confidants, but to my astonishment he didn't hold back in letting me know that it was all my fault because I, personally, should have done a full round of radio and press interviews to promote the concert. I told John that I didn't want to be in the spotlight, but he remonstrated with me, saying that I should put my own considerations aside and 'do it for Tony, Fran and Brian'.

He was right. I had been shy of the spotlight and it had nearly cost us the concert. It was time to do what I could to salvage things.

I began calling radio producers and newspaper columnists to request interviews, and I was even more terrified when they said yes. I had no confidence whatsoever, but John and Mike and Paul encouraged me and urged me on, and praised me after each interview, regardless of how I felt it went. Suddenly, I didn't have to call the media; they were calling me and I could hardly keep up with the requests. To my utter amazement, about ten days before the concert date, Bren Berry called me to ask if we would consider adding a second night at Vicar Street as the show was now completely sold out. 'It's the hottest ticket in town,' he said.

The logistics of organising a second night at such short notice were impossible, and we were more than happy to stick with our 'one night only' plan. The concert was a resounding success. Ireland's legendary impresario Jim Aiken, who had brought some of the world's leading musical acts to Ireland, later said that the Miami Showband's thirtieth anniversary concert was 'the greatest showband concert ever staged'. John Murphy's stern words that day gave me the confidence to speak up for my murdered friends.

12
Rubber Bullets

A blind man shows me how he changed the lives of thousands on the other side of the world through his own life-changing experience in an impoverished, working-class area of Derry.

In 2008, following the success of the 2005 anniversary concert and the 2007 publication of the book, we agreed to do a series of Miami Showband concerts. Des McAlea (also known by his stage name of Des Lee) fronted the band on lead vocals and saxophone, and it was great to have our original drummer, Ray Miller, with us too. I was on bass guitar and, as the band leader, I put the 1975 Miami Showband set list together, which included the hits of that time as well as the classic pop, rock and, especially, the soul music that Fran had made his own. I wanted us to sound as close as possible to the way we did back in the day. My aim was to be authentic without being a tribute to ourselves, so we had a fine line to tread. The veteran Belfast vocalist, keyboard and saxophone player Barry Woods was added to the line-up, along with an ancillary keyboard player for vocal harmonies. I also recruited my old friend, the legendary guitarist and vocalist Johnny Fean from Horslips, to complete the band.

Our first concert was scheduled for 16 September 2008, at Vicar Street. We had played there three years previously and we were confident of another great reception in Dublin. However, our concert at the Grand Opera House in Belfast, which was scheduled for the following night, had sold out very quickly and we were conscious that it would be very emotional, not only for the audience, but also for the band. We were determined to make our first date in Northern Ireland since the 1975 tragedy a very special and enjoyable occasion. Our guests were the showband legend Brendan Bowyer, as well as Ireland's first Eurovision Song Contest winner, Dana, and Les McKeown of the Bay City Rollers. We also augmented our brass section with the fabulous Kaye twins, Paul and Gerry, who had played with the Miami back in 1977. Des, Ray and I did not want the Belfast concert to be a commercial enterprise, so we decided to donate the profits. Having gone through a long list of charities, each one as deserving as another, we eventually settled on Children in Crossfire, subject to meeting its founder, Richard Moore.

In 1970 the Ministry of Defence (MoD) deployed the rubber bullet as a 'non-lethal' form of riot control on the streets of Northern Ireland. Designed to be aimed low or into the ground to reduce their velocity, rubber bullets were deemed more effective and less controversial than live ammunition, but, in reality, they were often fired at close range and directly at heads and upper bodies, so it wasn't long before they caused a fatality. In April 1972 11-year-old Francis Rowntree was killed when, without warning, a soldier firing into a crowd in West Belfast shot the boy in the head. Giving evidence at the inquest, Alan Hepper, a Ministry of Defence engineer, declared that there had been limited testing on rubber baton rounds before their introduction in July 1970. Just weeks after the killing of Francis Rowntree, a British soldier shot 10-year-old Richard Moore in the face at point-blank range with a rubber bullet, blinding him for life, as he ran home from school with his friends in the Creggan estate in Derry.

One evening after rehearsals on the outskirts of Antrim town, we went over to the Ramble Inn restaurant on the Lisnevenagh Road for dinner. We had arranged for Richard Moore to join us. Although the restaurant was very busy, I suddenly became aware of a powerful presence, as if an electric charge had gone through the room. Holding on to a companion's arm, Richard Moore moved confidently towards our table and, before I could stand up to shake hands, I was greeted with a hearty slap on the back. 'How's it going, mucker?' he said in an unmistakable Derry accent.

He pitched the idea for the Grand Opera House concert profits going to his organisation but, as far as we were concerned, he didn't need to make any pitch. He then invited me to visit his offices in Derry the following day, to learn more about the work of Children in Crossfire. When I got there the next morning everything had been meticulously prepared: slideshow, videos, brochures, etc. Even though Richard is blind, he can read the room better than most and after about fifteen minutes into the video presentation, he said, 'Stop the video. This is not really telling you what we do. Will you come to Africa with me and see for yourself?' My immediate answer was, 'When are we going?'

'You most certainly are not,' Anne said when I told her that I was going to Africa with a blind man. 'It's too dangerous. Who do you think you are – Indiana Jones?' But Anne didn't realise that I would have gone to the moon with Richard Moore. Moreover, I was fascinated at the thought of crossing the equator for the adventure of a lifetime with this remarkable man. I managed to persuade her, but only on condition that I took every insect and mosquito repellent available with me and got all of the required vaccinations. On the day of my departure, Anne presented me with a stylish straw hat that she bought for me at the upmarket Brown Thomas store in Cork to protect me from any dive-bombing bugs and off I went on a whistle-stop tour of Tanzania with Richard Moore and two other observers, Morris Crumb and Andrew Clenahan, and a few words in Swahili under my dapper new chapeau.

'You'll be put through the wringer every day,' Richard warned, 'but I promise you'll have a comfortable place to sleep at night.' He was true to his word. I certainly wasn't prepared for the awful poverty, suffering and destitution. At the Ocean Road Cancer Institute in Dar es Salaam, I met Dr Trish Scanlan, a brilliant young Irish doctor from Wicklow, who could have chosen a much easier and more lucrative life but had instead taken on the incredibly difficult task of treating Tanzanian children with cancer while running the only hospital in East Africa that provided chemotherapy free of charge at that time. Within just two years, the survival rate of children in her care rose from 27 per cent to around 60 per cent. It was a stunning achievement that might not have been realised without the support of people like Richard Moore and Children in Crossfire. We managed to visit eight projects during my visit and each one was heartbreaking, unique and inspiring. I found the orphanage in Dar es Salaam particularly upsetting as my own beloved father had been orphaned as a child.

At first I thought Children in Crossfire was somehow connected to child soldiers, but Richard told me that, although the name refers to the crossfire of poverty, it was inspired by his own experience. A child caught in crossfire himself, Richard, remarkably, insists that his blindness has been a positive experience because of the people in his life – his family and the people of Creggan, a nationalist area up on the hill overlooking the Bogside and Derry City. His memories of Creggan are particularly warm and wonderful. He breaks into a wide smile as he recalls being 'a football fanatic' growing up with other families as large as his own. In those days there weren't many cars, so the children had the whole street to themselves to play 'football and Red Rover and hide-and-seek'. While he claims he wasn't a natural academic, he says he was a very happy student, especially whenever he got a lift to school from his brother in Doherty Butchers' van. 'Even though it was only a couple of minutes' walk, it was fantastic to get a lift. I was a celebrity in a butcher's van,' he laughs.

Happy-go-lucky but increasingly aware that he was living in a war zone, Richard knew that Derry had changed. With burnt-out cars and barricades built of rubble, shootings and bombings, the city was tense. Bloody Sunday had happened in 1972, and three or four people living within a minute of his home were murdered on that awful day. He constantly saw IRA men with masks and rifles patrolling the streets and, as incredible as it sounds now, it seemed normal then that a young child could distinguish the different types of weapons they carried.

On the day he was shot, there was a heavy military presence in the area. Running home from school, Richard and his friends decided to sprint up the football field just as they had so often before. When the soldier fired a rubber bullet from the army lookout post built beside his school to watch over the nearby police station, it struck Richard on the bridge of his nose and the ten-year-old lost his right eye and was totally blinded in his left.

Richard's parents, devout Catholics who attended Mass every day, were apolitical and totally anti-violence. They did everything they could to protect their family from the Troubles. 'But it didn't matter,' he says, 'the Troubles found us.' His father, an unemployed shoemaker, was devastated by what had happened to his son. When the doctors told him Richard would never see again, he asked, 'Can I give him my eyes?' Years later, Richard recalled his father's words and called his autobiography *Can I Give Him My Eyes?* It was a statement of love that would sustain Richard for the rest of his life.

Despite his remarkable positivity, important questions remained. Why did it happen? Why did the soldier shoot him? For over thirty years, Richard developed his own narrative, imagining the soldier who shot him to be a squaddie, some naive teenager from England on the edge of a no-go area in Derry, scared out of his wits. But it was not a terrified boy who blinded him: it was a 34-year-old British army captain, Charles Innes, who discharged the lethal missile. This unexpected and inconvenient truth challenged Richard and led to a lot of torturous soul-searching. Why was an army captain firing rubber bullets at children that day? Where in the rules of engagement is a soldier permitted to use rubber bullets when there is no imminent danger? Clearly, it was an unlawful action by a British army officer who would later say that he fired the bullet to get the children to 'bugger off home'.

Years later, having finally tracked him down, Richard forgave Charles and now considers him a friend, 'a good friend'. It may be challenging for many, if not for most, to understand that, for Richard Moore, 'anger serves no useful purpose'. Nevertheless, while he forgives the soldier, Richard is quick to point out that 'it does not mean what Charles did was right'. Forgiveness, according to Richard Moore, is not justification. 'If a child throws a stone through a car window, you won't tell the child that it's right, but you will forgive the child, won't you?' he says. 'I am not saying my way is the only way, I'm just saying it worked for me. I am happy. We are good friends.'

When the files were eventually declassified in 2013, it was discovered that the Ministry of Defence knew that rubber bullets were far more dangerous than they had led the public to believe. Before they were used on the streets of Northern Ireland, tests on rubber bullets confirmed that they were lethal, but the MoD had stated otherwise. The British government has a responsibility to protect those who live under its jurisdiction, but in Richard's case it actually went out of its way to cover up evidence that proves it failed to protect him. 'I would be able to see today if those weapons hadn't been deployed on the streets. They shouldn't have brought them onto the streets. I'm alive to talk about it. Other children are not alive to talk about it,' he told the BBC in 2013.

During the Troubles there was no therapy or trauma counselling for children like Richard Moore or their families. It was his teachers, friends and parents who made it possible for him to realise his potential. Contemplating the children in Africa and South America who now have food, clean water and access to education, he says it is not because of him or Children in Crossfire, it's because of the people who showed him love and compassion at that terrible time. 'When you've been through the wringer, you'd be hard pushed not to learn from it, not to understand what worked and what didn't, what helped and what didn't. I've been lucky. I've been blessed.'

I was indeed put 'through the wringer' in East Africa, where I saw poverty and deprivation on a scale that I could never have imagined. The suffering I witnessed was overpowering. I was taken to the Ocean Road Cancer Institute on my very first day. As our small convoy approached the compound, Richard asked me if I could see the hospital, but I told him I could only see a few small, basic outbuildings, which I began to describe, but he smiled and said, 'We've arrived.'

The intense dry heat hit me the moment we stepped out of the Toyota Landcruiser. I couldn't believe that this was a hospital, let alone a cancer care centre. Dr Trish Scanlan was standing on the porch with a broad, welcoming Irish smile, surrounded by a cluster of little children, some holding her hands and others holding on to her doctor's white coat, and all excited and shy at the same time. There was an overwhelming sense of joy at Richard's arrival. We were soon inside the tiny ward that housed just fourteen beds for thirty-seven children. Some parents sat outside on the porch while others kept vigil at the bedsides of their children, some of whom, even I could see, were not long for this world.

I accompanied Richard and Trish as they stopped by every bed, offering words of comfort to a child or a parent. Even if I knew their language, I would have been tongue-tied, so all I could offer was an awkward smile. I was way out of my depth. I was just a bass player. All of a sudden, I felt a tiny hand wrap itself around my little finger. I looked down and saw a small boy, no more than 3 years of age, looking sideways up at me. Smiling, I immediately hunkered down to say hello, but as I did he turned his full face towards me and, for an instant, I recoiled in horror, then immediately composed myself. The child had a large cancerous tumour on the side of his face.

In that instant, I knew everything was connected. I picked little Edwin up and soon I was carrying an even tinier little girl around in my arms too. They were both beaming when Dr Trish came over to have a few words. I asked Trish how my new little buddies were doing and, like most Irish people, I expected her to tell me that they were doing very well and on the mend. The children didn't understand what we were saying and my Swahili extended only to a few simple words like *jambo* (hello), *ahsante* (thank you) and *kwaheri* (goodbye). Trish took the little boy's hand in hers and said, 'Ah, poor Edwin came to us too late, but we got madam here in time. The cancer was in her eye, which, as you can see, we had to remove and now she is doing very well indeed.' I was stunned, but I was also grateful for the doctor's candour. The little girl stretched her hands out to Trish, who took her in her arms, but Edwin was fixated by my new straw hat. When I placed it on his head, his eyes lit up, and I realised that I could actually help him to forget his woes for a little while just as we did in the dancehalls during the Troubles, so I gave him the hat that Anne bought me just a few days before and told him he looked really cool, and he smiled and put his little arms around me and hugged me. Although little Edwin has long since passed away, his strength and courage remain with me forever and I pray for him, and to him, every day.

Two days before we left Dar es Salaam, the Irish ambassador to Tanzania, Anne Barrington, invited us to dinner; she suggested meeting at O'Willie's Irish Whiskey Tavern, the only Irish pub in Tanzania at the time. I was physically and emotionally exhausted by our journey from Dar es Salaam to Mwanza and on up to Lake Victoria and from the distressing events and sights I'd witnessed along the way. I was looking forward to a relaxing evening, but to my utter dismay there was a huge banner over the main entrance of the pub, which read, 'O'Willie's Welcomes the Miami Showband'. To make things worse, the place was packed to the rafters with Irish, British, Australians, Americans, Canadians, New Zealanders and South Africans, among many others. After dinner I noticed musical instruments had been set up on the stage in the main lounge and that Richard, along with my fellow voyagers Morris Crumb and Andrew Clenahan, were tuning up and getting ready to play. Richard is a fine singer and a talented guitarist. Andrew knows his way around a fretboard too and Morris is an experienced keyboard player. I was conscious that since the Miami Showband featured on the big banner, I would be expected to front the band – but while I'm a bass player, I'm a long way from being a singer, so I made every excuse possible to avoid getting up on stage. However, when they presented me with a five-string bass guitar and a bass amp, I threw caution to the wind and went for it. I even sang a few rock and roll classics, and the place rocked and everyone said it was the best night's entertainment they'd ever had. *There's no accounting for taste*, I thought to myself.

The real Miami Showband got a fabulous reception at Vicar Street in Dublin, but we were conscious that our concert in Belfast the following night was going to be very special and emotional for the band and for the audience. To our delight, the moment we walked on to the stage of the Grand Opera House, the entire audience stood up and cheered. It was not just a standing ovation. It was an outpouring of love for the Miami Showband that the people of Belfast had held in their hearts for us for over thirty-three years.

13
The Savage Watch

Connecting the Troubles to the Second World War and a possible link between 'rank-and-file' terrorists and the upper echelons of society who the authorities remain determined to protect.

In October 2008 I received a call from a Northern Ireland journalist named Greg Harkin asking permission to pass on my contact details to someone called Ian Newell. He told me that Mr Newell was the son of a former RUC detective, Ally Newell, who, he said, had worked on the Miami Showband case. Ally Newell was in poor health, suffering from dementia and the effects of a number of recent strokes. He went on to say that Ian Newell had a watch, which he believed belonged to one of my murdered colleagues, and that he wished to return it to the family. Naturally, I gave him permission to pass on my telephone number. A few days later I received a call from Ian Newell. He sounded pleasant and friendly and explained that, while going through his father's things, he had come across a box that contained a watch labelled 'Miami Showband'. He did not make it clear whether it was the box or the watch that was labelled 'Miami Showband', but he was adamant that the watch belonged to 'the man on the cover of your book'. When I asked him to elaborate, it became evident that he meant Brian McCoy. I told him I'd ask Brian's wife, Helen, if this might be the case, but she assured me that Brian's watch had been returned to her by the RUC after his murder. I called Ian Newell and told him what she said, but he still insisted that the watch belonged to the Miami Showband and that he would like me to have it. I agreed to take it and to look into the possibility of it belonging to another member of the band.

I told Ian that we were scheduled to play at the Market Place Theatre in Armagh on Sunday 2 November and I'd be happy to meet him there. After the show, as was always the case at our concerts, the audience gathered around the band and we chatted and signed autographs and souvenir concert programmes and old Miami Showband albums and band pictures and posters that people had kept for years, and we also signed copies of my first book. When the audience finally left, I noticed a man still sitting in his seat towards the back of the theatre. As I suspected, it was Ian Newell. We spoke briefly and then he produced the wristwatch, which was clearly old and missing one part of its black leather strap. It didn't strike me as unusual, and I found it extraordinary that he could be so sure it was the same watch that Brian was wearing on the cover of my book, since Brian's watch isn't very clear in that picture. Nevertheless, I took him backstage to the dressing room and introduced him to the rest of the band. He was friendly and relaxed, and he chatted at length with the guys. We all discussed the watch and, although Des and Ray didn't recognise it, Ian Newell handed it to me in their presence. We all thanked him for his concern, and I promised I would do my best to check if it belonged to Fran or Tony, our other two murdered bandmates.

I took the watch home, where it remained on top of a filing cabinet in my office for a while, but after a few weeks I decided to make a renewed effort to establish the identity of the owner. I googled the make and learned through a website called Atlantik-Pirat.com that KM (Kriegsmarine) watches were issued to German naval officers during the Second World War. In correspondence with an administrator of the site, I also learned the specific model of the watch (KM592 Alpina) and that such watches often came into the possession of British military personnel while guarding prisoners-of-war when traded for cigarettes, extra blankets or other concessions.

I began to consider that the watch might belong to someone who was at the scene of the massacre other than one of the band members. It struck me that this curious watch might be a family heirloom and that it could contain some hidden clue to the identity of its owner. I examined it with a magnifying glass, but I couldn't find any tell-tale signs. I didn't want to open the back as I thought that should be left to an expert and so I contacted Keane's Jewellers in Cork city, who agreed to examine it. The engineer told me that there were markings on the inside of the back cover which, he said, indicated a previous repair and that the markings identified the repair shop along with the repairer's initials. Inscribed inside was 61, denoting the date of repair as 1961, and 890-N-50X along with mspg, which indicated that the main spring had been replaced. The letters EBTH were also found inside the back cover, though the last letter could be N. The engineer told me that the calibration was 592/1403 and also showed me the number 157 \ 1 \ 1 \ 5 \ \61.

After he screwed on the back cover, he said, 'I'm sorry I couldn't find a name inside the watch – but there is one on the outside.' I was amazed. I told him I'd examined it with a magnifying glass, but I couldn't find anything. 'You won't find it with an ordinary magnifying glass, but try this,' he replied, handing me a jeweller's loupe. To my astonishment 'G. Savage', written in a script lettering, was plain to see. At first we thought G might possibly be a C but the consensus was that it was in fact a capital G. The manufacturer's reference on the back of the watch was 323130.

As I walked out of Keane's, my mind was racing. I knew I had to have it photographed for the record, but how? I had hardly stepped onto Oliver Plunkett Street when I saw a man holding a sign advertising a new computer repair shop, close to where I had just emerged. The owner was very helpful, focusing a microscope on the back of the watch. He then placed his smartphone on the eyepiece and captured a number of crystal-clear, magnified images of the inscribed watch.

I went back home to my office and googled 'G. Savage' with 'Northern Ireland'. The very first search resulted in a name that corresponded with that of a prominent Northern Ireland individual. I felt that my research had yielded enough to enquire further into the matter so I handed it over to Margaret Urwin of Justice for the Forgotten for her advice, and she then contacted the Historical Enquiries Team (HET). Following a formal request, she passed it on to them. Margaret Urwin assured me that she received a receipt for the watch from the HET.

I decided to contact Ian Newell to tell him what I had discovered and I told him to expect a visit from the HET. I did so because I felt he deserved to be made aware of the situation. He sounded surprised, but thanked me for letting him know. He called me a few days later, telling me that his father had received many commendations for his police work and that he didn't want any aspersions cast on his father's reputation. I told him that while I regretted any inconvenience to him, my first duty was to my murdered friends and to uncovering the truth about their murders. I felt very uneasy about upsetting this man who, in all innocence, had attempted to do a good deed. However, given that his attitude on the phone was far from friendly, I was not surprised when he denied that he ever said that the watch or its container was labelled 'Miami Showband'. He insisted that the only reason he connected the watch to the murders was because it looked like the watch Brian was wearing on the cover of my book. This connection would stretch the imagination of any professional investigating team but, apparently, not that of the HET.

I later received an angry phone call from the journalist Greg Harkin, who echoed Ian Newell's assertion. I reminded him of his initial call and his tone softened, saying, 'If I thought there was a story here, I would be the first onto it.'

I eagerly waited for a report on the watch from the HET, but I was appalled to learn that their officers had returned it to Ian Newell. I called the HET officer and asked why this potentially important piece of evidence in the Miami Showband murder case had been given back to Mr Newell, but he said that they were satisfied with Mr Newell's story. I asked if they interviewed the high-profile person whose name corresponded with the name on the watch and I was told they had not. I told the officer that unless all avenues were seen to be explored and an acceptable reason for ruling out any further enquiry into the watch was given, any conclusions of the HET investigation into state collusion with terrorists could be open to serious, legitimate criticism. The HET investigator then agreed to retrieve the watch until we were satisfied that it could be safely ruled out of the investigation, but Ian Newell later insisted that the HET never asked him to return the watch.

In August 2016 Truth and Reconciliation Platform co-founder Eugene Reavey and I met with a BBC Northern Ireland reporter, Kevin Magee, in Newry. Eugene had told him about the 'Savage' watch and Kevin Magee was keen to feature the story on his radio show. Shortly afterwards, he contacted me and asked me to meet Ian Newell, in order to give him an opportunity to convince me that I was 'mistaken about the watch'. He added that the meeting would be recorded for his radio programme. I agreed and we met at the BBC in Belfast on 9 September. The meeting began pleasantly, but when Mr Newell realised that he wasn't making any headway, he resorted to insults, at which point I terminated the meeting. During the course of the conversation at the BBC, I asked Mr Newell if he would hand over the watch to the Police Ombudsman for Northern Ireland (PONI), but he wouldn't give a me a definitive answer. He also refused to allow Kevin Magee's producer to start recording the discussion for the radio programme.

I sent high-resolution images of the 'Savage' watch to our Belfast solicitor, Michael Flanigan, and also to a number of prominent national and international journalists. I also sent them to Jon Boutcher, the head of Operation Kenova and Operation Denton, which was investigating all of the Glennane murders including the Miami Showband massacre. On 7 November 2023, Jon Boutcher was appointed chief constable of the Police Service of Northern Ireland.

Below are the notes I made on the day that the watch was professionally inspected and photographed with the aid of a microscope which clearly showed the name 'G Savage' inscribed on the back plate:

> Why was this watch kept for thirty-five years, in a box marked 'Miami Showband', by a detective police officer who worked on the case in 1975?
> KM watches, according to a reputable collector, were issued exclusively to German Navy officers during World War II.
> Model Alpina 592
> Manufacturer's reference on the back 323130.
> G Savage inscribed by hand on the back.
> Calibration
> 592 /1403
> (592 over 1403)
> 157 \ 1 \ 1 \ 5 \ \61
> (Repair details written on the inside; 61 = 1961)
> 890-N-50X
> mspg (short for mainspring?)
> EBTH (last letter night be N)
> Shop initials and repairer initials.

The watch was examined at Keane's Jewellers, Oliver Plunkett Street, Cork, on Monday, 6 December 2010.

14
Truth and Reconciliation Platform

TaRP, the 'philosopher's stone' that turned the terrible trauma of victims into a powerful force for good.

I knew Michael O'Hare as a musician who played guitar and sang with the resident band at the Galtymore Dance Club in Cricklewood. The Galty, as it was affectionately known, was a home from home for the Irish in London since it first opened in 1952 until it finally closed its doors in 2008. Michael has a lovely, classic country-music singing voice – smooth as silk. While the Galty was primarily a country and Irish dance venue, especially in its later years, the management was mindful of the new wave of young Irish who emigrated to London in the 1980s and 1990s, and so the entertainment agency I had set up in 1990 was contracted to book suitable pop and rock bands for the venue on selected nights. Every so often I'd drop in for a chat with the manager, Michael Byrne, and to check that the bands were happy too.

I met Michael O'Hare in the upstairs café one night in 1999 after his band had finished their stint and the visiting Irish band had taken over, but he wasn't his usual affable self; in fact, he was visibly distraught. Over a coffee, Michael told me that the Reverend Ian Paisley MP had, under parliamentary privilege, falsely accused his neighbour and friend Eugene Reavey of having set up the Kingsmill massacre. He named Michael, along with some others including a

10-year-old boy, of 'having good knowledge' of what happened 'on that dreadful day'.[1]

I couldn't believe my ears. I didn't know Eugene Reavey back then, but I knew you couldn't meet a nicer or more decent person than Michael O'Hare. 'Well, you do know my background, don't you?' he asked, but, in all the years I'd known him, it hadn't registered with me that Michael's sister was Majella O'Hare.

On a warm summer afternoon in 1976, 12-year-old Majella O'Hare was skipping down the road in the tiny village of Whitecross in County Armagh on her way to confession when, having just passed a British army checkpoint, shots rang out from a machine gun and two bullets struck Majella in the back. Majella's father, Jim O'Hare, was cutting the grass at the village school nearby when he heard the gunfire. Jim ran to the road and broke through the soldiers only to find his precious child dying on the ground. The soldiers, all members of Britain's elite parachute regiment, verbally abused the distraught father. Close by in the little churchyard a young nurse, Alice Devlin, was praying as she placed flowers on the grave of her fiancé, Brian Reavey, one of the three Reavey brothers murdered at their home on 4 January 1976, the day before the Kingsmill massacre. On hearing the commotion she ran to the scene, where she tried to administer help. Eventually, a British army helicopter arrived to take the little girl to Daisy Hill Hospital in Newry. Throughout the short journey, Alice – one of the nurses who took care of me at Daisy Hill Hospital following the Miami Showband massacre – was subjected to vile abuse by the paras. Even as she cradled the dying child in her arms, the soldiers continued to abuse the young nurse, kicking her and spitting on her and calling her a 'Fenian bitch'. By the time they arrived at the hospital Majella was dead, but instead of allowing her father to carry his child to the hospital building, the soldiers deliberately flung the young girl's dead body out onto the grass.

At his trial in 1977 Michael Williams, a member of the parachute regiment, claimed he had opened fire in response to an attack by an IRA sniper in the ditch, and so he was acquitted of Majella's manslaughter. At the end of the trial Majella's broken-hearted mother, Mary, asked Williams why he did it, but he made no answer. In 2011 the Ministry of Defence formally apologised to the O'Hare family, saying that the soldier's version of events 'was unlikely'. However, Majella's family remains adamant that an apology without an investigation is not enough.

Furthermore, although it contravenes every human rights convention, the British government passed the Northern Ireland Troubles (Legacy and Reconciliation) Act of 2023, a law specifically designed to deny victims like Majella O'Hare's family access to justice through the law courts.

As part of his Irish studies programme at St Mary's University London, mature student Michael O'Hare created a project entitled 'Troubles, Tragedy and Trauma: Northern Ireland's Historic Legacy'. Scheduled for 30 January 2016 to coincide with the forty-fourth anniversary of Bloody Sunday, the project incorporated an event that featured contributions from a respected panel of journalists and analysts including former Irish army officer Senator Tom Clonan, Northern Ireland political journalist and author Eamonn Mallie, Jane Winter of Irish Rights Watch UK and *Guardian* journalist Owen Bowcott. The event was chaired by the visiting Professor in Irish Studies and former President of Ireland Dr Mary McAleese. Along with myself, the other three speakers or 'witnesses' were Alan McBride, husband of Sharon McBride who was murdered in the Shankill fish bar bombing in 1993, Joe Campbell, son of RUC Sergeant Joseph Campbell who was murdered at Cushendall in 1977, and Eugene Reavey, whose three brothers were murdered at their family home at Whitecross in 1976.

Alan McBride and I were interviewed together for a BBC Radio morning programme. We met for the first time in the hotel lobby after breakfast to travel together to Broadcasting House. It was a cautious meeting – a northern Protestant sharing a London cab with a southern Irish Catholic, both having had their lives changed forever by the Troubles. Alan's 29-year-old wife, Sharon, had been working in her father's fish shop, Frizzell's, on Belfast's Shankill Road at lunchtime on 23 October 1993 when two IRA men entered the premises carrying a bomb that exploded almost immediately. Nine people died as a result, including one of the bombers, and almost sixty people were injured. Sharon and her father, Desmond Frizzell, were among the victims that day.

Alan didn't know if I'd be bitter or angry or vengeful as a result of my experience, so he initially opted for what strangers in Northern Ireland often do and resorted to the tactic enshrined forever in the title of Seamus Heaney's poem, 'Whatever you say, say nothing.' Five minutes into the journey, however, he broke the silence. 'I believe you were in the Miami Showband. I wasn't old enough to know much about them, but I hear they were very good.' I asked him what music he liked. 'Bagatelle,' he replied without hesitation. A door opened. 'Really? Their lead singer, Liam Reilly, is an old friend of mine.' That was it, the talking began. Alan McBride and I chatted about 'Summer in Dublin' and 'Trump Card' and 'Raining in Paris Tonight' and 'The Streets of New York' and many more of Liam's brilliant compositions all the way to Broadcasting House. Once again, music proved to be the bridge that connects people and communities. As Fr Brian D'Arcy, the unofficial chaplain to the showbands, regularly reminds us, 'Both communities consider showbands part of their heritage.'

Michael O'Hare's 'Troubles, Tragedy and Trauma: Northern Ireland's Historic Legacy' event was a huge success. It was standing room only.

While the London event provided victims from different backgrounds with a platform from which to share intimate testimony of real-life experience, it also presented the audience with a rare opportunity to consider the appalling consequences of politically motivated violence. It was at once shocking and inspiring, but it was the highly emotional reaction of all present that left Eugene Reavey, Joe Campbell and I in no doubt that such a powerful experience had to be shared with a wider world, and so Truth and Reconciliation Platform (TaRP) was established to give every victim of the Troubles an opportunity to tell his or her own personal story.

From the very beginning, TaRP enjoyed widespread and enthusiastic cross-party and cross-border political encouragement, with messages of support coming in from everyone from Fianna Fáil's Micheál Martin and Fine Gael's Charlie Flanagan to the DUP's Sir Jeffrey Donaldson, Sinn Féin's Martin McGuinness and even the British government's Northern Ireland Office.

Initially, TaRP events attracted audiences of around fifty to a hundred people. Our intention was to develop and grow the events and fill larger venues across the island of Ireland, presenting discourse and testimony from a broad range of victims and panellists. However, word soon spread, and before long, Eugene, Joe and I, along with many of the witnesses who took part in the live TaRP events, were invited onto the national and international airwaves to tell our stories. The BBC and UTV featured counter-radicalisation testimony from TaRP witnesses, as did almost every national and regional newspaper. On Saturday 16 April 2016, the Al Jazeera television network recorded a special TaRP event at All Souls Church in Belfast.

Thanks to the support of Ireland's Department of Foreign Affairs' Reconciliation Fund, we were able to present TaRP events at venues across the island of Ireland and at schools and colleges where hundreds of students from both Catholic and Protestant communities heard first-hand accounts of the consequences of violence.

TaRP gave me an invaluable insight into the suffering of my fellow victims of the Troubles. Every event was riveting, shocking and intensely emotional. I had the privilege of meeting and interacting with the bravest of the brave. I watched men and women, most of whom had never spoken publicly before, open their hearts about their trauma and loss. There were countless occasions when there wasn't a dry eye in the audience. Most astonishing of all, I witnessed many who had previously considered themselves powerless, having stepped nervously onto the podium, go on to capture and hold audiences in the palm of their hands. TaRP convinced me, beyond any doubt, that there is not a more efficient deterrent to violence or a more effective antidote to radicalisation than the testimony of the victim.

Unfortunately, however, there are those who do not want victims to speak for themselves. Some want to control the narrative to suit their own personal bias or political agenda, others because they don't want to hear an inconvenient truth. Others still are so hurt or damaged by their experience that they denounce or even sabotage any attempt at dialogue. I have personally experienced the vitriol of some very vocal victims who chose to focus only on my interlocutor and to ignore what I said to them.

In July 2021 I took part in a webinar entitled 'Make Britain Keep Promise of Legacy Justice'. The discussion was organised by the Ancient Order of Hibernians (AOH) in the USA and hosted by the former Noraid director Martin Galvin, and included a senior Irish government official, Ciarán Madden, and a member of the Oireachtas, Neale Richmond, as well as members of the US government and judiciary, and relatives of murder victims of the Troubles. My opening statement was unequivocal in its condemnation of all violence. I thanked the organisers for the opportunity to tell my story, but added that 'horrific as it is, it should not be held up in isolation to use as a stick to beat any one community since terrible atrocities were committed against both communities and anyone who had hand, act or part in such atrocities must be held accountable'. Despite this, I was accused on social media of being 'aligned with terrorists' and, by association, our organisation TaRP was also vilified. This lie put my reputation and my life in danger. Bizarrely, while one high-profile victim was publicly defaming me, that same individual was privately emailing me to praise the great work I was doing with TaRP. (Needless to say, I have kept all of that person's emails.)

I subsequently wrote to the chief instigator who, curiously, didn't target the Irish or American government officials who had also taken part in the webinar or, by association, the Irish or American governments! Presumably, the fact that the Irish government was paying his wages seriously diluted his integrity. These are my words:

> Dear ...
> Instigating a hate campaign against me on social media because we differ on how best to deliver a message of truth and reconciliation to as broad an audience as possible, which I know is precious to both of us, is not right. But, even if you continue to enthusiastically direct hatred towards me, I will not, and would never, respond to you or to any traumatised victim in a negative way; I know only too well how it impacts, but I hope you will stop.
> God bless you and give you peace,
> Stephen.

Following a successful legal action taken against him by another person he had also publicly libelled, the chief instigator removed his posts against me from his social media account some months later.

The target, on that occasion, was a TaRP initiative called 'Victims of the Troubles Assembly' (VoTTA) that was designed to give all victims a collective voice as set out in the following email, and which was enthusiastically greeted by all except for a handful of recipients who, instead of just declining the offer to participate in the enterprise, decided to sabotage it:

VoTTA

A Truth and Reconciliation Platform Project

The reported meeting on legacy issues at Lambeth Palace, the Archbishop of Canterbury's official residence in London, between governments, intelligence agencies and representatives of paramilitary organisations in October 2020, resulted in a predictable outcry from victims and survivors of the so-called 'Troubles'. In the main, the discontent appeared to be due to the exclusion of victims' and survivors' representatives rather than to the inclusion of others but, either way, the absence of an effective, coordinated victims' and survivors' response to that event, or indeed to many other 'legacy issues' discussions, was not surprising since there are differing views and perspectives present even among those who share the all-too-common scars of victimhood.

With common purpose and determination, victims are capable of remarkable achievements; as witnessed recently in the heroic efforts of a group of intrepid victims from the WAVE Trauma organisation who succeeded in securing a 'victims' pension' but it would take a brave person or organisation to claim to *speak for* or *on behalf of* all the victims and survivors of the so-called 'Troubles'.

Truth and Reconciliation Platform (TaRP), was founded in 2016 by victims and survivors to enable victims and survivors to 'speak for themselves' and, continuing with that model, TaRP is currently in the process of establishing 'Victims of the Troubles Assembly' or VoTTA based on a Citizens Assembly where one hundred cross-community members (Chair + 99) will discuss and debate victims' and survivors' issues, respond to government proposals and relay the precise level of consensus within VoTTA to governments, to the national and international media and to other relevant bodies as well as to the general public.

TaRP does not 'speak for' victims or survivors; as its name indicates, it simply provides a platform which, in this case, will be the assembly and, regardless of the degree of divergence on any issue, the resulting ballot will be faithfully recorded and published. VoTTA aims to ensure that Victims and Survivors will never be sidelined or ignored on legacy issues again.

VoTTA is expected to be in operation by mid-September, 2021 and TaRP would like to offer you a seat on the 'Victims of the Troubles Assembly'.

Once established, the members will assume total control of the democratic victims' assembly.

We look forward to your reply.

Kind Regards,
Joe Campbell Chairman of VoTTA
Stephen Travers Chairman and Co-Founder of TaRP
Eugene Reavey Treasurer and Co-Founder of TaRP

Unfortunately, the lie they spread about me was reinforced by other 'self-righteous' victims, one of whom posted the following on social media: 'I write this with a heavy heart as I announce my withdrawal from the Victims Assembly. I will always support innocent victims from all sides of the Troubles but cannot be associated with those who align with and legitimise victim makers. My principals [sic] and morals are first.' Curiously, his principles and morals allowed him to denounce dialogue while, at the same time, basking in the comfort and safety of the peace that dialogue had delivered.

It came as no surprise, however, that, since the suffering of some of my most ardent and vocal detractors had been caused by republican violence, not one of them had criticised me for my well-publicised meetings with loyalist paramilitary representatives.

While I empathise and sympathise with fellow victims and understand their anger, they do not have the right to bully other victims who refuse to see the world as they do. My record speaks for itself. I have engaged with victims of all political and religious persuasions, with loyalist and republican organisations, with members and former members of the British security forces, with British and Irish government ministers and their officials and with members of the British royal family. I have sat at the table with the representatives of those who bombed and shot me and murdered my bandmates and I will continue to raise the case for justice for all at every opportunity regardless of any criticism or attempted character assassination by those who believe that they have a right to impose their bitterness on the world and choose to ignore the fact that, without such dialogue, the Belfast/Good Friday Agreement could never have been delivered.

Their smear campaign was amplified by trolls on social media and, consequently, TaRP did not continue with the VoTTA project, leaving victims, from all traditions, unprepared for the consequences that would emanate from 'the reported meeting on legacy issues at Lambeth Palace, the Archbishop of Canterbury's official residence in London, between governments, intelligence agencies and representatives of paramilitary organisations in October 2020', namely, The Northern Ireland Troubles (Legacy and Reconciliation) Act 2023, which denied all victims (including themselves and their own loved ones), from all traditions, access to justice through the courts.

I am convinced that there are even more sinister forces at work. In the summer of 2016, I noticed a tiny camera on the lapel of a former, discredited Northern Ireland politician when he was on what he claimed was 'a goodwill visit' to County Cork in an attempt to rehabilitate himself, which I was happy to facilitate. Surprisingly, he admitted, there and then, that it took a picture every thirty seconds. When I asked why he was using it, he just laughed and said photography was his hobby.

Later that summer I was invited to a meeting at his house where he carefully positioned me on a couch in his lounge before asking me to confirm that I had once made a derogatory remark about unionism – which I most certainly had not. Having worked with camera crews for decades, it was perfectly clear that I was being filmed, but his efforts were so amateurish that it was almost comical. I told him that I was having none of his nonsense and I walked out. As a result, he and his accomplice became markedly frustrated and angry. Fortunately, my friend Ken Murray was there to witness the entire farce.

It's easy to deliver a talk or present your book or show your film to a sympathetic audience. It's never a challenge to preach to the converted. TaRP, however, has facilitated the testimonies of victims of all political and religious persuasions at venues across the island of Ireland, even in places where such attestations are difficult to accept and, in some cases, even to hostile audiences. We have availed of every opportunity to highlight the reality of suffering and the consequences of supporting or employing violence as a political expedient or of accepting violence as a legitimate way to change society. These have included contributing to a documentary marking the twentieth anniversary of the Good Friday Agreement, attending the twenty-fifth anniversary memorial service for the victims of the Shankill Road Bombing and addressing the closing rally of the Bloody Sunday March Committee in 2020. We were always grateful for the opportunity to empathise and show solidarity with people whose courage and resilience have long been an inspiration to us.

In October 2019 I was honoured as 'Person of the Year' by the Irish Book Arts and Media (IBAM) organisation in Chicago. (Previous recipients of the award included Nobel Laureate John Hume and Richard Moore from Children in Crossfire.) At the IBAM gala dinner in Chicago, I assured six hundred of the great and the good of that city that the use of violence in pursuit of a united Ireland was entirely counterproductive.

It was the aim of TaRP to establish a purpose-designed 'peace centre' in Newry, County Down, to provide victims' groups, along with individual victims and their loved ones, with a secure place to work from and to facilitate dialogue and peace-building. Unfortunately, the COVID-19 pandemic put an end to those plans, but, thanks to the generosity and technical expertise of Tracy Dempsey, the Truth and Reconciliation Platform website was launched in July 2020, and became the home of the Miami Showband Peace Centre *Online*. It was named in memory of three young musicians of mixed religions, from north and south, who lost their lives in 1975 while working together in perfect harmony, to bring happiness and healing to everyone, regardless of social, religious or political background. That year, TaRP.ie began its online series 'Speaking for Myself' to give every victim of the Troubles an opportunity to tell their stories in their own words. Those testimonies have been viewed thousands of times around the world.

TaRP changed my life. Meeting with and hearing the testimonies of victims was an education for which I will be eternally grateful. 'Truth is stranger than fiction' certainly rings true, for I have heard many true stories of pain and loss and sorrow and sacrifice and courage that even the most ambitious authors of fiction would regard too outrageous to invent. I have personally seen how quickly precious lives can be extinguished but I have also seen how slowly, often over many decades, their fathers, mothers, siblings, children, partners, husbands, wives and companions take to die from the same bomb or bullet that killed their loved ones. Too often, the courage and sacrifices of those left behind, to 'live' with the consequences, go unacknowledged. I have seen countless examples of such strength, many of which continue to resonate so intensely with me that they have become part of my own experience.

15
The King and I

A hierarchy of victims and the inequality of acknowledgement.

Monday, 19 September 2022. The streets of London were shrouded in mourning. The eyes of the world were on the state funeral of Queen Elizabeth II. It was a fitting burial for a decent woman who deserved a good send-off, but it was difficult for me to watch the spectacle without mixed feelings. Soldiers in dress uniforms paraded bold as their shining brass across our television screens. Up and down familiar streets they marched to the tune of 'Rule, Britannia!'. Britannia waives the rules, I found myself muttering. Though the pageantry was extraordinary, for me it was nothing more than hollow symbolism. Yet this was still a nation that spawned so many of my heroes: artists, musicians, composers, writers, inventors, business colleagues and some of the best friends I have ever known.

As the cameras focused on the face of the new king, I was drawn back to the day I met him at a peace event high up in the beautiful Wicklow mountains back in 2019. When it was first proposed that I meet the then Prince Charles, I was less than enthusiastic. I had no interest in the Colonel-in-Chief of Britain's elite parachute regiment that murdered innocent people at Ballymurphy and again, less than six months later, on the streets of Derry on Bloody Sunday. Of course I knew that Charles was not personally responsible for those atrocities, but, given his stature and his status, I felt he should acknowledge the terrible wrongs committed by that regiment. Television commentators speculated that he might have inherited the credibility and tact of his mother. I hoped so.

As rows of decorated dignitaries filed past at the Queen's funeral, I was reminded of my friend John Teggart, who was just 11 years old when his father, Danny, was murdered by the parachute regiment as they swept through the Ballymurphy area of West Belfast to round up 'suspects' following the introduction of the British government's notorious 'Internment without Trial' in Northern Ireland on 9 August 1971. Over the course of three days, ten innocent people were shot dead, each of them unarmed. None of them posed any threat whatsoever; yet, for half a century, they were all branded as terrorists. To reinforce the official lie, some of the murderers from that 'elite' regiment were subsequently decorated with medals and received royal citations from their monarch.

I know John Teggart, I know some of the Ballymurphy families and I know how extraordinarily difficult their struggle for justice has been and how brave and strong they had to be to keep on fighting, decade after decade, to clear the names of their loved ones. As John has repeated many times, 'There were twenty-seven murders across the north that week in August 1971. The Ballymurphy massacre families have spent years knocking on doors, taking statements, meeting with all sorts of politicians and doing everything we can to try and clear our loved ones' names.'

I also know that, had I not survived to tell the truth of what happened at the Miami Showband massacre, I would also have been condemned as a terrorist by the British and, probably, by the rest of the world too.

I couldn't see any point in meeting Prince Charles, but the hosts suggested that since his grand-uncle, mentor and 'honorary grandfather' Lord Louis Mountbatten, along with his 14-year-old grandson Nicholas Knatchbull, Doreen Knatchbull and Paul

Maxwell, a teenage boy from Enniskillen, had been murdered by the IRA at Mullaghmore in County Sligo in 1979, we could meet as 'fellow victims on a journey of understanding and reconciliation'. So, in that context, I agreed to meet Charles.

Regardless of my utter distain for Mountbatten, when Charles extended his hand to me I offered my condolences on the loss of his relatives. But when he replied simply, 'Thank you very much,' I was disappointed – for him – that he had missed a historic, symbolic 'reconciliation' opportunity by not offering his condolences on the loss of my murdered bandmates. Instead, he just made small talk, and so did I. Nevertheless, I had a contingency plan; handing him a copy of *The Miami Showband Massacre: A Survivor's Search for the Truth,* I said, 'Maybe you'll find time to read this.' He glanced at the book, passed it to his aide and said, 'I will indeed.' I don't know if he ever did read it, but he should.

Charles commented on 'the tremendous work' of TaRP and wished me every success before moving on to my TaRP co-founder Eugene Reavey, who was standing next to me. As Camilla and I were shaking hands, Eugene and Prince Charles were shaking hands too. In his unmistakable, booming South Armagh voice I heard Eugene thunder, 'Well, you're a fine cut of a man!' Still holding onto Charles's hand, he gave him a friendly thump in the chest with his left fist and continued, 'There can't be much between our ages.' With each word, Eugene continued his friendly thumping. He finished with a bizarre and unforgettable challenge: 'I'll arm-wrestle you for a fiver!' As I counted the five friendly thumps, I expected security to jump in and wrestle Eugene to the ground, but Charles shook Eugene's hand all the more and they both laughed. Camilla and I exchanged pleasantries and everyone had tea. When I asked Eugene what it was all about, he just shrugged his broad shoulders and said, 'Ah, I was just having the craic with Charlie.'

Eugene Reavey is a joyful man, intelligent, funny and strong as a bull, and often on the frontline between survivors who want to know the truth and those who fear it being exhumed. On 4 January 1976 his three younger brothers, Brian, John-Martin and Anthony, were in the living room of the family cottage in Whitecross, County Armagh, watching *Celebrity Squares* on TV, when three masked gunmen walked in and opened fire on them. John-Martin and Brian were killed outright. Anthony, although badly wounded, managed to take cover but died under suspicious circumstances less than a month later.

With over a thousand people gathered at the Reavey brothers' wake outside the family home, local republican leaders saw a recruitment opportunity. They arrived in a big black car, but before they could get a foothold Eugene's mother, Sadie Reavey, held her ground and asked everyone to kneel and say a decade of the rosary for her sons. The recruiting officers got back in their car and left.

Eugene is often asked why he didn't join the IRA; indeed, some have tried to shame him for not 'avenging' his three brothers. The pressure to prove himself was immense. Vivid memories of lifting one of his dead brothers from the fireplace with cinders still burning his flesh will haunt him forever, but he insists that he could never put anyone else through such pain. On the day following the murders, Eugene's father, Jimmy, spoke directly to the TV cameras and said, 'I want no retaliation against the people who killed my sons.'

It is worth remembering that it was the first such televised appeal and would be echoed almost twelve years later by Gordon Wilson who told on-the-scene BBC reporters that he forgave the IRA for the Remembrance Day bombing at the Enniskillen Cenotaph as his beloved daughter Marie lay dying in the rubble. Mr Wilson said he would pray every night for the men who murdered her. Until the day she died, Sadie Reavey lit a candle in the window every night for the men who murdered her three sons.

Before he died, Jimmy Reavey made his sons swear on the family Bible that they would never seek revenge. Eugene was true to his word, seeking only the truth – not revenge – but the anger remains. He is a man haunted by the murders, especially by what happened on the road home from Daisy Hill hospital where he and his mother had gone to officially identify the bodies of John-Martin and Brian.

It is not difficult to imagine the awful atmosphere in the car that evening. Eugene's mother was distraught with grief. She was tightly clutching a bag of her murdered sons' bloodied clothes when they were stopped at a British army checkpoint. The soldiers ordered them to get out of the car and, while Eugene was held at gunpoint by one soldier, another soldier began sexually abusing his traumatised mother to the cheers of his depraved comrades. While his comrades-in-arms laughed heartily and danced on the blood-soaked clothes that they wrenched from her arms, the degenerate British soldier fondled the bereaved mother in front of her son. Throughout her terrible ordeal, the dignified lady kept her eyes firmly focused on Eugene, silently begging him not to give her abusers an excuse to murder yet another of her sons if he ran to her rescue. Eugene recalls that the young soldier pressing a machine gun into his back was 'shaking like a leaf'. To this day, he is tormented by guilt for not being able to protect his beloved mother.

Following the murder of his three brothers, Eugene Reavey, then just 27 years old and with a wife and young family, eventually returned to work. On his first day back, the British army stopped him just down the road from where his brothers were murdered and ordered him out of his car. The soldiers proceeded to ransack the car. They even removed the wheels and threw them over the hedge into a field. Assaulting Eugene with the butts of their rifles and calling him a terrorist, they repeatedly forced his head into the freezing river until he almost drowned. This harassment continued for weeks, but when I asked him why he didn't take a different route to work, he said, 'I wouldn't give the bastards the satisfaction.'

The Reverend Ian Paisley died on 12 September 2014 without retracting the false accusation he made against Eugene Reavey under parliamentary privilege. However, in 2010, a police Historical Enquiries Team (HET) report cleared Eugene of any involvement in the Kingsmill massacre. The Reavey family sought an apology from Paisley, but he refused. Over the years, Eugene lobbied anyone he thought might be able to assist in having the House of Commons statement expunged or corrected, but his pleas fell on deaf ears. Paisley's death in 2014 put paid to any hopes that Eugene or his family had of the firebrand cleric correcting his false statement or apologising.

However, on 11 November 2020, the Labour Member of Parliament for St Helens North, Conor McGinn, told a parliamentary committee in Westminster that Paisley's allegation 'caused incredible pain' and that 'it was and is completely and utterly false'. Mr McGinn went on to say, 'Eugene Reavey had no involvement whatsoever in Kingsmills and I think it's right the record is corrected here today.' Minister Robin Walker, the Conservative MP for Worcester, responded shortly afterwards and said, 'I thank the honourable member for St Helens North, in particular, for the important intervention he has made on this matter and note that the PSNI's Historical Enquiries Team found no wrongdoing whatsoever by Eugene Reavey in the incident that he raises.'

16
Survival

All too often, the suffering and the heroism of those left behind goes unrecognised.

Kate

On 26 June 2018 a Truth and Reconciliation Platform event, organised by Denise Johnston and chaired by one of the great negotiators of the Good Friday Agreement, Seamus Mallon, took place at St Patrick's Parish Hall in Lisburn. The witnesses were Kate Carroll, Eugene Reavey, Alan McBride and me. At this point, Eugene, Alan and I were well accustomed to speaking at TaRP events, but, as it was Kate's first Truth and Reconciliation Platform testimony, she was, understandably, quite nervous. Eugene took me to meet Kate at her home a few weeks prior to the event where she told us her heartbreaking story.

Settling into a new life following her divorce in 1983, Kate was enjoying a new-found independence in the little Banbridge flat she shared with her son Shane. As the months passed, her friend Anne thought it would be good for Kate to enjoy a night out and convinced Kate to go with her to the Front Bar. However, when Anne's boyfriend and his friend Steve sat down at their table, she began to suspect that she had been set up. While Anne and her boyfriend danced, Kate and Steve chatted, and the more he talked, the more she liked him. He was sporty and fit, a happy-go-lucky guy, but, when he offered to buy her a drink, her guardedness immediately resurfaced. 'No, thank you,' she replied. 'I can buy my own.' Undaunted, Steve persevered. He liked her and he wanted to see her again, but Kate wasn't ready. 'I like you too, but I'm just not ready for a relationship. Let's take our time.' In fact, Kate did everything to discourage him. She was ten years older than Steve and she worried that the age difference could be a problem as they got older. There was also a risk that his job might require him to go to England, so she felt they had no future together. 'I'm not getting my son involved with anyone who'll just get up and go.' Nevertheless, Steve persisted, and they were soon inseparable. A year later, on St Patrick's Day 1984, Kate said yes when he proposed.

Following their marriage in 1985, Steve began looking for a career change. He enjoyed his work in the Royal Military Police but wanted to stay in Northern Ireland with Kate and so he took a security job at the airport. Meanwhile, he applied to join the Harbour Police as well as the Royal Ulster Constabulary. The interview with the RUC took place first, and, although his expectations were low, he was successful. Steve was hired as a police constable on 13 March. Kate felt it was a good omen as they'd met on 13 July and their first home together was number 13, so, as far as she was concerned, it was meant to be.

It was a dangerous time to be a policeman. On 28 February 1985, the Provisional IRA launched a heavy mortar attack on the RUC base at Corry Square in Newry, which killed nine RUC officers and injured almost forty others. It was the highest death toll ever suffered by the RUC. Naturally, Kate was afraid. Steve was an RUC rookie at a time when there were few Catholics in the security forces. Steve had told her how he struggled with the hatred he experienced at work and in the community; he was often referred to as 'the Micky Brit', a reference to the fact that he was born in England and lived there until he was 8 years old before moving to Newbridge in County Kildare. Although the name may have been used in jest, Kate felt it was 'a Northern Ireland joke with a jag'. The couple never experienced anything like that in England or south of the border. 'Even today, when I travel over the border to go to County Mayo,' she says, 'a huge weight lifts off my shoulders. I don't have to worry about being Catholic or Protestant and I can say "My name is Kathleen Carroll" and nobody questions my religion.' This was not the case at her husband's workplace. Steve always wore a small crucifix, a treasured gift that Kate gave him for protection, but, emerging from the shower at work one evening, he was challenged by an RUC colleague: 'What's that around your neck? Get it off immediately,' the man demanded.

Kate felt like a second-class citizen. 'With Steve being Catholic, it almost felt worse. Nobody wanted you. Your own side didn't want you and the other side didn't trust Catholics. It was terrible.' Half-Irish, half-English and a Catholic serving in the RUC, Steve was a target. 'He was always a target, no matter where he went. He wasn't allowed to wear his uniform outside. We weren't allowed to go to Newry or Dundalk or to any other "high-risk" places. Our lives were dictated.'

Once again, Kate was no longer in charge of her own life. 'Our lives were completely mapped out,' she recalls. As a policeman's wife, she was constantly fearful, and Steve regularly checked underneath their cars to make sure there were no bombs attached. He would vary his route to work and make sure that nobody followed him. Even at home, Kate was vigilant. When she did the laundry, she would take care not to hang Steve's uniform on the washing line in case neighbours saw the RUC insignia, and she lied to people about what he did for a living. It was easier to say he was a PE teacher than to tell the truth and put him at risk. 'I couldn't be a normal person. I was a policeman's wife. There were places we wanted to go, but we couldn't because Steve might be recognised as a police officer. When we went away, it was usually down south. I was never one hundred per cent happy except when we were on holiday in Mayo or when we went to Canada. Part of me was always on high alert. I lived with a gnawing dread.'

By 2009 Steve was planning early retirement. He was focused on completing a degree in sports science and looking forward to working from home. It was over a decade since the Good Friday Agreement was signed and, despite sporadic attacks, a delicate peace prevailed in Northern Ireland until Saturday 7 March when, as Steve watched football on TV, the news broke that two young British soldiers had been shot dead at the Masserene army base in Antrim, just hours before they were due to fly out to Afghanistan. They had walked out to the gates to collect a pizza delivery where two gunmen were waiting for them with semi-automatic rifles. In an instant, her worst fears and forebodings resurfaced, and Kate was terrified that Steve might be the next victim. That ordinary Saturday, which began with the couple choosing furniture at IKEA for Steve's future home office, ended in despair. Neither of them could silence their inner warning voices. Over dinner that evening, Kate told Steve she never wanted to experience what the families of the two British soldiers were going through. Contemplating their own mortality, Steve said that, should violence return to Northern Ireland and anything happen to him, he wanted 'Pie Jesu' sung at his funeral. Kate told him to stop and, to lighten the conversation, she said, 'If you go before me, I want you to stand at the gates and keep St Peter busy while I climb over the wall.'

Kate's anxiety following the killing of Quinsey and Azimkar – the first soldiers to be murdered in Northern Ireland since the Provisional IRA ceasefire in 1997 – intensified. The next day they took a trip to Silent Valley near Newcastle and, looking out over the beautiful Mountains of Mourne, Kate thought again of the two soldiers and their families. 'I'm so lucky I have my husband with me. I just want him to be safe.'

Steve sensed her unease as he left for work the next day and, as always before leaving, he told her he loved her. 'Give me a kiss. Give me another one now. That'll keep me right all day. If I die now, I'll die a happy man.'

Upset and not wanting to hear that kind of talk she replied, 'I just want you to be safe and come home to me. I love you and I'll see you tonight.'

When Kate came home from work, she found three Post-it notes. He always left notes on the door, little assurances he felt she needed to get her through the worrying times. 'I love you.' 'I'm sorry if I upset you.' Underneath, she wrote, 'I love you.' She knew he wouldn't be home until midnight and so, expecting him to call or text by 9.30 p.m., she settled down to watch a documentary about meerkats. When the phone call didn't come, she assumed he was working late and returned to her documentary. However, when she spotted the lights of an approaching car, she thought he'd come home early for a change of clothes, so she put the kettle on and returned to see the familiar policeman's silhouette at the door. Wondering why Steve hadn't come in, she opened the door to see a policeman and a policewoman standing there. It was an eventuality, her husband had told her, which meant the worst had happened. Instantly, she recoiled. 'I begged them, over and over, not to tell me he was dead.'

'Kate, can you please sit down?' She didn't want to sit down. She didn't want to hear that Steve had been shot at 9.42 p.m. She didn't want them to calm her. She recalls the tidal wave of emotions as she paced back and forth, listening to words she didn't want to hear. 'It was like they were talking in the distance and my eyes were staring down this long black tunnel. My mind was racing. What was I going to do without him? Who's going to take me shopping? Oh my God! I hope they didn't hurt him. I hope he didn't feel anything. How will I get by? All this, all at once. I remember I didn't even cry. I couldn't. I ran to the wash basket and picked up one of his shirts and pressed it to my face so I could smell him. Then I walked into the conservatory and looked down at the floor. A little woodlouse had made its way inside. I picked it up and took it outside. I couldn't even kill a woodlouse, yet somebody had lifted a gun and killed my husband.

I couldn't even kill a fly. I had to write a note to myself to tell me my husband was dead. It was the worst I had ever felt in all my life.'

Just 48 years of age, Constable Stephen Carroll was the first member of the PSNI to be killed since the signing of the Good Friday Agreement. He was ambushed and shot in the head when he and a colleague were called out to respond to an emergency call in Craigavon. Carried out by a republican splinter group, the Continuity IRA, the attack was intended to lure police into the area. His murder united politicians of all persuasions. There was an outpouring of sympathy. Representatives of Sinn Féin and the DUP attended his requiem Mass. But the same questions were being asked on both sides of the Atlantic: why was Stephen Carroll murdered and who gained from his killing? How could he have been murdered now when we were promised peace?

While Kate tries to pick up the pieces of her shattered life and move on, every anniversary is difficult. In many ways, she feels she's being punished more than those who were convicted of Steve's murder. 'I don't want this cancerous feeling eating away at me. I forgive for myself, but I can't forgive for others. The years have been dreadful. I'm still suffering at their hands.' More than fifteen years on, she vividly recalls the excruciating grief and trauma of that time. 'We were so close. I recall one particular night during that first year, I was inconsolable. The loneliness was indescribable. It was just before Christmas. Snow was on the ground. I longed to embrace him, to feel my hand on his chest. I could see the graveyard from my garden. I got up at two o'clock in the morning and I went out to the shed and got a shovel. I was almost at my gate when I fell to my knees. I set the shovel down asking myself, "My God, what would people think?" but nothing mattered, only Steve mattered to me.' She was alone, traumatised and suffering, unaware and unprepared for the devastating reality that the bullets that killed her beloved husband would continue to travel and create even more pain.

Unable to recover from the loss of his stepfather, Kate's son Shane fell into a deep depression. Driven to avenge his father's death, he told his mother, 'I wish I could cry like you. I'm telling you, when they get out, I'll be there. If they get out of jail, I'm going after them. Where was God when my dad was murdered?' Kate worried that he was stuck in that awful moment when the police came to their door with the terrible news. Over the years, she took him to several specialists and she began to think that he was turning a corner and getting past his depression. Aged just 48, and by then a loving father himself, Shane was the same age as his stepfather when he died. He went to bed one night and never woke up. 'Maybe it was an overdose. Maybe he was trying to kill himself. I don't know if he meant to do it. I just know he couldn't go on.' Kate believes that the men who murdered Constable Stephen Carroll are also responsible for her son's death.

Today, from her bedroom window, Kate looks out at the cemetery where her son and her husband are buried. 'All taken away over a piece of ground, over a piece of an island that fell apart.' For Kate Carroll, an unwavering advocate for peace, 'Kindness is the easiest thing carried.' She is encouraged by the response from children when she shares her story in schools across Ireland. Nevertheless, since the attack on Detective Chief Inspector John Caldwell in February 2023, together with renewed threats against the families of police officers, she worries about the future. Kate is quick to remind us that peace is fragile and must never be taken for granted.

Kate's Truth and Reconciliation Platform testimony in Lisburn in June 2018 was extraordinarily powerful. Her gentle, sincere disposition immediately connected her with the audience and it continues to do so wherever she speaks. However, Kate's presentation to a large group of students at a TaRP counter-radicalisation 'border counties schools' event at Cavan County Museum five months later was nothing short of miraculous. The spellbound teenagers hung on to every word she said and they surrounded and hugged her when the event ended, prompting one of their teachers to remark, 'It looks like they've found a new hero today.'

Rosemary

I first met Rosemary Campbell on 14 September 2018, when we were holding a TaRP event in Cushendall, County Antrim. I thought I knew her story reasonably well since her son, our colleague Joe Campbell Jr, has been an integral part of TaRP from the very beginning. I was aware of her long and difficult fight for truth and justice for her beloved husband, Joseph, whom she married in May 1955, but Rosemary exceeded all of my expectations. From the moment I met her, it was clear to me that she was a formidable lady of remarkable dignity, courage and strength.

Joseph Patrick Campbell was born in Rathmullan, County Donegal, on 26 October 1928. Following in his father's footsteps, Joseph, along with his brother, George, cycled to Monaghan town in 1963 to join An Garda Síochána, the national police service of Ireland. However, to their dismay they discovered that there was a temporary moratorium on Garda recruitment and so they decided to try their luck over the border in County Fermanagh, where Joseph joined the RUC and was subsequently stationed in Moneymore and Crossmaglen.

Joseph Campbell was held in high regard by both the Catholic and Protestant communities and, on being promoted to sergeant, despite a petition with a thousand signatures asking that he be kept in Crossmaglen, he was transferred to the picturesque village of Cushendall in the green glens of Antrim, where he was equally well-liked and respected. Sergeant Joseph Campbell was essentially a community policeman some four decades before that role was officially recognised and, as such, he didn't always wear his police uniform.

Locals would regularly knock on the Campbell family's door if they had a problem. For him, success was not about the number of arrests he made, it was about how peaceful the village was under his watch. Joseph understood country folk and their day-to-day concerns such as the pub closing times and opening hours on Christmas Eve or Good Friday. He served his community as the quintessential glens man: affable and approachable. He enjoyed grouse-shooting with his dog, Franz – the runt of the first litter of Hungarian Vizsla pups in Ireland – that he'd brought home in a box one evening and who automatically became the ninth child of the Campbell family. It was an idyllic life.

Although he was just one of a small number of Catholic policemen in Northern Ireland, Joseph and Rosemary had never experienced any animosity towards themselves or their family. He avoided bringing his work home with him, having told Rosemary on the day they got engaged that his job would never be of any concern to her. He didn't share any case details with his wife, so she never really felt there was anything to worry about.

Nevertheless, by 1977 tension in Northern Ireland was at boiling point and Sergeant Campbell had changed. His family noticed that he was quieter at home, sometimes even irritable and preoccupied, but there was no indication that his painstaking police work had uncovered a major loyalist paramilitary arms-smuggling operation and that members of RUC Special Branch, together with the army in collusion with loyalist paramilitaries, were responsible for a spate of terrible atrocities. Sergeant Joseph Campbell knew too much and he was fearful for his life and for the safety of his family. Worryingly, there had been a number of threatening phone calls to the family home. On one occasion Rosemary answered the telephone to hear a menacing voice say, 'We wouldn't like to see you cry when they put a bullet in his head.' The male caller went on to say that her husband should 'mind his own business'. It was a nightmare that, until then, only seemed to happen to other people.

On the evening of 25 February 1977 Joe was off duty at home with Rosemary when he received two phone calls, the details of which he kept to himself. Looking up from her sewing, Rosemary watched as he put on his hat and opened the door. 'I'm away now,' he said. He didn't say why he was going out, but he took his police-issue firearm with him. Sergeant Campbell knew he wouldn't return. Rosemary recalls that her son Joey had already gone to the police station on an errand, and as he was coming out, he met his father on the way in. Joseph told his son to get back to the house quickly, so after driving two of his friends to the nearby village of Waterfoot and dropping them off outside the pub, Joey headed straight back, but by the time he got home, it was all over.

Just a few minutes before nine o'clock, a shot rang out through the village. Standing in her kitchen, Rosemary thought she was hearing a car backfire, but it was the sound of her husband being shot in the back of the head as he was locking the main gates of Cushendall Police Station.

Word spread quickly, and soon Fr White and a family friend were at Rosemary's side. At first, they advised her against going to see Sergeant Campbell at the hospital, but she was adamant and so they agreed to take her. 'You'll have to be very brave, Rosemary,' they told her. Her husband's lifeless body was covered with a white sheet and his head was wrapped in a bandage. Rosemary wept as Joey tried his best to comfort her. 'Mammy, you've no need to cry. Nothing to be sorry for. We only have to be proud of who Daddy was.'

In an instant Rosemary Campbell was a widow with eight children. The expectation was that she and her family would just have to 'get on with it'. 'We didn't know any better,' she reflects. 'While the Police Welfare Unit people were very nice, we didn't even know what help to ask for. It was our new reality. We were in the depths of pure survival.' Although, years later, she would come to regret it, she sent her children to stay with her sisters in Derry for a few nights. 'I feel now that it was wrong. Perhaps they would have been better with me.' Decades later she clearly remembers her two youngest children holding hands and saying, 'Mummy, why did you not tell us the truth? Why didn't you tell us that Daddy's head was blown off?' Other children at school and people in the community knew some of the harrowing details that had been withheld from Rosemary. They knew that Sergeant Campbell had been shot through the head and that the bullet had 'gone round and round his brain before it exited'. Although Rosemary saw the bandages around her husband's head, she didn't know how to explain it to her children. 'How could I tell the two little ones that? Looking back, maybe it would have been the right thing to do.' Some weeks later one of her sons wrote in a school essay that his daddy went out that night to save the rest of them.

Left to navigate the aftermath of the atrocity without any of the mental health resources that would become available a few decades later, the whole family was deeply traumatised. Her daughter Mandy explains: 'We didn't realise it was real. I can still see myself kneeling in the chapel, in the front row, as all these people paraded by. I clearly remember asking myself, why are all those people doing a plenary in the chapel? At 16, I didn't have the language to tell people how I felt. None of us had the language. Everybody just rallied – my mother, my grandmother, friends in the community. Everyone.'

Although the RUC assured Rosemary that they would provide assistance, they only gave her £1,900 in compensation. Typically, following the death of a policeman there would have been an immediate payment of £5,000, but Rosemary, with eight children, was subjected to questioning by Welfare about how much she spent 'on this and that'. For Rosemary, the RUC focused more on what the family might know about the murder rather than the help she needed to raise eight children on her own. The grief-stricken Campbell family was forced to deal with the trauma and loss as best they could. The gnawing, heartbreaking question for them was why Joseph Campbell was murdered. For Mandy, her father's mantra, 'Two wrongs don't make a right', still endures. 'Daddy always said that and it has stuck with me down the years. We've all had good lives, but at any given moment, it's nine o'clock on that terrible evening in 1977. A part of me is forever fixed in that 16-year-old. It is visceral and immediate. Unresolved.'

Wrestling with the fact that he and his siblings were just like any other family, raised to 'respect law and order, teachers, religious and political leaders', Joe has questions that have remained unanswered for decades. 'If the people who did this wanted to make an impact, they were successful. Where do you go with that? Where do you go with your grievances?' His father's murder permanently changed many lives: the family's – four girls and four boys – the extended family's and, to some extent, the spirit of the entire community. Cushendall, which until then had been a peaceful place, was changed too, with a much heavier police presence. Unable to cope, Joe Jr left Northern Ireland six months after his father's murder. 'Following an inquest that took just one day in October 1977, I didn't want to do anything that might cause problems,' he said. 'I decided to channel my efforts into finding the truth and then justice.'

Compounding the devastating loss of her husband, the truth about his murder continued to elude Rosemary Campbell. Afraid that her children would grow bitter, she made sure that their Catholic faith remained strong. 'We would kneel down at night and pray for those who killed Daddy. I don't know if I did that for the right reasons. I did want to see them held to account.' Why did the RUC allow this to happen? Why were those responsible allowed to walk away from Joseph Campbell's murder when his widow and children were not? Rosemary still tries in vain to get answers. She knew that his employers, the RUC, were aware that he was under threat. People in positions of power were refusing to provide any answers. 'They knew, but they did nothing. If my Joe couldn't be safe, then how could anyone expect to be safe? Why should anyone expect justice?' Initially, those powerful people blamed the IRA, and when that didn't work, they falsely claimed that Joseph was murdered because he was an IRA sympathiser.

Two years later, when Rosemary Campbell went to Belfast to ask the chief constable for the official documents from the criminal investigation into her husband's murder, she was presented with a file of no more than four sheets of paper. 'There would have been more paperwork for a sheep lost on the side of the mountain,' she said. Coupled with the lack of co-operation from the RUC, harassment and hostility were directed at the murdered policeman's family. Unnecessary, re-traumatising security stops and checks on the roads became a daily ritual for Rosemary and her children. While they became accustomed to the bullying and intimidating intrusions, their distrust of the police increased with every encounter. Rosemary related how one of her sons, still reeling from the murder of his father, was walking through the village when a policeman blocked his path and told him that he would go the same way as his dad.

One evening in March 1981, on their way home from a St Patrick's Day hurling match at Croke Park in Dublin, Rosemary recalls that there were army jeeps on the road just as they entered the glens. They had to stop, and Rosemary and her son Peter were ordered out of the car. Her youngest son, Philip, was having an asthma attack and, with all the car doors open, the interior was getting wet, so Rosemary asked the soldiers if they would close the doors, but they refused. Instead, they harassed Rosemary and demanded to know why there was a hurling stick in the boot of the car. They then proceeded to verbally abuse her about an encyclopaedia she had just bought to help with the children's studies. Worried about Philip, she finally snapped and said, 'Shoot me if you have to, but I'm not standing here anymore.' Exasperated and exhausted, she got back in the car. The soldiers responded by banging loudly on the roof. 'We were so used to it, we didn't even realise how cruel they were. Their cruelty had reached an acceptable level.'

Repeatedly denied answers and disappointed over and over again, Rosemary Campbell has somehow found a path to forgiveness. 'It took me a while, but I forgave the person that shot my husband, but it isn't just one person that you must forgive. After forty-six years, no public official will tell me who murdered my husband or why he was murdered.' There isn't a day that Rosemary doesn't ponder these all-important questions. 'I want to know what it is that they don't want me to know. Not knowing shattered my life and the lives of my family and my friends.'

Bullied by the operators of the very system that should have protected them, Mandy says it continues to be an unjust and gruelling journey and that every day is physically and emotionally exhausting. 'We know they are playing the long game and just waiting for us to die.' Having lost two brothers in the past six years, the family is concerned that their beloved matriarch may not live to see justice delivered. Despite all the evidence, there are still those who say that her father got what he deserved, 'so we all talk about Daddy and how lovely and decent he was and that we must protect his legacy', Mandy continues. 'Forgiveness always places the onus on the victim to grant absolution to those who did you wrong, but I believe that not hating someone is forgiveness.' Nevertheless, Mandy remains resolute and dignified in her determination not to give up on the truth. She will never give up on her father. 'Now that my eldest son is a father, I am more determined than ever, and with Joseph and Rosemary's new great-grandchild comes a guarantee that, down through the generations, we are never going away.'

17
Rock Royalty

*I get on with my life and fill every day to the brim leaving
no room for the past to intrude.*

In July 2006 I was still commuting every week between Cork and London. I'd leave my home in Cork on Monday morning and return on Thursday evening. It was a hectic schedule. I recall one particularly busy week when I also had to attend a meeting in Dublin, a round trip of more than 500 kilometres from home. My business in the city centre finished shortly after 4 p.m., so if the lights were with me, I had an outside chance of beating the traffic to Newlands Cross at the start of the M7 motorway before rush hour. Dublin, however, kept its own schedule and I soon found myself bumper to bumper by the side of the Liffey heading at a snail's pace towards Kilmainham. Just as I was passing City Hall, the monotony was broken by Johnny Winter's 'Rock and Roll, Hoochie Koo' guitar riff, which I'd set as my phone's ringtone. My friend Clem Walsh was calling from Craughwell in County Galway, and since the traffic was barely moving I answered the call. To say that Clem was a music enthusiast would be a gross understatement; he was a music fanatic. He got straight to the point and asked me to produce an album for a young rock band from Athenry called the Deans. I duly responded in kind and told him I had no interest in his proposal, especially when he said that the lead guitarist and main vocalist, Gavin Dean, was only 16 years old. Clem, a successful businessman who didn't give up easily, patently ignored my refusal and asked where I was, and when I told him I was slowly making my way out of Dublin, heading for Cork, he said, 'I'll meet you in Portlaoise, I'll be there in an hour and a bit.' When I got to the hotel, Clem was already there and ready with his pitch and, over several coffees, he convinced me to check out the band when they played in Cork city the following week. To my surprise the Deans – Gavin Dean on guitar and vocals, Gary Dean on bass guitar and vocals, and Martin Sheanon on drums and vocals – proved to be an excellent band with a great image and commanding stage presence. When I spoke with them after the show I was intrigued by their extensive knowledge of the blues, classic rock and rhythm and blues, and their appreciation of artists and bands such as B. B. King, John Mayall's Bluesbreakers, Rory Gallagher, Chuck Berry and the Yardbirds.

Clem Walsh was right: they were special, but, in an age of gimmickry, hyperbole and synthetic pop, I felt that if I were to make an album to introduce them to the world, the album would have to be unique and special too. While their original material was promising, we agreed that I would produce an album of blues and rhythm-and-blues classics for them and, to give it a distinctive boost, I would ask some of my old pals to guest on their album. We decided to make it at Sun Street Recording Studios in Tuam, County Galway, just thirty kilometres from Athenry where Gary and Gavin Dean lived, since it had everything we required and the in-house engineer, Ken Ralph, came highly recommended.

My first phone call was to my old friend Henry McCullough. Henry played lead guitar with Joe Cocker at Woodstock and later with Paul McCartney's Wings, but I knew him from his showband days when he played at the Ormond Ballroom in Carrick-on-Suir in the early 1960s, with a showband called Gene and the Gents. Although my friends and I were too young to go to the dance to hear the band, we would wait for them to arrive in the afternoon and 'help' them carry their equipment from their bandwagon to the stage. When the equipment was set up, Henry would sit on the front of the stage and show us the guitar riffs and chords to the trickier hit records of the day. Later, when the band started playing, we'd sit outside the side door of the ballroom and listen, especially to our hero's guitar breaks.

Henry was curious, but he was also cautious about being associated with a young band he'd never heard, so when I told him I'd be in Portrush the following week, he asked if I'd call to his house on my way home. It was only a twenty-minute drive and, as I drew close to Henry's cottage just outside Ballymoney, I spotted his wife, Josie, picking berries from the bushes and hedges along the roadside. Her beautiful French accent made the welcome even more special as she proudly showed me a basketful of berries, which she promised we'd have for desert. Henry met me at the door and immediately ushered me into the room where he kept a collection of rare instruments. He was eager to show me his latest acquisition, a beautiful old F-Style Scroll Top mandolin, which he proceeded to play with the enthusiasm of a teenager. After a leisurely, very French lunch, Henry and I strolled around his garden among the goats and the peacocks. I felt as if I'd walked into the sleeve of a 1960s psychedelic rock album. Eventually, as Josie prepared the pot-bellied stove for the evening, we got around to listening to a rough recording of the Deans. Henry smiled and nodded his head in approval. He liked what he heard and I knew I had my first special guest for their album.

I first met Belfast-born Jackie McAuley in London in 1982, but I was already aware of his reputation as a talented vocalist, guitarist, keyboard player and songwriter. Jackie played keyboards with Van Morrison in Them and shared stages and dressing rooms with the Beatles, the Rolling Stones, the Who and the Kinks and many others. When Van Morrison left Them, Jackie joined Paul Brady's Dublin band, the Kult. By 1982 he was a prolific songwriter and, together with John Gustafson of Roxy Music, wrote the hit song 'Dear John' for Status Quo. When he wasn't touring in Europe with his own Celtic rock band, Poor Mouth, Jackie played on the burgeoning Irish-themed pub circuit around the UK with his brother, Brendan, in the acclaimed super-duo the Navigators. However, it was his time as musical director, guitarist and fiddle player for the legendary Lonnie Donegan that fulfilled a bucket-list wish that most musicians of his generation only dreamed about.

I worked with Jackie in 1997 when the Navigators were booked to record two tracks for a compilation album of Irish folk and trad groups entitled *A Traditional Taste of O'Neill's*, which I was producing at Red Bus Recording Studios in London to showcase some of the most popular groups on O'Neill's Irish-themed UK pub circuit. The album, which was sponsored by Guinness, featured bands with varying experience of the recording process. Some had never been in a professional recording studio before, while for others, like Jackie and Brendan McAuley, recording at the highest level was second nature. When Jackie and Brendan arrived at Red Bus studios, however, they explained that they had to get away as quickly as possible for an engagement outside London and so there would barely be enough time for a quick soundcheck. Furthermore, while they wanted me to play bass on their tracks, there would be no time to run through the musical arrangements with me. The engineer was excellent, and as he was already set up for their instruments, he 'got' their sound very quickly. Since they were both playing acoustic instruments, I was acutely aware that, to anticipate the unique timing of seasoned folk musicians and to 'feel' the emotional nuances in their playing without any rehearsal, my best hope was to stand face to face with Jackie and watch his eyes rather than his fingers. They were in a hurry and I was on a tight schedule so we went for it and hoped for the best. We did both tracks in one take and they were on their way.

Jackie McAuley was also an old friend of Henry McCullough so, with Henry already on board to guest with the Deans, I was confident of getting Jackie too. My hunch proved to be right and before we finished the first cup of coffee in Jackie's kitchen in Dundalk, he was already contemplating the tracks he intended to record. I had my second star guest for the Deans' album.

Almost every guitarist I knew learned the iconic solo that Eric Bell played on Thin Lizzy's 'Whiskey in The Jar'. The Belfast-born guitarist's stunning fretwork on Lizzy's first three albums, *Thin Lizzy*, *Shades of a Blue Orphanage* and *Vagabonds of the Western World*, has guaranteed him a permanent place in rock and roll history. I've always loved the unique and passionate way Eric sings and plays the blues, so I was determined to include him among the elite group of musicians on the Deans' debut album. Eric and his band had done some work with my entertainment agency in London, so when I called him about the Deans' project, he was intrigued and asked if I would drop some of their recordings over to his London apartment on my way to Heathrow the following day. On first listening, he said Gavin Dean's guitar playing sounded like a cross between Rory Gallagher and early Johnny Winter, and before I left Eric's apartment we had settled on a recording date.

The Deans idolised Horslips' phenomenal Celtic rock guitarist Johnny Fean and were very excited at the prospect of working with him on their album. Following on from two excellent guitarists, Declan Sinnott and Gus Guest, 21-year-old Johnny Fean joined Horslips in 1972 and brought with him a unique blend of rock, blues and Irish traditional music that gave the band an edge similar to that which Joe Walsh would bring to the Eagles three years later. Even Johnny's banjo and mandolin playing had a 'danger' that captivated O'Carolan and Hendrix enthusiasts alike.

Every year from the early 1960s onwards, radio stations and newspapers around the country invited their listeners and readers to vote for their favourite Irish and international artists across a range of musical categories – showband, country, folk, rock and so on.

The biggest of these were the *Spotlight Magazine* Annual Awards in Dublin. *Spotlight Magazine*, which later changed its name to *New Spotlight* and then to *Starlight Magazine*, was the most influential music publication during the showband era, and its journalists, especially the columnist Julie Boyd, could make or break a band. Julie's weekly gossip column entitled 'Boyd's Eye View' was the first page every musician nervously opened to see if they had inadvertently provoked her ire during the previous week. Happily, although we didn't always see eye to eye, Julie and I got on well and, for no apparent reason, I was even named her 'Super Boy of the Week' on a number of occasions. The 1976 *New Spotlight* Awards ceremony was a star-studded affair that featured the reformed Miami Showband, the Bay City Rollers, Chris de Burgh, Rory Gallagher, Joe Dolan, Brendan Grace, the Swarbriggs, Big Tom, Philomena Begley, Marianne Faithful, the Chieftains and some members of Horslips among others.

The event, which was held at the Country Club in Portmarnock in April 1976, was presented by Radio Luxembourg's star DJ, Tony Prince. The show was scheduled to begin at 8 p.m. sharp, and when I arrived at around 6 p.m. quite a few of the other award recipients were already there and chatting among themselves. Although we criss-crossed each other on the road week after week, awards concerts were among the few occasions that we got to socialise with other artists, so I was looking forward to catching up with old friends as soon as I hung up my immaculate white band suit in our dressing room. There was a stern-looking security man standing guard at the entrance to the corridor that led to the dressing rooms, but when the production manager nodded to him, he stepped aside and I soon found a door with 'Miami' emblazoned on a large gold star. Ray Miller was already inside relaxing on a couch, and as I entered he said, 'I see you got past Godzilla. Those poor lads are cooped up next door since they arrived.'

'Who?' I asked.

'The Bay City Rollers,' Ray replied. 'They're not allowed out. What an awful life,' he added, shaking his head. Just then, there was a knock on our door, a reminder that it was our turn to do a soundcheck, so Ray and I headed back down the corridor towards the stage where our bandmates were already plugging in and testing their microphones. The soundcheck lasted all of ten minutes, and, as I was carefully putting my bass guitar back in its case, I heard a familiar, lilting Cork accent. 'That has to be the nicest Rickenbacker bass I've ever seen. It's beautiful. Here, Steve, let's have a look.' I'd known Rory Gallagher since 1970 when we were both regular customers at Crowley's music shop on Merchant's Quay in Cork. In fact it was Rory who convinced me to buy a Marshall bass amplifier when I was deliberating whether to go for a Marshall or a Hiwatt. He was right – my blonde Rickenbacker 4001 stereo bass guitar with its gold Grover machine heads and chequered binding was stunning, and so we sat at the side of the stage while Rory gave my bass a thorough road test. As we were chatting, Rory spotted his friend Johnny Fean and called the Horslips virtuoso over to see my bass. I was well aware of Johnny's reputation, but we had never met. When Rory introduced us that day, neither of us imagined that Johnny and I would work together, live and in recording studios, and remain the best of friends up until his untimely death in 2023.

Horslips split in 1980 and the band members went their own way. Johnny formed the Zen Alligators with Horslips drummer and lyricist Eamon Carr to play a blues, rock and soul set, much of which was original material. In 1984 they were joined by their former fiddle player, Charles O'Connor, to form the Host. Meanwhile, Horslips' bass guitarist Barry Devlin worked on a solo project which he called *Breaking Star Codes*, an album based on the signs of the zodiac. Barry hired some of the best musicians of the time to play on his album, including guitarist Greg Boland and drummer Paul McAteer from the Dublin band Supply, Demand and Curve, as well as bassist

Tommy Moore. The recording engineer was Brian Masterson, who had also played bass with Supply, Demand and Curve. In 1980 I had formed an original group called the Crack with the Belfast guitarist/vocalist Tommy Lundy, drummer Martin McElroy and keyboard player Ronan O'Callaghan. We were managed by Arthur Walters, who also managed Johnny's band, the Zen Alligators. Arthur had been the Irish booking agent for Horslips and also for Thin Lizzy in their early years. As we had signed a record contract with CBS Records, and particularly because there were very strong Beatles and Wings echoes in our original material and Tommy's voice sounded uncannily like Paul McCartney, Barry Devlin was curious. When he heard us in Carlow, he asked me to play bass on the remaining four tracks of his solo album, *Breaking Star Codes*. I liked the album concept and also his songwriting, so I agreed to finish his album. However, the credits on the album sleeve are actually incorrect since I played bass on 'When Two Stars Collide', 'Let The Scales Decide', 'Aquarian Girls' and 'Love with a Sting in Its Tail'. We recorded it at Windmill Lane Studios in Dublin, and I used my Wal Pro II E bass guitar on all four tracks. Sadly, my friend the late Tommy Lundy wasn't given any credit for playing rhythm guitar and singing backing vocals on those four tracks.

Anne and I sold our home in Portmarnock in 1982 and moved to West London. We bought a house in Hillingdon where we would stay for almost twenty years. Like so many Irish musicians of that period, Johnny Fean and his wife Maggie also decided to emigrate, and they moved to London in 1986. Our paths crossed again in 1991 when he played with a band called the Treat at a concert I was producing at London's Wembley Arena, but it would be another five years before we finally formed a band together. In 1996 Johnny and I recruited the Dublin drummer/percussionist Danny 'Bongos' Smith and Irish keyboard player Dave Lennox, who had played with some of the greatest artists in the world including the legendary drummer Ginger Baker from Cream. Apart from a short Irish tour, none of us wanted to travel far from London, so we drew the line at Southend and Bournemouth, where we attracted large crowds to the popular O'Neill's venues. It was a straightforward, good-time, classic rock/Celtic rock band that didn't require any real effort or rehearsal and suited the crowds that flocked to the Irish-themed venues springing up all over the UK at the time. We called the band the Psycho Pats, which clearly indicated that we didn't take ourselves too seriously, and it afforded us a welcome break from the more demanding projects we had been involved with. We rarely mentioned our past lives. Anonymity suited us. As far as the non-Irish audiences were concerned, we were simply a very good band, but there was no hiding Johnny's unique Celtic rock trademark guitar sound. Furthermore, whenever I wore my record producer's hat, Johnny Fean was always my first-call studio guitarist for electric or acoustic.

It was no surprise that the Deans were excited about having him on their album. I called Johnny, and, without even hearing the young band, he agreed.

I had secured some of the greatest living Irish guitarists to play on an unknown teenage band's debut album but I regretted the fact that the late great Rory Gallagher, who had passed away in 1995, was not on the list. However, as the old saying goes, 'where there's a will, there's a way', so I called Rory's brother Donal Gallagher, who had seen the Deans at the Rory Gallagher Festival in Bundoran, and I asked him if he would loan us a couple of Rory's multi-track recordings for the project. We arranged a meeting with Donal at a restaurant in Chelsea and he kindly agreed to have two of Rory's multi-tracks, 'Walk on Hot Coals' and 'Hands Off', sent from France, where they were stored, to Sun Street Studios in Tuam, County Galway.

Everything was set, and so I headed up west to begin recording. Clem and Mary Walsh invited me to stay at their beautiful home in Craughwell, just a thirty-minute drive from the studio, so I got a good night's rest before I was due to start work. I planned to get two tracks recorded with each artist, but, as I had never used this studio before, I was eager to meet the owner/engineer Ken Ralph and to check out the equipment and the facilities.

Martin Sheanon was the first to arrive and had already set up his kit in the drum booth when Gavin and Gary Dean showed up. By lunchtime, the mics and D.I.s were connected and I was able to hear a rough mix of the instruments. I was keen to keep their raw, teenage energy, which I felt would inject new life into the classic rhythm and blues we were about to lay down with my seasoned rock and roll friends. While the musicians were excited about meeting and working with their heroes, they certainly were not daunted. Gavin, Gary, Martin, Ken and I spent a few long days and nights getting the basic tracks and guide vocals down as tight as possible so that the guests would slot in comfortably when they came to do their thing.

To ensure that the structure worked, we recorded the songs as if it were to be just the band on their own. I got Gavin to play two guitar solos on each track with the intention of replacing one with a guest solo and likewise with the vocals. It was beginning to take shape, and I felt confident that my friends would be impressed with the band. However, while all of the tracks, so far, had been built from the ground up, I knew that the Rory Gallagher tracks had to be approached differently. Multi-track recording allows artists to assign each instrument or vocal to a separate track so that they can be individually worked on without interfering with the other recorded components and their sound levels to be adjusted to blend in the mix as the producer sees fit. Rory's tracks were already complete, and I had to replace his drums and bass with Martin and Gary who, although intimate with all of the nuances on the tracks, had to play 'with' Rory rather than to 'follow' him and that was no easy task. While we were able to mute the original bass guitar on the multi-track, we included just enough of the original drums into Martin's headphone mix to sync the timing without distracting him, and I sent Martin's drums, without the original drum tracks, to Gary and Gavin's headphone mix. After a number of takes and the successful removal of all the original drums and bass guitar, we had it.

Our next task was to clean Rory's vocal tracks as there was some guitar 'spill' on them, but Ken Ralph was more than up to the task and he also successfully brought them up to the contemporary sound levels. Late one evening as Ken and I were working on the Rory Gallagher tracks, it felt as if the great man were alive and well and in his prime on the other side of the recording studio glass. Rory's energy and charisma filled Sun Street Studios that night – it was pure magic. I still get goosebumps listening to Rory Gallagher sharing vocals and swapping guitar solos on those tracks with 16-year-old Gavin Dean and the driving bass and drums of Gary Dean and Martin Sheanon solidly underpinning them.

I had allocated two days to record two tracks with each of our guests and Jackie McAuley was the first on my roster. As expected, Jackie breezed through his chosen tracks, 'Caldonia' and 'Dust My Broom'. His vocals and slide-guitar playing were sensational. One evening Jackie even treated us to some of his own original compositions, accompanied by his beautiful acoustic guitar playing.

We spent two days with Eric Bell during which the original Thin Lizzy guitarist rocked Sun Street with a brilliant version of 'Johnny B. Goode'. Eric followed the Chuck Berry classic with 'The Things I Used To Do', which reminded us why he is regarded as one of the finest blues artists on our side of the Atlantic Ocean. He gave us 'King Bee' as a third track when I mentioned that it was the first blues number I ever played when I started on bass aged 15.

Johnny Fean was the personification of cool. The King of Celtic Rock was the most unassuming guitar hero you could possibly imagine but his astonishing riffs on 'Dearg Doom', 'Trouble With A Capital T' and 'Sword of Light', along with many others, lit a fire under a generation that will burn forever in Irish rock lore.

Johnny chose 'Shakin' All Over' and 'I Wish You Would' and he added the Robert Johnson classic 'Ramblin' On My Mind' as a bonus track. Gary, Gavin and Martin were mesmerised.

I was sitting at the mixing console with Ken early one morning, working on a rough mix of the Deans' recording of the Chuck Berry 1958 classic 'Around and Around' when two long bony hands landed on my shoulders and a familiar Northern voice behind me asked, "Bout ye?' I smiled. I didn't have to look around. Within minutes Henry McCullough, the man with one of the most impressive CVs in rock history, was sitting beside me, tapping along with the track and nodding his head in appreciation of the young Galway band's rendition of 'Around and Around'. Ironically, it was the first song he'd taught my friends and I at the Ormond Ballroom in Carrick-on-Suir when we were teenagers. The wheel had turned full circle. Henry's other choices included Robert Johnson's 'Crossroads' and a very slow blues version of 'Sick and Tired', which I had first heard on a 1957 recording by Chris Kenner.

Wings' original lead guitarist was a dream to work with. Henry had brought his red Gibson 335, his Fender Stratocaster and his Gibson Les Paul Goldtop. In 1965 I was just 14 years old when I fell in love with the sound of Mike Bloomfield's 1956 Gibson Les Paul 'Goldtop' and I was very keen for Henry to use his on one of the tracks, but he seemed content to use the 335 on every take, so I'd say, 'Sounds great, Henry, we'll keep that … let's get another one for safety.' Eventually, I said, 'Let's do one with the Goldtop … what do you think?' Imagine asking a superstar who had toured with Pink Floyd, the Move, the Animals, Soft Machine and Jimi Hendrix to change guitars in the middle of a recording session! The rock legend who played lead guitar on the original 1969 *Jesus Christ Superstar* album and lead guitar with Joe Cocker at Woodstock that same year – Paul McCartney's first lead guitarist after he left the Beatles and formed Wings. Nevertheless, Henry, gracious as always and without

Stephen in 1970, aged 19. On the right, he is playing his 1965 Fender Precision with the Cowboys.

Left: Liam Dwyer with Stephen in 1973, *Clonmel Nationalist*.
Right: Stephen with his Dan Armstrong bass guitar in 1973. This bass guitar was completely destroyed in the explosion at the Miami Showband massacre in 1975.

A TOPLINE BAND · MAKES ALL THE DIFFERENCE

TOPLINE PROMOTIONS

DICKIE'S BAND · MIAMI
INDIANS . TWEED

55 PARNELL SQUARE (W)
DUBLIN 1.
PHONES: 47830 — 42203

Thursday September 19th 1974.

Mr. Steve Travers,
4, Gregg Road,
Carrick-on-Suir,
Co. Tipperary.

Dear Steve,

Harry Holt gave me your name and address. We will have a job vacant in a couple of weeks for a good bass player in 'The Miami', so if you are interested in an audition would you please ring me right away, and we can arrange a day.

Looking forward to hearing from you.

Kindest Regards.

Yours Sincerely,

Joe Tyrrell.
Joe Tyrrell.

● LISTEN IN TO THE TOPLINE SHOW · RADIO EIREANN · TUESDAYS 11.15 p.m.

Stephen's first invitation to audition for the Miami Showband, dated Thursday, 19 September 1974.

St Anne's Park, Raheny, Dublin, May 1975.
L to R - Tony Geraghty, Fran O'Toole, Ray Miller, Des (Lee) McAlea,
Brian McCoy, Stephen Travers.

Miami Showband fans, 1975.

Wreckage of the band VW minibus on the morning of the attack, 31 July 1975.

Buskhill Road on the morning of the attack, 31 July 1975.

The new, re-formed Miami Showband playing at the TV Club in Dublin, 1976.

Stephen with wife Anne Travers, Carrick-on-Suir, 1976.
Courtesy of Pat Cashman, *The Irish Press*.

Left: Stephen playing his Wal Pro II E bass in London, 1984.
Right: Stephen with Aubrey Oaki, bass player with Hugh Masekela, London, 1986.

L to R: Stephen with Maurice McElroy and Andy Richardson, London, 1985.

Above: Former Taoiseach Albert Reynolds with Stephen at the launch of his first book, Dublin, 2007.

Left: The hat Stephen gave to Edwin in the Ocean Road Cancer Institute, Dar es Salaam, 2008.

Below: Promotional photo of Johnny Fean with Stephen, 2005, ahead of the Fean and Travers Irish tour.

Truth and Reconciliation Platform event in Cushendall, October 2019.

Bass player to bass player: U2 bassist, Adam Clayton, with Stephen's Steinberger XL-2 during a break in the filming of *Ballroom Blitz*, 2024.

any hesitation, replied, 'Good idea, Steve, let's get it. I think that'll work great with this track.' Within minutes, Henry was unclasping the distinctive contoured Gibson case, and there it was in all its glory. Lifting it out of its slumber, he handed it to me and said, 'I played the solo on Paul's "My Love" with this. Most people think I did it on the 335 but that was just for the video.' It was a surreal moment, which for me crystallised, in my mind, the truly amazing journey that the young guitarist who played in Carrick-on-Suir with Gene and the Gents showband when I was a kid, had actually travelled. It was also profoundly humbling to witness the genuine modesty of a musician who really had done it all and seen it all.

The session went very well. We were both delighted with the results, and Henry was in top form at dinner in the hotel that evening. He was recounting some of his adventures, so I asked him, 'If you could relive any one musical day of your life, what would it be?' He thought deeply about the question for a while, and then his face lit up with a smile that seemed to come from a long way back in time. He put his hands behind his head, leaned back in his chair and directed his closed eyes towards the ceiling. I wondered if he was back at Woodstock with Joe Cocker in '69, basking in the adulation of half a million adoring fans as he bent the intro of 'With a Little Help from My Friends' across the fretboard of his Les Paul – or was he transported to January '72 when he joined Paul McCartney in Wings? On our many late-night telephone conversations over the years, Henry had told me so many fascinating stories that there were surely countless contenders for his 'A Day in the Life' top spot, but I wasn't prepared for the answer he gave me that evening in Tuam. 'Ah, I can see it now,' he smiled. 'It's a beautiful summer day. I'm just a wee cub sitting on a low stone wall by the side of our road with me band suit beside me and me guitar leaning against it and I'm looking down the road every couple of minutes to see if the Skyrockets Showband are on their way up to collect me to play at the dance.'

Of all the magical musical moments Henry could have chosen, he chose the most innocent, carefree, uncomplicated time of his life as the happiest. Henry passed away in the summer of 2016, and I'm sure, somewhere in the great timeless consciousness, he dons the band suit now and then and teaches some wide-eyed kid the intro to 'Around and Around'.

Unfortunately, for various reasons, the 'Deans And Friends' album featuring Rory Gallagher, Jackie McAuley, Johnny Fean, Eric Bell and Henry McCullough has never been released, but I still have the recording studio masters, should things change.

If I could relive any one musical day of my life, what would it be?

Over the years, I've played to millions of people in the biggest venues, concert halls, ballrooms and sports stadiums in Ireland. I've played at some of the most prestigious festivals and with headline acts at wonderful auditoria such as London's Royal Albert Hall. I've had storming gigs on both sides of the Atlantic and even on both sides of the equator, but when I was asked this very question I replied, without hesitation: 'The summer of 1974 with Liam Dwyer and the Sinners at the Kickham Inn in Carrick-on-Suir.' I was the first to leave the New Miami Showband in 1976, and my initial instinct was to go back to Carrick and form a new local band with Liam. I was sure I could get my life back again, but after two years of trying, I realised it was impossible, and so Anne and I embarked on the long journey of reconstructing and re-establishing new lives. Through the years, I always kept in touch with Liam. He visited us in London and I called to see him whenever I was home on holiday. When we moved back to Ireland in 1997, Liam and I got together regularly, and we even played at a few fundraisers and special events whenever an opportunity arose.

Liam and I made plans for the official launch of his album, *Heartfelt*, a project that had been on his bucket list for decades, but we decided to wait until he was 'feeling better'. He led me to believe that he needed to recover from a recent fall at his home, but in December 2022 William, the eldest of Liam's three sons, called me with devastating news: 'Dad's been diagnosed with pancreatic cancer,' he said. Even though I'd seen enough death to last ten lifetimes, I was distraught. William told me that his dad had about a month to live, but added that 'some people could live as long as three months'. Part of me hoped Liam wouldn't last three months because I knew it would cause him great suffering. I made preparations to see him the following week, but William called me again the following day to say his father only had a week to live and was asking to see me.

I got to the hospital in Clonmel as quickly as possible. 'Stephen is here,' William said quietly. Liam opened his eyes and slowly stretched out his arms. As I hugged him, I realised how much I loved him. I told him that this was not the end, that he was just going through a change and all the pain would be gone. William left us alone for the best part of an hour, during which I said, 'You've got over a thousand likes on YouTube for our song "Annie".' Though he was barely able to talk, his eyes lit up and I felt his fingers gently tap the three-four rhythm of the song on the back of my hand. I put my arms around him and told him I loved him and said goodbye. Liam died peacefully the following day and he was buried on New Year's Eve.

18
The Jigsaw

A picture begins to emerge.

The Historical Enquiries Team (HET) was a unit of the PSNI set up in September 2005 to review all files on Troubles-related deaths that occurred within the borders of Northern Ireland between 1969 and 1998. The Miami Showband massacre falls within that timeframe. The HET first made contact with Justice for the Forgotten (JFF) regarding the Miami Showband murders in May 2007. Subsequently, JFF held two meetings with the two survivors and the O'Toole and McCoy family members in 2007 and in 2008. The HET interviewed me and Des McAlea separately in 2009. The HET then held a meeting with JFF regarding the Miami Showband in 2011, and draft reports were completed later that year. The HET subsequently held two more meetings with the survivors and the families in the same year at which HET officers read the overall report to the two survivors and the families.

All present listened attentively as the report was read out, but Des and I were horrified that the HET concluded that the upper-class English voice we heard at the scene of the massacre was, in their opinion, that of the murderer, James Roderick Shane McDowell, who, they contended, spoke with a more 'refined' voice than the others because he was an 'optical worker from Lurgan' and was therefore 'better spoken' than the other murderers. It was ludicrous in the extreme to claim that McDowell's strong Northern accent could be mistaken for a posh English accent by Des McAlea and Brian McCoy, both of whom were born and reared in Northern Ireland. Moreover, as professional musicians, we all had finely tuned ears that could not easily be tricked.

When the HET officer finished reading the report, I immediately protested at such an absurd conclusion, but my protest was met with scorn by all present with the exception of my fellow survivor, Des McAlea. One person actually shook their head when I mentioned 'the British army officer' and exclaimed wearily, 'Oh, not that old chestnut again.' Another, who was sitting beside me, criticised me under their breath for my 'ingratitude' at being 'handed the smoking gun'. I was shocked. When I left the room, two HET officers followed me out onto the landing, saying, 'We don't know when you first introduced the British officer into the narrative; there's no record of you mentioning him in any of your statements.'

When I got home, Anne asked if I was happy with the report. I told her that the HET had effectively accused me of introducing the British officer into the narrative at a later stage and that, unless I had proof that I mentioned his presence from the beginning, they could justify dismissing it altogether. As always, however, Anne came to my rescue with the aid of an old scrapbook filled with newspaper clippings. There it was in black and white, indisputable proof that, while I was still in my hospital bed, I told the *Evening Herald* in an interview with Tony Wilson, published on 14 August 1975, of Brian McCoy's assertion that 'the British army' was in charge at the murder scene. Since the interview took place some days before it was published, Anne had produced irrefutable evidence that I had been telling the public about the presence of the British officer from the very beginning. I immediately scanned the newspaper article and emailed it to the HET, asking them to reconsider their conclusions, but they claimed they couldn't download the image to their system and, outrageously, left the report unchanged.

The HET officers who worked on the Miami Showband report were all former English police officers and part of the 'White Team', which reviewed cases where there were allegations of collusion. Steve Morris, formerly of the London Metropolitan Police Service, was the leader. His boss Dave Cox was director of the HET. The White Team also reviewed other Glenanne cases.

A statement was read out to the waiting press at Buswell's Hotel on Kildare Street on 14 December 2011, in response to the findings of the Historical Enquiries Team into the murders of Anthony Geraghty, Brian McCoy and Francis O'Toole, and my attempted murder.[2]

Reaction was swift. The former assistant chief constable, Alan McQuillan, stated: 'If what has been reported is true then it's horrendous and this needs to be followed up, properly examined, properly investigated to see what was going on and who was involved. When you joined the police in those days just as now you swore an oath of allegiance which is to uphold the law. The use of agents saved thousands of lives in Northern Ireland including many of our politicians who wouldn't be alive today if we hadn't had agents reporting people who were planning to kill them but that's no excuse for some of the things that seem to be alleged in this report.'

The following quote from the HET report made headlines across Ireland: 'To the objective, impartial observer, disturbing questions about collusion and corrupt behaviour are raised ... no means to assuage or rebut these concerns and this is a deeply troubling matter.' Unsurprisingly, it wasn't covered by the British mainstream media.

A formal complaint was subsequently sent to the Office of the Police Ombudsman for Northern Ireland (OPONI) in relation to the Miami Showband murders:

Robin Jackson:
A critical finding in the HET report on the murders of three members of The Miami Showband: Anthony Geraghty, Brian

McCoy and Francis O'Toole and the wounding of members Stephen Travers and Desmond McAlea on 31st July 1975 at Buskhill, Co. Down, concerns the involvement of former Ulster Defence Regiment member and UVF murderer, Robert (Robin) Jackson.

Jackson was arrested on 5th August 1975, five days after the murders, but was released without being charged with any crimes two days later. There is no record of any RUC interviews conducted with Jackson.

The following year, on Tuesday, 18th May, former B Special and Ulster Service Corps member, Edward Tate Sinclair, was arrested following the discovery of firearms, ammunition, explosives and bomb components on his farm at Canary, near Dungannon.

The following day, Sinclair was allowed home, ostensibly to milk his cows. In his presence, police discovered a Luger pistol, along with a homemade silencer wrapped in black adhesive insulating tape hidden behind a wall fan in the milking parlour.

A forensic examination of the gun, silencer and tape revealed two fingerprints, matching Jackson's, on the silencer's metal barrel.

While the silencer was not attached to the Luger when they were found, a scientific examination established that the muzzle end of the gun had been drilled to accept the fixing grubscrew on the silencer.

The location of Jackson's fingerprints was originally misquoted as being found on <u>both</u> the silencer and the insulating tape.

This error was repeated in the fingerprint department's report, dated 28th May 1976.

Police made several abortive attempts, between 20th and 30th May, to arrest Jackson.

On 31st May, Jackson was finally arrested.

On the same day, the corrected information reached Detective Superintendent Ernest Drew that Jackson's fingerprints had been found on the barrel of the silencer only and <u>not</u> on the insulating tape.

D/Constable William Elder interviewed Jackson on two occasions on the day of his arrest but no record of these interviews could be found by HET.

On the following day, D/Superintendent Drew and D/Constable Elder interviewed Jackson who denied he had ever been to Sinclair's farm (while admitting he knew him through the Loyalist Club in Portadown).

D/Superintendent Drew then placed the Luger, the silencer and magazine (but not the tape) on the interview table.

Jackson denied handling them.

Drew asked Jackson if he could offer any explanation, should his fingerprints be found on either the pistol or the silencer, or both.

Jackson again denied he had handled the items but then volunteered the unsolicited information that, one night at the Portadown Loyalist Club, Sinclair had asked him for some tape.

Jackson told his interviewer: 'I gave him part of the roll I was using in the bar.'

D/Superintendent Drew had intentionally held back the information that the silencer had been wrapped in the black tape, yet, without prompting, Jackson revealed that he knew about the tape and provided an explanation as to how his fingerprints could be on it.

Jackson then made a statement in which he said that a D/Superintendent and a D/Sergeant had told him on 24th May (a week before his arrest) that his fingerprints had been found on tape on a silencer.

He refused to disclose the names of the officers or in what town or place the conversation had taken place.

He went on to say that these officers had told him that he 'should clear as there was a wee job up the country I would be done for and there was no way out of it for me'.

On 2nd June Jackson was charged with possession of a firearm, magazine, four rounds of ammunition and a silencer with intent to endanger life.

The 9mm calibre Luger semi-automatic pistol model PO8, serial no. 4 and serial no. 655, recovered with the silencer was 'quickly identified' as being one of the guns used in the attack on the Miami Showband.

This weapon was also one of two pistols used to murder John Francis Green in Co. Monaghan on 10th January 1975, six months before the attack on The Miami Showband.

Despite this significant new evidence, Jackson was not questioned regarding The Miami Showband attack.

There is no evidence that The Miami investigation team was even informed of these developments.

Because of his earlier arrest, the investigation team obviously considered Jackson as a likely suspect. Now significant new evidence had been found, which could have provided reasonable grounds to justify Jackson's re-arrest.

I do not know if the Gardaí were informed in relation to the murder of John Francis Green.

Clearly concerned, D/Superintendent Drew's prosecution report stated that Jackson had known, before his arrest, that his fingerprints had been found and was claiming that two senior RUC detectives had tipped him off about a week before his arrest.

This confidential internal RUC report stated that, if the allegation were true, it constituted a 'grave breach of discipline and police confidentiality on the part of the officers concerned'.

Drew sent a report on that aspect of the case to the Complaints and Discipline Department of the RUC for investigation and sent a full report on the case to his Divisional Commander, Chief Superintendent William Harrison at Armagh on 19th July 1976.

On 29th July, Chief Superintendent Harrison submitted D/Superintendent Drew's report, including his own supporting recommendations, to RUC Headquarters.

At HQ, the report was allocated to Superintendent William Thompson to assess the evidence and make his recommendations prior to its submission to the Office of the Director of Public Prosecutions.

Superintendent Thompson drew up a report, in which he failed to address Jackson's allegations, confining his recommendations to Jackson's criminal liability.

The clear inference must be, therefore, that RUC Headquarters allowed Jackson's allegations about the two detectives to drop.

This gives rise to serious concerns that senior RUC officers were involved in a conspiracy to pervert the course of justice. I am requesting OPONI to investigate this grave issue.

Also, HET has found no evidence that the RUC Complaints and Discipline Department instigated any criminal or disciplinary investigation. I am also requesting OPONI to investigate this matter.

To summarise:
The fingerprints of Robin Jackson were found on the silencer of a gun used in The Miami Showband murders (and the murder of John Francis Greene);

There is no evidence that this information was passed to the Miami investigation team;

Jackson was aware that his fingerprints had been found <u>before his arrest and had an explanation ready</u>;

He claimed that a D/Superintendent and a D/Sergeant had tipped him off and advised him how to avoid arrest;

There were only 12 officers of this rank in the RUC at that time – only a very small number were in Special Branch;

There is no evidence that RUC headquarters investigated these serious allegations.

The HET conclusion on this issue reads:
'To the objective, impartial observer, disturbing questions about collusive and corrupt behaviour are raised. The HET review has found no means to assuage or rebut these concerns and that is a deeply troubling matter.'

These findings by the HET indicate strongly that Robin Jackson was an agent of RUC Special Branch and that he was involved in The Miami Showband murders.

If this was the case, the really disturbing implication is that the security forces may have known in advance that the attack was planned and permitted it to go ahead.

The issues around Jackson are the main concerns of the bereaved families and survivors of the attack on The Miami Showband. However, there are other disquieting issues, which require investigation by OPONI:

Interview notes relating to those arrested during August 1975 could not be located by HET (with the exception of those convicted of crimes);

There are no records that detail the specific grounds for Jackson's arrest on 5th August 1975;

On 6th June, just eight weeks before the attack on The Miami Showband, police had stopped Thomas Raymond Crozier, Samuel Fulton Neill and Robin Jackson in Banbridge, Co. Down, in possession of shotguns. HET were unable to locate any further records in relation to this incident – they cannot tell if the three men were arrested, reported for prosecution or charged with any offences. However HET states that detectives interviewing Crozier on 7th August were clearly aware of the association between the three men. The absence of records regarding this incident is troubling.

There was a failure to conduct any forensic examination of the three green berets recovered at the scene of The Miami Showband murders, apart from an examination for firearm residue;

The unidentified fingerprints recovered from the Ford Escort are no longer available;

There is no indication as to whether Samuel Fulton Neill's Triumph was examined for fingerprints;

There is no indication as to whether the recovered weapons were examined for fingerprints;

HET states that no fingerprint records were held for either William Wesley Somerville or Harris Boyle prior to their deaths. This is very surprising as both men had been charged previously with other subversive crimes;

A part-time UDR soldier from Moygashel, seen with Wesley Somerville on the night before The Miami murders, was never arrested or questioned. This information came from an intelligence source;

It is believed that at least 10 men were involved in the attack on The Miami Showband. Only three were convicted while two died in the bomb explosion at the scene. Therefore, at least five others were never charged or convicted.

One of the weapons recovered at the scene was an Enfield Albion MK11 Smith & Wesson .38 calibre revolver, serial no. C5381. This weapon was one of several stolen on 23rd October 1973 from E Company, 11 UDR depot, Fort Seagoe, Portadown, when 12 armed men tied up the guards and bypassed the internal security system. The circumstances of the raid prompted suspicions that there must have been inside knowledge and assistance. HET states that there is nothing within the case papers to indicate whether McDowell or Crozier (both serving members of 11 UDR) were interviewed about the arms raid;

An HET report on the murder of Portadown man, Martin McVeigh, shot dead on 3rd April 1975, says Jackson and two others, Edward Philip Silcock and Robert (known as John) Thompson – both Portadown loyalists – were found in possession of the murder weapon (a .38 calibre Enfield revolver, serial no. ZJ3691) when they were stopped in a car on 9th October 1979 at Mourne Road, Lurgan.

They were arrested when balaclavas and gloves were found in the car and subsequently pleaded guilty on 20th January 1981 to unlawful possession of firearms and ammunition for an unlawful purpose and were each sentenced to seven years in jail.

Like the Enfield Albion found at the scene of The Miami Showband murders, this weapon had been taken during the raid on the UDR base on 23rd October 1973. In this case HET were even more explicit: 'There are grounds to suspect that those responsible were helped by members of the UDR.'

Jackson was arrested for questioning about this raid on 7th November 1973 after 79 rounds of 7.62 ammunition was found in his home in excess of his permitted limit as a UDR soldier.

Jackson was not charged with possessing this ammunition because his explanation, that he had forgotten to return it, could not be disproved, but he was discharged from the UDR on 4th March 1974.

Jackson, Silcock and Thompson were caught red-handed in possession of the weapon used to murder Martin McVeigh six years after the raid and more than four years after his murder, but none was questioned by police about Martin's murder.

The HET says:
'It is inexplicable that Jackson and his co-accused were not interviewed about Martin's murder while they were detained for the possession of the .38 revolver . . . their UVF associations and possession of the murder weapon were factors that should have resulted in their interview over the murder.' (HET RSR concerning the murder of Martin Anthony McVeigh, p. 26).

This information reinforces the implication that Jackson was a Special Branch agent and is very alarming indeed.

It is disturbing that only one of the men, convicted for the murders, John J. Somerville, was charged with my attempted murder.

It now concerns me greatly that, during the preliminary trials in Newry and the trials in Belfast, both the prosecution lawyers and the attending police officers told me that the difference in the berets, cap-badges and uniforms of the soldiers present at the murders was irrelevant and 'not worth mentioning'. I didn't see the presence of the English officer in charge as unusual or significant at that time although I had already flagged it up publicly in the national press* within two weeks of the massacre, i.e. while I was still in hospital. It was not until the English officer's presence was denied that I began to suspect a cover-up.

Copies sent to OPONI and HET.
Stephen Thomas Travers

19
The Long and Winding Road to Justice

The fight-back begins.

Following the HET report, Des McAlea and I, together with the widows of Fran O'Toole and Brian McCoy, decided to explore the possibility of taking legal action against the British state. At a meeting convened by Margaret Urwin of Justice for the Forgotten, I was disappointed to be told that Tony Geraghty's family could not join with us in the litigation. I was surprised too that Brian Maguire and Ray Miller, both of whom were, and remain, severely traumatised by the murders of their friends and colleagues, were not participating in the lawsuit. Des's brother-in-law Dan Daly, a successful Belfast businessman, recommended the Belfast solicitor Michael Flanigan, and having met him in Dublin in March 2012, all four parties agreed to engage him. My barrister was Eilis McDermott.

On 23 May Michael Flanigan wrote to me to confirm that he had issued writs on my behalf against the British Ministry of Defence and the Police Service of Northern Ireland. The writs issued included claims for assault, trespass, conspiracy to injure, negligence and abuse of public power. Both aggravated and the more punitive form of exemplary damages were also sought. The High Court proceedings centred on the collaboration between terrorists and military personnel to carry out the killings. In the proceedings, the following matters were being litigated:

That the MOD policy of admitting loyalist paramilitaries to the UDR and giving them training and access to weapons was a reckless policy.

That such vetting of membership applications as did take place was carried out negligently.

That the MOD was aware of infiltration by the UVF and UDA for many years before the attack but failed to address it.

That the loss of weapons from the UDR to loyalist paramilitaries was not properly investigated by the then RUC and that UDR members colluded with loyalists in the loss of their weapons.

I was about to set out upon a new journey which, at the outset, excited me and crystallised an overwhelming life experience that hitherto made no sense to me at all. Until then, I was an effusive jumble of haphazard bewilderment, a random medley of emotions which I had little or no understanding of. I had been conferred with an embarrassing, bizarre celebrity that I had no idea what to do with or how to escape from, but now I had a focus for what I thought would be the next eighteen months or two years at the outside. My line of sight would be paved with truth and damning evidence and revelations that I was sure would shock the world, expose wrongdoing and deliver justice that would be appreciated and welcomed by all right-thinking people. Every single drop of momentum generated by that exuberant naivete would be required to run the ten-year gauntlet to the doors of the High Court in Belfast.

I set about preparing. I rummaged through bulging boxes in the attic for medical records and psychiatric reports that I thought I'd never have to read again. I made new appointments and attended doctors and psychiatrists and specialists for up-to-date reports and assessments. I filled folders and ring binders with proof-of-earnings documents that went back all the way to 1975 and beyond for my forensic accountants. I awaited every request from my solicitor and read and logged every update. I made notes and tried my best to read the body language of every conversation I had with my lawyers. I was a man in a hurry up against a system that was a world champion of the long game. Britain's well-practised 'deny, delay and death' policy has served it well for centuries.

However, the defendants' immediate response was not surprising. In relation to Robin Jackson, they said, 'We cannot confirm nor deny his position as an agent.' Also – and true to form – they pleaded that our cases were 'statute barred' due to the length of time that had elapsed since the murders, but we pointed out that crucial evidence had just been unearthed and given to us by the HET. My 'statement of claim' was as follows:

2012 No.

IN THE HIGH COURT OF JUSTICE IN NORTHERN IRELAND
QUEEN'S BENCH DIVISION

BETWEEN

STEPHEN THOMAS TRAVERS

Plaintiff:

and

MINISTRY OF DEFENCE

First Defendant:

and

CHIEF CONSTABLE OF THE POLICE SERVICE OF NORTHERN IRELAND

Second Defendant:

STATEMENT OF CLAIM

The parties

1. The plaintiff was born on 12 January 1951 and was at all times material to this claim a professional musician.

2. The first defendant is the Ministry of Defence, and is liable for the acts and omissions of officers referred to below (whose identities or descriptions, save where stated otherwise, are unknown to the plaintiff) in, or purportedly in, the course of employment, or which are so closely connected to it that it would be fair and just to hold the employer liable.

3. The second defendant is the Chief Constable of the Police Service of Northern Ireland, and is liable for the acts and omissions of officers and agents referred to below (whose identities or descriptions, save where stated otherwise, are unknown to the plaintiff) in, or purportedly in, the course of employment, or which are so closely connected to it that it would be fair and just to hold the employer liable.

Background

4. The plaintiff left school aged 17 years, and in February 1969 became a trainee broker with the firm of Price Forbes in London. He was at the same time playing music with bands in London, and on returning to Ireland in 1970 obtained work playing with the Cowboys. He developed a reputation as a musician, working consistently and with successful bands, until he secured the position of bass guitarist for the Miami Showband following a competitive audition.

5. In 1975 he was a member of the band together with Francis (Fran) O'Toole, Anthony Geraghty, Brian McCoy and Des McAlea (Des Lee). At that time the Miami Showband was one of the most popular showbands of the period. They were based in Dublin and had played in Northern Ireland at least once a week for the previous six years. The members of the Miami Showband were employees of a limited company operated from Dublin by Topline Management, and received a weekly wage.

The attack on the Miami Showband

6. On 31 July 1975 at approximately 0200 hours, while travelling back to Dublin in the band's minibus after a performance in Banbridge, County Down, the above members of the band were stopped on the

A1 between Banbridge and Newry, close to the junction with Buskhill Road. They were stopped at what appeared to be a vehicle checkpoint, ostensibly being operated by members of the Ulster Defence Regiment (UDR) and located in the vicinity of a UDR shooting range.

7. In fact, the checkpoint was being operated by a paramilitary patrol including members of the Ulster Volunteer Force (UVF). Many of these persons were dressed in military uniforms; items recovered in the course of the investigation included three green army berets.

8. The five members of the band travelling in the minibus were asked to get out and line up at the side of the road, and did so. One 'soldier', dressed differently from the others, appeared to take a position of authority, and spoke with what was perceived to be a well spoken English accent. As the band's details were being taken a bomb exploded, killing two men who had been attempting to place the bomb in the band's minibus.

9. The blast blew the five band members into a field. Other members of the patrol then opened fire, killing three members of the band (Francis O'Toole, Anthony Geraghty and Brian McCoy) and seriously injuring the plaintiff, who was struck by a 'dum-dum' bullet.

10. It is understood that the original intention of the perpetrators was to hide a bomb on the Miami Showband minibus; the members of the band would have been killed on explosion of the bomb, and could have been wrongly portrayed as having been involved in republican terrorist activity, and having been killed by a bomb they were transporting. It is plain that the effect of such a deception, had it been successfully executed, would have been to inflict enormous damage upon trust and community relations, and further to destabilise the political situation.

11. Within twelve hours of the murders a UVF press statement indicated that the two men killed (William Wesley Somerville and Horace Harris Boyle) were members of the organisation.

12. Two other members of the patrol (Thomas Raymond Crozier and James Roderick Shane McDowell) were convicted in October 1976 of offences including the murders of three members of the Miami Showband and the attempted murder of the plaintiff. A third member of the patrol (John James Somerville) was similarly convicted in November 1981.

13. Both Crozier and McDowell were members of the 11th Battalion of the UDR (11 UDR). Crozier was an associate of prominent loyalist paramilitary and Special Branch agent Robert 'Robin' Jackson (who in June 1974 was included on an 'excluded' list, exempting the named persons from targeting for British Army Intelligence psychological operations). On 6 June 1975 Crozier and Jackson (together with Samuel Fulton Neill) had been stopped by police in Banbridge in possession of shotguns. Both Jackson and Neill were arrested on 5 August 1975 on suspicion of involvement in the Miami Showband attack. Jackson's fingerprints were later found on a metal silencer found with, and compatible with, a 9mm calibre Luger semi-automatic pistol used in the Miami Showband attack.

Subversion in the UDR

14. It is now possible to assess the relationship between the UDR and loyalist paramilitary organisations in the mid-1970s in light of declassified government documents, and relevant reports of judicial and other inquiries. Notably, a British Army report in 1973 entitled Subversion in the UDR indicated that:

> "It seems likely that a significant proportion (perhaps 5% – in some areas as high as 15%) of UDR soldiers will also be members of the UDA, Vanguard Service Corps, Orange Volunteers or UVF. Subversion will not occur in every case, but there will be a passing on of information and training methods in many cases, and a few subversives may conspire to 'leak' arms and ammunition to Protestant extremist groups" (para 10).

15. The report indicated that since the beginning of the current campaign, the best single source of weapons (and the only significant source of modern weapons) for Protestant extremist groups had been the UDR. It was concluded that:

   "There can be little doubt that subversion in the UDR has added significantly to the weapons and ammunition stocks of Protestant extremist groups" (para 18).

16. Using the UDR as a case study, and having considered a range of government documents, Paul O'Connor and Alan Brecknell have concluded that:

   "[S]uccessive governments tolerated an illegal and deadly relationship between paramilitaries and security forces as part of a counter-insurgency policy".[1]

17. Vetting of prospective UDR members was undertaken by the second Defendant, with significant involvement of Sergeant Andrew (Drew) Coid of Special Branch. In 1975, Coid sought and obtained a number of British Army uniforms (10 or 12) through an officer attached to the Special Military Intelligence Unit; these were obtained from a UDR quartermaster in a manner that did not see Coid associated with their possession.

Historical Enquiries Team investigation

18. The case of the Miami Showband has now been re-investigated by the Historical Enquiries Team (HET). That investigation has considered six weapons identified as having been used in the attack: between them, these are linked to thirteen other murders and one attempted murder.

19. A Sterling Sterling 9mm calibre sub machine gun originally held at RUC Central Stores before being transferred to the Ulster Special

---

[1] 'British counter-insurgency practice in Northern Ireland in the 1970s – a legitimate response or state terror?' in *Counter-Terrorism and State Political Violence: The 'War on Terror' as Terror* (Routledge, 2012).

Constabulary (precursor to the UDR). It was reported stolen in 1970 from Donaghmore, Newry, in apparently unexplained circumstances in respect of which no records of investigation have been found.

20. Another Sterling 9mm calibre sub machine gun used in the attack was linked to murders of which William Thomas Leonard – a member of 8 UDR at the time of the murders on 7 May 1974 (and an admitted member of the UVF) – was convicted on 3 December 1975.

21. An Enfield (Albion) Mk II Smith and Wesson .38 calibre revolver was stolen on 23 October 1973 from E company 11 UDR depot Portadown, County Armagh in suspicious circumstances. Twelve armed men tied up the guards and bypassed the internal security systems. The raiders, who told the guards they were UVF, escaped with 4 self-loading rifles, two sub machine guns, five pistols and 150 rounds of ammunition. Connecting doors that should have been locked were left unsecure, a fence that would normally be overlooked was cut without any alarm raised and the raiders knew the combination of the cabinet containing the armoury keys. No charges followed investigation of the arms raid.

22. Although this weapon was recovered at the scene of the Miami Showband attack in respect of which 11 UDR members McDowell and Crozier were arrested, there is no indication that either was interviewed about the arms raid during that detention only 21 months later.

23. A 9mm calibre Luger semi-automatic pistol used in the attack was linked to the murder of John Francis Green in County Monaghan on 10 January 1975.

24. Robert 'Robin' Jackson had been arrested on 5 August 1975 as a suspect in respect of the Miami Showband attack, and was later linked by fingerprints to a metal silencer found at a dairy farm in Dungannon with the Luger pistol (with which it was compatible). There is however no indication that Jackson was re-arrested and interviewed further about that matter, or that those investigating the Miami Showband attack were advised of this significant development.

25. Interviewed by police in relation to the firearms allegation, Jackson alleged that a senior detective and junior officer provided him with information that enabled him to evade arrest and potentially obstructed justice by providing him with an alibi. His allegations were reported to RUC Headquarters, but no record of any further investigation has been found.

26. The attack on the Miami Showband was pre-planned and co-ordinated. Those involved had access to UDR weapons and uniforms. The attack was militarily executed by UDR soldiers operating in collusion with UVF associates. Those associates included Robert 'Robin' Jackson, who was linked to the Luger pistol used in the attack by his fingerprints. Jackson was a Special Branch agent, given the protection of placement on an 'excluded' list over a year before the Miami Showband attack.

27. Furthermore, the investigation and prosecution of offences disclosed by, or related to, the attack on the members of the Miami Showband was undermined or impeded by police. An arms raid in suspicious circumstances, that yielded a weapon used in the Miami Showband attack, was not properly investigated. Police failed to further interview a suspect (Jackson, who was a Special Branch agent) on receipt of important new evidence linking him to a weapon used in the attack, and were alleged to have instead assisted him in evading arrest.

28. By reason of the above, the plaintiff has suffered personal injuries, loss and damage. The said personal injuries, loss and damage were caused by reason of:

    i. the assault, battery and trespass to the person, wrongful interference with goods, misfeasance in a public office, intentional infliction of harm, conspiracy to injure and negligence of the first defendant, its servants and agents, and

    ii. the misfeasance in a public office and negligence of the second defendant, his servants and agents as follows:

PARTICULARS OF ASSAULT, BATTERY AND TRESPASS TO THE PERSON OF THE FIRST DEFENDANT

a) Conspiring to attack the Miami Showband.
b) Using weapons in the attack on the Miami Showband.
c) Causing an explosion on the minibus of the Miami Showband.
d) Causing injury to the plaintiff by, or as a result of, an explosion.
e) Causing injury to the plaintiff by, or as a result of, the use of a firearm.
f) Attempting to kill the plaintiff.
g) Discharging a firearm with intent to kill the plaintiff.

PARTICULARS OF WRONGFUL INTERFERENCE WITH GOODS OF THE FIRST DEFENDANT

The plaintiff repeats the above particulars of the foregoing tort as particulars of wrongful interference with goods.

a) Damaging or destroying the property of the plaintiff by, or as a result of, an explosion.
b) Damaging or destroying the property of the plaintiff by, or as a result of, the use of a firearm.

PARTICULARS OF MISFEASANCE IN A PUBLIC OFFICE OF THE FIRST DEFENDANT

The plaintiff repeats the above particulars of the foregoing torts as particulars of misfeasance in a public office.

a) Tolerating and permitting the UDR membership of persons who were also members of, or strongly supportive of, paramilitary organisations.
b) Tolerating and permitting the UDR membership of persons likely to use UDR knowledge, skills, and / or equipment to further the aims of paramilitary organisations.
c) Failing to identify and / or remove from the UDR persons who were members of, or strongly supportive of, paramilitary organisations.

d) Allowing the use of UDR weapons, uniforms and / or equipment by those involved in the attack on the Miami Showband, with the intention of bringing about the plaintiff's death or serious injury, or with reckless indifference to the illegality of so doing, and in the knowledge of, or with reckless indifference to, the probability of causing the plaintiff's death or serious injury.

e) Colluding in a terrorist attack on the Miami Showband with the intention of bringing about the plaintiff's death or serious injury, or with reckless indifference to the illegality of so doing, and in the knowledge of, or with reckless indifference to, the probability of causing the plaintiff's death or serious injury.

f) Attacking the Miami Showband with the intention of bringing about the plaintiff's death or serious injury, or with reckless indifference to the illegality of so doing, and in the knowledge of, or with reckless indifference to, the probability of causing the plaintiff's death or serious injury.

g) Injuring the plaintiff with the intention of bringing about the plaintiff's death or serious injury, or with reckless indifference to the illegality of so doing, and in the knowledge of, or with reckless indifference to, the probability of causing the plaintiff's death or serious injury.

PARTICULARS OF INTENTIONAL INFLICTION OF HARM OF THE FIRST DEFENDANT

The plaintiff repeats the above particulars of the foregoing torts as particulars of intentional infliction of harm.

PARTICULARS OF CONSPIRACY TO INJURE OF THE FIRST DEFENDANT

The plaintiff repeats the above particulars of the foregoing torts as particulars of conspiracy to injure.

a) Conspiring to cause economic harm to the plaintiff.
b) Conspiring to cause economic harm to the Miami Showband of which the plaintiff was a member.

PARTICULARS OF NEGLIGENCE OF THE FIRST DEFENDANT

The plaintiff repeats the above particulars of the foregoing torts as particulars of negligence.

a) Allowing members of paramilitary organisations to join and remain in the UDR.
b) Failing to operate a reasonable recruitment policy.
c) Failing to ensure that inappropriate persons were not engaged in service with the UDR.
d) Failing to ensure that inappropriate persons were not removed from service with the UDR.
e) Allowing the acquisition of weapons by those involved in the attack on the Miami Showband.
f) Failing to prevent the acquisition of weapons by those involved in the attack on the Miami Showband.
g) Allowing the acquisition of military uniforms and / or equipment by those involved in the attack on the Miami Showband.
h) Failing to prevent the acquisition of military uniforms and / or equipment by those involved in the attack on the Miami Showband.
i) Allowing members of the UDR to collude with terrorists in an attack on the Miami Showband.
j) Failing to prevent members of the UDR colluding with terrorists in an attack on the Miami Showband.
k) Allowing members of the UDR to attack the Miami Showband.
l) Failing to prevent members of the UDR attacking the Miami Showband.

PARTICULARS OF MISFEASANCE IN A PUBLIC OFFICE OF THE SECOND DEFENDANT

a) Conspiring to attack the Miami Showband.
b) Causing the attack on the Miami Showband to proceed, notwithstanding the availability to the second Defendant of information from an agent or agents of Special Branch.

c) Allowing the attack on the Miami Showband to proceed, notwithstanding the availability to the second Defendant of information from an agent or agents of Special Branch.
d) Assisting in the attack on the Miami Showband.
e) Failing to prevent the attack on the Miami Showband, notwithstanding the availability to the second Defendant of information from an agent or agents of Special Branch.
f) Engaging in collusive behaviour in relation to a terrorist attack on the Miami Showband and offences related thereto, with the intention of frustrating the interests of justice in terms of the apprehension of the plaintiff's assailants, or with reckless indifference to the illegality of so doing, and in the knowledge of, or with reckless indifference to, the probability of frustrating the interests of justice in terms of the apprehension of the plaintiff's assailants.

PARTICULARS OF NEGLIGENCE OF THE SECOND DEFENDANT

a) Failing adequately to investigate the theft of weapons from the custody of the UDR and / or Ulster Special Constabulary.
b) Further to (a) or in the alternative, failing to interview arrested members of 11 UDR about the theft of weapons from the custody of the UDR following recovery in the course of investigation of the Miami Showband attack of a weapon stolen from the custody of 11 UDR.
c) Failing to arrest and further interview a person suspected of the Miami Showband attack on receipt of significant information linking that person to a weapon recovered in the course of investigation of the Miami Showband attack.
c) Failing to advise relevant officers of significant information linking a suspect to a weapon recovered in the course of investigation of the Miami Showband attack.
d) Providing a suspect with information that enabled him to evade arrest.
e) Providing a suspect with an alibi.
f) Failing adequately to investigation allegations of misconduct against officers alleged to have engaged in collusive behaviour.

g) Failing to operate a reasonable vetting policy in respect of prospective members of the UDR.

h) Failing to ensure that inappropriate persons were identified as such in order that they be precluded, or removed, from service with the UDR.

i) Failing to ensure that members of paramilitary organisations were identified as such in order that they be precluded, or removed, from service with the UDR.

j) Failing to ensure that information available from an agent or agents of Special Branch was obtained, disseminated, and acted upon.

k) Failing to prevent the Miami Showband attack.

In proof of the torts alleged the plaintiff will rely on such facts as are within the knowledge of the defendant and his witnesses but not of the plaintiff, and on such facts as may appear from the evidence for the defence at the trial of this action.

27. [sic] By reason of the aforesaid acts and omissions the plaintiff has sustained personal injuries, loss and damage, has suffered loss of income, and in the circumstances the plaintiff claims damages for personal injuries, loss and damage including aggravated and exemplary damages.

PARTICULARS OF PERSONAL INJURIES

The plaintiff underwent a laparotomy, involving an incision approximately 7 inches in length, at Daisy Hill Hospital, Newry, on 31 July 1975. Approximately 2–2.5 litres of blood was found in the peritoneal cavity, and about 12–15 holes in the small bowel. There was a hole in the left dome of the diaphragm, through which blood was coming.

Haemostasis was effected by identifying and ligating bleeding mesenteric vessels. Segments of the small bowel were resected and anastomosed end to end. Other small holes in the small bowel wall and mesentry were repaired in two layers.

The plaintiff remained in Daisy Hill Hospital for approximately two weeks, and was then transferred to hospital in Dublin for a further two weeks before being discharged.

Examination of the plaintiff shows evidence of sensorineural hearing loss affecting both ears at the higher frequencies, a proportion of which would be due to his involvement in the explosion on 31 July 1975. The plaintiff also suffers from mild – moderate tinnitus, the majority of which would be due to the explosion on 31 July 1975. This tinnitus affects both ears and is constant in nature, and can affect the plaintiff's daily activities (such as by delaying the onset of sleep at night for up to 20 minutes).

Following assessment by Dr M. G. Kelly (Consultant Psychiatrist) on 4 November 1976 it was concluded that the plaintiff was suffering from a chronic disabling anxiety depressive state, directly attributable to the trauma, particularly psychological, of the massacre of the Miami Showband. The prognosis for recovery was at that time poor.

Following assessment by Dr Maria O' Kane (Consultant Psychiatrist and Psychotherapist) on 13 October 2012 it was concluded that the symptoms described by the plaintiff were in keeping with a diagnosis of Enduring personality change after catastrophic experience (such as can occur after exposure to life-threatening situations such as being a victim of terrorism). This condition is recognised as irreversible and is not amenable to treatment.

PARTICULARS OF LOSS AND DAMAGE

Following the attack on the Miami Showband, the plaintiff lost the income he had attained with the band. Attempts to continue playing with a new line-up of the Miami Showband and thereafter with a new band (Starband) ended in or about 1980: the plaintiff experienced difficulties both with his hearing and with performing in the aftermath of the attack, feeling that the survivors had come to be viewed as a spectacle. The plaintiff moved to London with his wife in or about 1982 and started to work in the newspaper industry. He returned to Ireland in or about 1997.

The plaintiff has subsequently been involved in music production, but is hampered in the mixing process because of hearing difficulties with higher frequencies.

[Details of loss to follow]

PARTICULARS SUPPORTING AN AWARD OF AGGRAVATED AND / OR EXEMPLARY DAMAGES AGAINST THE DEFENDANTS

a) Involvement and / or collusion in unlawful violence against civilian targets and / or in interference with the course of justice, in furtherance of a political agenda.

And the plaintiff claims damages and interest thereon pursuant to section 33A of the Judicature (Northern Ireland) Act 1978.

EILIS McDERMOTT QC
DONAL SAYERS

20
Demons

I visit Hell.

On 13 October 2012 I drove to Belfast for an up-to-date psychiatric report, after which I was very tired. With a long drive to Cork ahead of me, I headed towards the city centre in search of a McDonald's for a sugar hit. One large coffee, a vanilla milkshake and a chocolate McFlurry later and I was ready for the road. I pointed my car in the direction of the motorway, but I was hardly behind the wheel when I came upon a line of six or seven cars backed up in front of me. My Toyota Landcruiser afforded me a clear view over the other cars and I could see a PSNI police officer diverting the traffic down another street. I fully expected him to tell me to follow the others, but as I approached him, he looked at my Irish registration number plate and, to my surprise, waved me on. Glancing in my rear-view mirror, I could see that I was the only vehicle allowed to go through, but then I noticed thick smoke coming from what looked like a small fire on the street up ahead, which was reducing visibility, so I slowed down. As I got close, through the smoke I could see about a dozen young men who appeared to be setting up a roadblock over which they were placing a sizeable union flag. I was concerned for my safety, but fortunately the smoke obscured my number plates and I drove straight through without stopping and safely onto the main Belfast–Dublin road. Travelling down the motorway, I kept thinking, 'If only we had driven straight through the roadblock on 31 July 1975. Having recounted and relived the massacre with the psychiatrist just a few hours earlier, I wondered if I was exaggerating the perceived danger.

Road signs displaying placenames, long burned into my mind, flashed past me as I sped down the A1. Rathfriland, Banbridge, Lough Brickland, and suddenly, standing on thin, green iron legs were two words that are forever printed large on my soul in black-on-white lettering: Buskhill Road. As if with a mind of its own, my black SUV slowed, turned left, then instantly turned right and came to a halt at the very spot where we were ordered out of our minibus all those years ago. Just as I've done on many occasions when I can find no peace, I had returned to the holding cell between my two realities. The darkness and the silence, and especially the timelessness, would afford me a weightless, out-of-body freedom to wander through the screams and the noise and the flames. I knew what was to come and so I turned off the engine and the lights and tilted my seat back and closed my eyes and I waited for them.

Robin 'The Jackal' Jackson was the first to speak, 'Ah, there ya are, big man ... lookin' fit ... but yer not as fit as ya let on now, are ya?'

Standing beside him was the horribly disfigured, mutilated carcass of his faithful lieutenant, Harris Boyle, who, almost inaudibly, blood-gurgled, 'Carryin' all that oul stuff around in yer head, sure it must be doin' ya in, what di ya say, Wesley?'

'Ah for fuck sake, Stephen, sure didn't we do yer three mates a fuckin' favour puttin' em outta their fuckin' misery? You'd be better off goin' with them, so ya would, big man ... an' yer well up for it, aren't ya?' Somerville added.

Jackson moved closer to me. 'Course ya are, big man, instead a wakin' up at all hours, wishin' ta fuck ya were dead and tormentin' yerself and yer poor wife an' child. Sure you're fuck all good to 'em now anyway.'

Boyle raised his voice almost to a wail. 'Aye, an' what's all this bollocks about goin' on the fuckin' radio an' mouthin' off about us after we makin' ye fuckin' famous? Sure ye'd all be well forgot by now if it wasn't for us.' His putrid breath sprayed into my face.

'Ungrateful shower of fuckin' bastards,' retorted Wesley Somerville angrily.

I turned to walk away, but Boyle pushed past me, his tormented features rapidly disintegrating.

'Ya haven't much ta say for yerself now, ya wee bastard, have ya?' Jackson screeched, clearly in terrible pain. 'Don't you dare turn your fucking back on me.'

Holding out a long, filthy rope hanging from his one remaining shattered bloody forearm, Harris Boyle's voice softened. 'Here ya are, mate, this'll make it all stop right now this minute,' he said, pointing at the tree overlooking the killing field.

Jackson and Somerville drew closer, imploring me, 'Go on, Stephen, end the fuckin' thing now and everyone can move on.'

Suddenly my phone rang and I sat bolt upright in my seat. It was Anne. 'Just checking how close you are to Cork,' she said.

'Ah, I pulled in for a rest, I was exhausted after the day. I'm fine now, love, but don't wait up. I'll probably stop again on the Naas Road for a coffee.'

21
Heroes

Murder on the road.

In 2014 the two survivors of the Miami Showband massacre, Des McAlea and I, received an invitation to meet the Lord Mayor of Belfast, Máirtín Ó Muilleoir. The meeting was arranged for 3 p.m. on 13 May at Belfast City Hall by our solicitor, Michael Flanigan. We had been told 'get on with your lives and forget you have a case', but that was impossible. It had become central to our lives and foremost in our minds from the day we began so we were happy to do anything that was case-related because it felt like progress. It was a good opportunity too to keep our civil action in the public consciousness as the meeting would be covered in the press. We were also due to meet our barrister, Éilís McDermott, for the first time later that afternoon at the High Court. At the onset, we naively believed that the case would take about two years but, at this stage, almost three years on, the defendants still hadn't served their defence.

In the meantime I had received a call from Gerry Byrne, a long-time friend of Eugene Reavey, who I'd met a few times in Cork when he came down from Armagh to visit his partner's daughter. Gerry asked if I would meet his friend Alan Black, who, although critically wounded and left for dead, had miraculously survived the Kingsmill massacre. I was curious to meet a man whose experience is remarkably similar to mine. I arranged to go to his home in Bessbrook with Gerry before my appointment at City Hall.

Alan welcomed me warmly. It was obvious that he and Gerry shared a special bond since Gerry was one of the first to come across the carnage at Kingsmill, where Alan had been shot and left dying among the butchered bodies of his friends and workmates. Almost on arrival, he asked if I would watch a documentary that he did for TV rather than having to recount his painful story. Gerry and I watched the DVD in silence while Alan made the tea before joining me and his faithful little dog on the brown leather sofa in his living room. When the film finished, we talked about the striking similarities between Alan's experience and mine and how we've both tried to cope with life ever since. It was fascinating, too, to hear Alan express his heartfelt gratitude to Gerry for saving his life that day.

At 5.25 p.m. on the evening of 5 January 1976, Gerry Byrne and his brother-in-law Charlie Hughes were driving a lorryload of timber towards the small south Armagh village of Whitecross. Charlie was at the wheel chatting when, through the darkness and the light rain, Gerry spotted what he thought was a cow lying across the road beside a Ford Transit minibus up at the brow of the hill. At first they thought the minibus had crashed into one of the local farmer's herd but, as they got closer, they realised they were looking at human bodies, piled up on top of one another. Charlie stopped the truck but left the headlights on. Both men got out, and as they walked forward, each step further revealed the most horrific scene either of them could possibly have imagined. In the headlight beams, they could see steam rising up from the strewn bodies through the silent, misty rain. It appeared to Gerry that everyone was dead, but when he heard a groaning sound coming from the back of the minibus he went to investigate and found a body on the road, its head against the rear wheel of the bus. Alan Black had been shot eighteen times and the force of the gunfire had knocked him back under the Ford, wedging his head in beside the back wheel. Gerry dragged Alan by his heels from underneath the vehicle and placed him in the recovery position on the road. Alan seemed to be going in and out of consciousness, so Charlie whispered an act of contrition in his ear while Gerry ran the 400 metres down the road to Henry Magee's farmhouse to raise the alarm. Having received a number of threats, the Magee family had parked their farm tractor in front of the house with one of the larger wheels across the front door for security. Shouting at the top of his voice, Gerry managed to bang on the door with his fist and when a startled Lottie Magee opened the upstairs window he told her to call the police and ambulance services. According to Gerry, the first ambulance arrived about twenty minutes later, by which time a sizeable crowd had gathered at the scene of the slaughter. One of the first cars to approach from the Whitecross direction was Eugene Reavey with his father and mother on board. They were on their way to the Daisy Hill Hospital morgue to collect the bodies of two of his brothers, John-Martin and Brian, who had been murdered at their home in Whitecross the previous evening. Eugene got out of his car and walked up to the minibus with Gerry, but, coupled with the dreadful trauma that he and his family had endured just twenty-four hours earlier, he could barely stay on his feet. Manifestly distraught at the carnage on the road, he had to be helped back to his car. The ten men who were murdered by the IRA that evening were John Bryans, Robert Chambers, Reginald Chapman, Walter Chapman, Robert Freeburn, Joseph Lemmon, John McConville, James McWhirter, Robert Samuel Walker and Kenneth Worton.

For many years, Alan Black wondered about the young man who saved his life that night, but it wasn't until 2013 that he and Gerry Byrne finally met. Alan also told me how grateful he was for the extraordinary generosity shown to him by Sadie Reavey, the mother of the Reavey brothers who had been murdered the evening before. He also spoke of his friendship with her son, Eugene.

I left Bessbrook and headed towards our mayoral reception at Belfast City Hall with a lot to think about. I was happy to meet Alan, but what he swore to me as 'the gospel truth' that morning, in the presence of the man who had saved his life at Kingsmill, left me in shock, and it continues to trouble me greatly to this day.

22
Diversion

I receive information from an unexpected source.

The first Truth and Reconciliation Platform (TaRP) event took place on 15 April 2016, at 7.30 p.m. at Tí Chulainn in Mullaghbawn, Co. Armagh, and was chaired by the local historian Kevin Murphy. The format was modelled on Michael O'Hare's 'Troubles, Tragedy and Trauma: Northern Ireland's Historic Legacy', which we had taken part in that January, in London. We didn't have any government funding at that stage so had to get the word out as best we could. Nevertheless, we were satisfied with the turnout and with the reaction from all present. Just a few days prior to the event, we were told that if we could arrange a TaRP presentation for the following evening, the Al Jazeera TV network would be keen to record it. It was a big challenge at such short notice, but it was also a huge platform on which the testimonies of victims from all sides of the conflict could reach a large international audience. Fortunately, the Rev. Chris Hudson came to the rescue and gave Al Jazeera permission to film a special TaRP event at All Souls Non-Subscribing Presbyterian Church, close to Queen's University Belfast. That event was chaired by the writer and broadcaster Eamonn Mallie. At the end of the evening, I was asked if I would speak with a 'staunch, loyal Orangeman' who had come along to tell me something that had been playing on his mind since the night of the massacre.

The Orangeman wasn't tall but he was strong and stocky. He didn't smile or engage in any small talk and he appeared anxious to get to the point, but 'not in the old church'. He suggested that we might go to a restaurant or 'somewhere we can talk'. I told him that my friend, John Travers, from Kilkenny was with me and that we had a long journey ahead of us. I explained that, although John and I shared the same surname, we weren't related, but that I'd known him since we were teenagers and he could be trusted to be discreet about anything he might hear. He was happy to include John and we settled on a nearby late-night café.

He began by telling me that he was a farmer and that he lived south of Banbridge, close to the border. I didn't know what to expect because, quite often, people simply want to tell me that they heard ambulance or police sirens on the night of the murders or that they met their future partners at one of our dances. However, the Orangeman got my undivided attention when he said that he was at the Miami dance in the Castle Ballroom in Banbridge on the night of 30 July and that, later, he was 'parked at the lakes for a bit of a court' with the lady he subsequently married, when the explosion happened. He went on to say that, although it was a few miles away, it 'lifted' the boot, or tailgate, of his car, whereupon he 'immediately drove the car onto the road towards Newry, but within a couple of minutes' they were stopped by security forces and diverted down another road, thus avoiding the area where the killings would still have been in progress.

It would have been impossible for the security forces to put a diversion in place that quickly, and over the years I had often wondered why no vehicles drove past us on that busy main road while we were stopped and being questioned by the murderers. In the absence of any other explanation, it would appear that there was an 'out-of-bounds' order in place to allow the 'operation' to proceed uninterrupted. Such an order would have required authorisation from high up the chain of command.

I told him about the civil action I was taking against the chief constable of the PSNI and the Ministry of Defence and asked if he would give a statement to my solicitor in Belfast, but he said he wouldn't as he felt he'd 'be in danger'.

However, when I arranged to meet with him again in Belfast with Eugene Reavey, he told us to go to a very busy street in the city centre where he would pick us up in a small camper-style van and that we were to waste no time getting in when he arrived. He was on time and he flashed his headlights as he approached. Eugene and I had no sooner entered through the sliding side door when he set off again, but, to our surprise, he pulled into a parking space just around the corner on an equally busy street, opposite a large carpark. He left his driver's seat and joined us in the back of the van, but before he sat down with us at the fixed table, he took our phones and put them into a small microwave oven and closed the door, an exercise I have become used to over the years.

I was glad that Eugene was there because, although they said they'd never met before, he and the Orangemen were both farmers and a few comments about the weather broke the ice. He was much more relaxed than when we first met and he began by telling us about his background, which made me wonder all the more why he would want to tell me about the traffic diversion on the main Belfast–Dublin road at the precise time of the murders. However, he explained that his Christian faith compelled him to tell the truth to the innocent victims of such a terrible outrage.

He repeated the story exactly as he had related it to me in Belfast, but on this occasion, when I asked if he would make a statement to my solicitor, he said he 'would consider doing so'.

With his permission, I passed his name and contact details on to Michael Flanigan. I also gave his name and contact details to Jon Boutcher, who was head of Operation Kenova and Operation Denton at the time. Jon Boutcher was appointed chief constable of the Police Service of Northern Ireland in 2023.

23
The Fox in Charge of the Hen House

The betrayal of victims and a monumental conflict of interest.

Our scheduled 'end of June 2018' recap meeting at the Canal Court Hotel in Newry with Seamus Mallon, Anthony Reavey and other Truth and Reconciliation Platform colleagues was concluded by midday, and Eugene Reavey asked if I'd accompany him to Banbridge to collect his new iPhone. He was no sooner set up and connected to his network when a slew of missed calls, desperate voice messages, despairing text messages and emails from victims of British security forces and loyalist paramilitary organisations began to register thick and fast. Eugene's face was ashen. He didn't say a word. He didn't have to. He just handed me his phone. Although it had been flagged for weeks, I could hardly believe my eyes. The appointment of Jeremy Andrew (Drew) Harris OBE as Ireland's new garda commissioner had been officially confirmed by the Irish government on 26 June 2018.

The garda commissioner is the head of An Garda Síochána, and is appointed by the government of Ireland on the recommendation of the minister for justice. The commissioner reports to the minister, who is in charge of the Department of Justice of which An Garda Síochána is a state agency. The garda commissioner sits on the Irish government's National Security Committee and is responsible for Ireland's domestic state security apparatus.

Back in the phone shop, Eugene remained shocked. He had always maintained that the Dublin government would not proceed with the appointment of someone who had let down so many seeking justice for the victims of state collusion. 'Dublin has betrayed us,' he said quietly.

I had no answers for Eugene. The situation was unprecedented.

John O'Brien, a retired detective chief superintendent and former head of the International Liaison Protection section in Garda HQ, perfectly summed up the Irish government's astonishing decision when he declared: 'No country that I'm aware of would have an officer that is directly connected with the security of another state running its security service. I know of no state security organisation in Europe, or elsewhere, that would do it that particular way.'

After the Miami Showband massacre, my only goal was to get back to normal. I wanted my old life back. I had no interest in conspiracy theories. I didn't want to believe that the Britain I admired had slaughtered my friends and tried to murder me. However, in 2005, having been shown incontrovertible documented evidence of widespread collusion between British security forces and paramilitary organisations, I could no longer maintain my denial. I watched in horror as leak after leak dripped into the public arena. Overall, the accumulated pool clearly confirms collusion on an industrial scale.

At one stage the RUC carried out its own dirty work, which became known as its 'shoot-to-kill' policy. In the early 1980s John Stalker, the deputy chief constable of the Manchester police, was tasked with investigating a series of deaths at RUC checkpoints and elsewhere. In response, MI5 and other dark forces vilified this honest and principled British police officer and removed him from the inquiry. The man in charge of the RUC at the time, Sir John Hermon, had threatened Stalker after his arrival in the North. Hermon once told the British government not to outlaw the UDA. The RUC Special Branch continued to engage in a conspiracy to murder using proxy assassins.

In 1989 John Stevens, who later became Metropolitan Police commissioner, was appointed to investigate claims of collusion between State forces and loyalist paramilitaries in numerous other killings. His investigations lasted fourteen years, during which his HQ in Belfast – 'protected by the RUC' – was the subject of an arson attack. Despite these and other obstacles, Stevens managed to unearth some of the truth about collusion.

The victims of the Glenanne Gang and their families brought pressure to bear on the State to investigate the activities of that alliance and, in particular, the issue of collusion. Figures vary as to how many people were murdered by the so-called gang, but the number is widely believed to be in excess of one hundred. Incredibly, the door was slammed in their face in 2010 by Drew Harris, who wrote to the campaigners informing them that an investigation into the wider questions raised by the activities of the Glenanne Gang, i.e. collusion with the State, would not proceed. The families were aghast. Drew Harris and the RUC were unilaterally subverting a decade of assurances furnished by the UK government to the Committee of Ministers of the Council of Europe that investigations into State killings would be carried out independently and would examine patterns and links to reveal systematic violations by the State of 'the Right to Life', which was enshrined in Article 2 of the European Convention of Human Rights.

The HET, a vehicle designed to carry out such an inquiry, was already in place. The HET was a unit of the PSNI set up in 2005 to investigate the 3,269 unsolved murders committed during the Troubles, specifically between 1968 and 1998. It had established a unit that was purportedly independent of the RUC and the PSNI. While it was run by police officers, the HET had a modicum of credibility among the more optimistic of survivors and families of murder victims as it was based in England and had no members that had served in the RUC or the PSNI. The HET had been sold to the European oversight mechanism as a creditable response to European Court judgements in a range of State killing cases in 2001. It was presented as an operationally independent body as it did not have to seek leave from the PSNI in relation to its investigations and it had its own finances although the Relatives for Justice group (RFJ), for example, never accepted the HET's assertions of independence from the State. Their position was vindicated in 2014 when Her Majesty's Inspectorate of Policing found that the HET was lacking in independence and had acted illegally when examining cases where the State was implicated. Yet Drew Harris and the top brass of the PSNI were not even prepared to let the HET look at the question of collusion between the RUC and the UVF. The only conclusion I can draw from this was that the pile of collusive dirt was so large there was no carpet big enough under which to sweep it all.

Originally, in 2009, the PSNI had provided assurances of the independence of the HET to the Committee of Ministers. It was after this that Drew Harris made his move. In 2010 he brought the HET under his control as head of the Crime Operations Branch of the PSNI. He removed investigative functions from HET officers, which meant that they could no longer arrest and question suspects. Harris took control of their budget and closed down their thematic investigation unit that cross-referenced the individual investigations for links, patterns and systems drawing out the involvement of RUC personnel and wider collusion. Victims' families took Drew Harris to the High Court in Belfast, and in 2017 Mr Justice Treacy gave his devastating assessment, accusing Drew Harris of an 'extreme' abuse of power in closing down this exercise in analysing collusion, making it clear that 'the State is not genuinely committed' to addressing the concerns of families despite all its claims to Europe. This move made a mockery of the new PSNI since it had been sold to the public as the 'new beginning to policing' in the North. To make matters worse, the PSNI was exposed as having been guilty of endemic disclosure of information failures in cases involving allegations of RUC–loyalist collusion. The PSNI, it emerged, had habitually failed to provide disclosure to inquests and in civil cases. One of these 'failures' related to a group of UVF agents involved in killings and in the attempted murder of a man called John Flynn.

Drew Harris was severely criticised by the families and survivors of UVF atrocities. Relatives for Justice stated that: 'It is surely time for [Harris] to resign. He is a reminder of the political policing of the past and the contamination of current policing by the cover up of the past. His role in this case is the last straw.' However, Harris did not resign. Instead, in October 2014, he was promoted to the post of deputy chief constable, i.e. second-in-command of the PSNI.

By now, retired RUC officers had banded together under the banner of the Northern Ireland Retired Police Officers Association (NIRPOA). The body opposed inquests into killings involving the RUC. It had ongoing access to the top tier of the PSNI at what were called 'legacy seminars'. At one of these seminars, Harris's predecessor as deputy chief constable, Judith Gillespie, told her former colleagues that 'our interests are similar' and 'the PSNI is determined to play our part in the defence of the RUC'. Drew Harris, still an assistant chief constable, assured them that 'we don't dissociate ourselves from what happened in the past. I have a great pride in my RUC service.' The senior legal advisor of the PSNI, also in attendance at a meeting, confirmed during a Q&A: 'The bedrock of what we are trying to do is to protect our people. To protect the reputation of the organisation and to protect people's security.'

In 2013 a retired US diplomat, Dr Richard Haass, chaired talks in an effort to resolve a string of issues dividing the political parties in Northern Ireland. The talks, which took place over several months, included issues such as parades, flags and allegations of collusive murder during the Troubles. The NIRPOA made submissions to

Haass in 2013 in which they castigated inquests into controversial State killings as nothing more than show trials of police officers and British soldiers.

In November 2014 Drew Harris found himself in the witness box at an inquest into the killing of six people by the RUC. The deaths were those probed by John Stalker before he was removed from his inquiry by RUC dirty tricks. Harris was obliged to answer questions about the length of time it had taken to hand over records relating to three RUC 'shoot-to-kill' incidents. By now, the PSNI had access to the most powerful computers available to any police force in the world. In fact, the RUC and PSNI had been at the cutting edge of information retrieval for decades. Yet, as a frustrated John Lecky, the senior coroner, pointed out to Harris, the PSNI's engagement in the disclosure process had lasted 'longer than the Second World War'.

In the witness box, Harris was asked about the submissions made by his former colleagues at the Haass talks. He claimed to have no knowledge of their hostile attitude. Drew Harris was asked about the tone of seminars arranged to brief NIRPOA members on inquests and other legacy matters. He had previously sought to describe these as informal and focused on practical information and support. He had claimed that there were no notes of the proceedings. Yet notes, which had recorded the discussions, had emerged. The record now pointed to an entirely different agenda. Harris was asked about the occasion when he, Gillespie and the PSNI senior legal adviser had reassured former RUC officers that the PSNI would defend the legacy of the RUC and put its activities in the best possible light through the inquest process. The relevant quotes (outlined above) were put to Harris. When challenged about his own contribution, Drew Harris replied that he had no recollection of the recorded words.

The unit responsible for control of the files relating to RUC–UVF and RUC–UDA collusion at this time was the Legacy Support Unit (LSU), under the control of Drew Harris. It was responsible for redacting sensitive information prior to its release to the families of victims. It emerged that all of Harris's key staff were former RUC Special Branch officers. Harris refused to accept that his staff were being too cautious in what they wished to cover up. As lawyers pointed out, this system contravened European case law, which required mechanisms investigating State killings to be independent and to be seen to be independent. A barrister put it to Harris that, by employing former RUC Special Branch officers in all the key positions, he had deployed people with a 'corporate allegiance' to the reputation and name of the RUC. The PSNI, under Harris, continued to drag its feet.

In 2018 Drew Harris resigned from the PSNI in order to take up his new role in the Republic of Ireland as Garda Commissioner at the request of the Irish government.

On Tuesday evening, 26 June, Denise Johnston from the SDLP party, presented an event at St Patrick's Parish Hall, Chapel Hill, Lisburn, entitled 'The Bomb and Bullet Legacy'. It was chaired by Seamus Mallon and, along with Eugene Reavey and me, the guest speakers were Kate Carroll and Alan McBride. Driving back to my hotel afterwards, I accepted an invitation from the RTÉ Radio 1 flagship programme *Morning Ireland* to be interviewed by Audrey Carville the following morning about the appointment of the new Garda Commissioner. The transcript is as follows:

> Audrey: *Drew Harris will be the new Garda Commissioner. He's Deputy Chief Constable of the Police Service of Northern Ireland (PSNI) who began his career in the old RUC (Royal Ulster Constabulary). He's the first non-citizen of the Republic to fill the post. For several years Mr Harris was Assistant Chief Constable in command of the PSNI Crime Operations Department – that incorporated everything to do with intelligence gathering plus serious crime. He was promoted to Deputy Chief Constable four years ago. We'll hear Sinn Féin's reaction to his appointment in a moment.*

But first, I've been speaking to a survivor of the Miami Showband Murders – three members of the band were taken from their tour bus and shot dead on a country road after a gig in Banbridge, Co. Down, in July 1975.

They were travelling back to Dublin when a fake British Army patrol made up of UDR (Ulster Defence Regiment) soldiers and UVF (Ulster Volunteer Force) members stopped them at a bogus checkpoint outside Newry. In 2011 a report by the Historical Enquiries Team (HET) raised collusion concerns around the involvement of an RUC Special Branch agent. Well, Stephen Travers survived the attack. He told me a while ago why he was angry about Drew Harris's appointment as the new head of An Garda Síochána.

Stephen: Well, I believe that it's putting the fox in charge of the hen house. As a survivor of The Miami Showband Massacre, I'm part of a civil action against the Chief Constable of the PSNI and the British Ministry of Defence. And during the past eight years, since our action was started, the Office of the Chief Constable, of which Drew Harris is the second most senior officer, has blocked, delayed and frustrated our every effort to access the files on those who murdered our three lads and who shot me. And just last week they gave us notice that they're seeking a Public Interest Immunity certificate to block us from getting their files on the notorious RUC Special Branch agent and mass murderer, Robin Jackson, often referred to as 'The Jackal'. Now can you imagine our new Garda Commissioner being questioned in relation to the Miami Showband Massacre and its cover-up? This new appointment is a hammer blow to every victim of collusion between British security forces and loyalist terrorists. This new appointment is not progressive. It's a massive step backwards and it's certainly not helping reconciliation.

And while every effort is being made, and rightly so, in reconciling both communities and understanding that no side has a monopoly on suffering or loss, it's certainly not right to reach out to one community and slap the other community in the face like this. The damage it will *do to our government's relationship – hard-won relationship – with the nationalist community in the North will be catastrophic.*

Audrey: And yet Drew Harris is someone who, despite his own personal loss and personal tragedy, continued to work with Republicans during his time in senior roles in the Police Service of Northern Ireland. He's seen as a trusted part of a modern, senior PSNI management and he says that there will be no conflict of loyalties when he takes up his new role.

Stephen: Well, he can swear allegiance to uphold our constitution as many times as he likes, but I would prefer if he just held up his hands and said: Here are the files. We will no longer block the files on the people who are responsible for the Miami Showband Massacre and, indeed, the Dublin-Monaghan bombings.

I think that perhaps we should be talking as well to people like Joe Campbell – whose father was Joseph Campbell, an RUC sergeant, a decent man, who was shot and murdered in Cushendall by the Glenanne Gang of which Jackson was the leader. We should be talking to him and getting his opinion on how badly treated he and his family – and, indeed, his widowed mother – has been treated by the PSNI/RUC. Being a victim does not qualify him to take over our Garda – the Garda Commissioner role.

Audrey: That was Stephen Travers there who survived the Miami Showband Murders in July 1975.

I had other concerns about Harris. At the time of his appointment as our garda commissioner, Drew Harris was a deputy chief constable, i.e. the number two position in the PSNI. He had several years as the man in command of the Crime Operations Department under his belt, which ran all PSNI intelligence-gathering operations as well as serious crime. Put simply, Drew Harris dealt with MI5 on a daily basis. One of MI5's tasks is to recruit members of An Garda Síochána as British agents, i.e. to get them to betray Irish State secrets to British intelligence. Harris admitted his close working relationship with

MI5 when he attended a session of the Smithwick Tribunal (set up to inquire into allegations of Garda–IRA collusion) in Dublin while he was still serving in the PSNI.

Various Irish governments have requested that the British government release the files it holds about the UVF, especially those relating to the May 1974 Dublin and Monaghan bomb atrocities. All efforts proved utterly fruitless because the British government, through the Ministry of Defence, Home Office, NIO and FCO, have a lot to hide. They were the architects of the collusion: they used the UVF as proxy assassins and bombers. The UVF members involved in the 1974 bombings were their agents. Ironically, Drew Harris probably knows more about what is in the relevant files than most in the PSNI. The Garda inquiries into the 1974 and other atrocities are still open. At the time of writing, Drew Harris is in overall command of all ongoing Garda inquiries. In my opinion, this amounts to a monumental conflict of interest.

24
Netflix

We break through the iron bars of censorship and containment and onto the world's biggest streaming platform.

We had been working on a sensitive Truth and Reconciliation Platform project in February 2017 when my phone rang late one afternoon. I hoped it was the green light we'd been waiting for to progress our objective, but it wasn't the call I was expecting. It was an American number and the caller, Bill Wheeler, said he was contacting me on behalf of a production company called All Rise that was exploring the possibility of making a documentary for Netflix about the Miami Showband massacre.

Bill explained that there was great interest in our story and that it was under consideration for inclusion in an eight-part series entitled *ReMastered* that combined music, politics and trauma. The other subjects were Bob Marley, Johnny Cash, Jam Master Jay, Sam Cooke, Victor Jara, Robert Johnson and Solomon Linda. Anne happened to come into my office while I was on the phone and whispered that my tea was almost ready. Twenty minutes later I was still on the phone. She was curious to know who I was talking to for so long. 'Some man in America,' I whispered. 'He wants to make a film about us and Johnny Cash and Bob Marley and . . .' But Anne just rolled her eyes and smiled.

As the conversation went on, I began to think that the caller might actually be serious. When I asked how he'd heard about us, he explained that it was during a discussion he'd had with Brian Warfield of the Irish ballad group the Wolfe Tones. Brian felt that his group was ideal for the project. During his pitch he'd said, 'But for the grace of God we could have suffered the same fate as the Miami Showband', which instantly piqued Bill's interest and led him to research the massacre and report his findings to the series producers. That first phone call with Bill lasted almost three hours; a call the following day was just as long.

I quickly realised that Bill wasn't just some guy doing a podcast from his bedroom. It was clear that he had thoroughly researched our story so, when he suggested that we should meet, I said, 'Well, if you're ever in Ireland, give me a call. You have my number.' He replied, 'I'm in Washington right now, but we're based in California. How about next week?' I was scheduled to do a TaRP event in the North the following week so I suggested that we could meet up there. When I made my usual booking at the Canal Court Hotel in Newry, I had no idea just how important that meeting would turn out to be and how much it would change my life and impact the lives of many others too.

The Academy Award-nominated film director and screenwriter, Stuart Sender, was eventually appointed as director and the Emmy Award-winning producer and writer, Alexandra (Allie) Orton, was appointed as producer.

During the first round of filming, Allie was still producing multiple films within the *ReMastered* series and juggling shoots and booking interviews across multiple continents. She monitored from afar while the field crew filmed the first round of interviews and visited the site of the bombing on a sad, grey day. Allie would wake early to emails detailing the latest adventures: new locations that needed to be booked, new details in the case or possible witnesses who needed to be located and contacted, hotels that needed to be changed by the logistical crew. There was so much to do, and the eight-hour time difference so punishing, that she stayed awake for forty-eight hours attempting to arrange signed releases from across the ocean. The strange part about television is that, amidst the excitement and glamour, there remains enough paperwork to stymie the best accountant. Filmmakers ask subjects to tell their most personal stories to an international audience. They try to create safe spaces and to live in the moment, yet the moment is often interrupted: a light is ticking and ruining the sound; someone wants to red-line a single piece of paper that has to be signed before the following day's shoot; the on camera contributor has a flat tyre, and can't get to set on time; the cameraman has food poisoning. Though most people think of filmmaking as a primarily creative experience, over half of a filmmaker's energy is spent on managing chaos and keeping the day on schedule.

In between the first and second shoot, the production team made great strides in booking interviews. With the key cast in the can, they could focus on supporting voices who would broaden and deepen the story. The second shoot was scheduled for September, and it involved MPs Michael Mates and Ken Livingstone, whistleblowers Colin Wallace and Fred Holroyd, and a former head of RUC Special Branch, Raymond White. It was important to get the facts straight, so Allie flew out to London in advance of the shoot to do some research.

Her years on *Who Do You Think You Are?* had taught her a lot about archives in the United Kingdom, which she subsequently applied to all projects that ran through the UK. During *Framing John DeLorean*, she had gone to the National Archives at Kew and located troves of documents pertaining to the funding of the DMC plant, Prime Minister Thatcher's decision to pull funding, and the subsequent legal battles over missing millions. In the UK, records are released through freedom of information laws after thirty years. If a researcher can access the records in the narrow window after the records have been released to the public but before they are heavily studied, they can sometimes get lucky and nab a document the government subsequently decides to pull or redact. Allie had had luck with the DMC document dump. When the time came to visit the National Archives for records connecting to the Miami Showband, she consulted research activists for tips.

The UK National Archives are held in a large building in Kew in southwest London. Researchers are welcome, but they are not allowed to bring a scanner or laptop into the reading room. They leave all their possessions save their phone in a locker and are issued short pencils and paper for notes. Once they are issued IDs, they are ushered into the reading room to review documents. Archivists pull the requested documents from the stacks and issue them to researchers in small batches. Most folders are stacked with ephemera, so locating pertinent information takes close reading or a commitment to photographing hundreds of pages and poring over them later. Either way, a trip to Kew takes at least a day. Allie pulled what government records she could, though in the end the most important documents to the story were released during filming.

Her next research errand required a train ride to the coast. Former military intelligence officer Fred Holroyd had agreed to meet with her before filming. He graciously shared the documents he had painstakingly secured from his personnel file. Holroyd had served in Northern Ireland in the 1970s and observed operations that did not sit well with his conscience. He began taking notes, and when he reported his findings to his higher-ups, he was sent to a mental hospital. For years, he insisted that his stint in the hospital was trumped up by powerful men who needed to discredit and silence him. He maintained that his personnel file would bare the truth, that he had no recorded history of mental illness, and that he had always been evaluated as mentally fit before he was suddenly and unceremoniously carted away. Finally, after decades of legal action, Holroyd finally had his military medical file. He showed Allie the papers. They matched his testimony. Finally, Holroyd had been vindicated.

She was impressed by his resilience and moved by the evident trauma he had endured. Allie understood why this was such a victory. Even after all the books she had read and people she had interviewed, it seemed impossible to believe that members of a government in a so-called free society would frame whistleblowers for murder and insanity to cover up their crimes. She felt as if she had tumbled into the pages of a le Carré novel. Her brain knew these things were possible, but she couldn't grasp how individuals could make such craven and cruel decisions about other people's lives. Allie realised that, for someone who had spent her life fascinated by political intrigue, she remained almost hopelessly naive.

Each night, Stuart Sender and Allie would go over the interview questions for the following day. The interview days were long. Even though each interview contributes only a few minutes to the run time of the final film, the raw interviews are hours of footage. The filmmakers don't always know what details will prove critical in the edit bay, so they have to ask about everything.

In order to connect with international audiences, comprehensibility and context were essential. Too often the stereotypical, clichéd characterisation of 'the Troubles' is of a clear-cut conflict between Catholics and Protestants in the North of Ireland and that the British authorities were simply honest brokers caught between the warring factions. The producers understood that it was much more complicated than that and so focused on individuals who had been directly affected by the massacre of a Catholic and Protestant band, from north and south of the border, to make sense of it.

It would be a major achievement to get someone who was directly involved in the Miami Showband killings on screen, but the convicted murderers, Thomas Raymond Crozier and James Roderick Shane McDowell, have kept a low profile since their release from prison. (The other murderer, John Somerville, died of cancer in 2015.)

In our first book, *The Miami Showband Massacre: A Survivor's Search for the Truth*, my co-writer Neil Fetherstonhaugh and I had a lengthy conversation with a senior representative of the UVF codenamed 'the Craftsman'. The purpose of our meeting was to ask him why the attack had taken place. I wanted him to convince me, and our readers, that violence was finished. Agreeing to a precondition that he would not be meeting with us as an official spokesperson of the UVF but that he would be speaking in a personal capacity and only advancing his own opinions, the meeting, which was originally planned to last no more than thirty minutes, actually lasted five hours. We discussed the politics, education opportunities and economics that impact on his community, as well as our respective personal journeys, and we found common ground on many issues. At one stage, the Craftsman deviated from his prepared notes and said, 'There is a code of honour; you don't discuss past operations. We have a saying, "Those who know, don't talk, and those who talk, don't know."' He went on to say that he was proud of what he had done: 'I'm satisfied that everything I did – or was involved in – was right, but there have been incidents carried out in my name, or rather in the name of my organisation, that we are not proud of. The Shankill Butchers and the Miami Showband are right up there at the top of that list.'

Naturally, from the filmmakers' point of view, to capture such a meeting on film would be groundbreaking. For my part, I felt it would offer great hope to victims if such a conversation were to be recorded for public viewing. Notwithstanding the difficulties involved, I immediately bought into the idea that it just might be possible. After all, I reassured myself repeatedly, my track record is solid. I've never betrayed a confidence of anyone I've engaged with over the years.

Before we went to print with our first book, we sent the Craftsman the relevant chapter via the mediator to ensure it represented the meeting accurately, and he confirmed that it did. I was acutely aware that an opportunity to publicly ask if the UVF would engage with victims of political violence had never happened before. I didn't expect them to compromise themselves or those they represented but I did want a commitment that they would enter the kind of dialogue that could lead to some form of healing. The director and producer certainly felt that this would be powerful, but I cautioned, 'If you think you'd just be a fly on the wall, you're mistaken – in fact you'd be part of the story.'

In January 2018, in a Belfast city-centre hotel, Stuart Sender and Allie Orton stared anxiously at Stuart's iPhone, waiting for the UVF to call. The messenger app on the producer's phone was open to Burbank, California. The camera and sound crews were ready. Finally, the call came through with an address, but it was accompanied by strict, unexpected conditions; the meeting was on, but to everyone's astonishment and dismay, there was to be no filming. Having travelled over 5,000 miles and spent two years preparing, the producer was told, 'no recording'. The director was flabbergasted. Allie remained cool and instructed the crew to stand by at a minute's notice if she called them.

We set off towards the given address in two SUVs – mid-journey, the caller changed the destination. When we finally arrived at the meeting place twenty minutes later, an eerily quiet but well-lit, large, modern building, I considered how much the balmy early summer morning when I first encountered the organisation I was about to meet again contrasted with the cold night frost that now sparkled on top of a fresh sprinkling of snow. However, my musings were short-lived when my friend, Pat Hynes of the Glencree Centre for Peace & Reconciliation, who had facilitated the meeting, purposefully rapped the window of our SUV and wasted no time ushering us in past 'security'. Upstairs, two senior UVF representatives stood up and one of them, the more senior, walked directly towards me. We shook hands. The Craftsman was not present.

As we talked, the director's focus was on the interaction between me and the two men. It was a cordial exchange that lasted almost an hour, and at the end one of them remarked, 'That was constructive. It's a pity it wasn't filmed.' Stuart instantly responded, 'Oh, we have our film crew on standby at the hotel,' but his hopes were dashed when his suggestion was met with a sharp 'Perhaps in six or eight weeks.' The filmmakers knew that such a delay could cause them to miss their deadline, but it was out of their hands. There was no point in arguing. The producer and director realised that their only hope depended on the exceptional mediating skills of Pat Hynes. While Stuart and Allie were disappointed that a golden opportunity had evaded them for the moment, they now realised the enormity of what was at stake and that it was crucial not to rush the process. I believe it was then that they understood what I meant when I said they would be 'part of the story'. The UVF is ultra-cautious and suspicious of all mainstream media. Nevertheless, our parting was promising well beyond my greatest expectations. Pat was the last to leave.

Back at our hotel, Allie immediately began working her way through this unexpected turn of events. While the rest of us were trying to make sense of what had just taken place, she was on her laptop liaising with the producers back in California, updating the relevant people and rescheduling the *Game of Thrones* technicians who were augmenting her production crew. I have rarely seen such efficiency. She knew too that they would have to return to the States and convince the Hollywood moguls to extend the budget for yet another trip to Ireland.

The question still remained whether the UVF would actually co-operate in the making of the film. I was aware that there were serious risks involved for all concerned, but with courage, trust and goodwill from all sides, we agreed that the risks were worth taking.

Stuart and Allie got their extension and a filming date was agreed by all the parties.

When I arrived, Stuart was in full director mode and the camera and sound operators were setting up and checking and testing and adjusting and fine-tuning their equipment and hanging on his every word. Allie, too, was totally focused. Nevertheless, for me it was surreal. The state-of-the-art technology all around me seemed light years away from the blood-soaked field, and yet I knew that not only was this bizarre juxtaposition essential to convey to the world the obscenity that had occurred, it was also an opportunity to reach a global audience.

Although the Craftsman was present, Stuart was informed by an intermediary that he would not be taking part in the recording. Instead, the UVF was providing a 'spokesperson', the prominent loyalist Winston 'Winkie' Irvine. I wasn't surprised, but Stuart was incredulous. 'The Craftsman must take part,' he insisted. 'They've presented us with a camera-ready substitute.' But insistence was futile – and dangerous. Resigned, Stuart set up the cameras so that Winston and I were facing each other. The Craftsman sat on a chair off-camera but in full view of Winston Irvine. Filming had barely commenced when Winston advanced the view that 'nobody was supposed to be killed that night', but I pointed out that the forensic evidence clearly showed that was not the case. However, I immediately suggested that there was no point in arguing about such matters and that our focus should be on a better future, and Winston agreed.

I felt that the recording could not have gone any better, in no small part due to the skill and courage of everyone involved. The UVF representatives had committed to the organisation talking to its victims which, in itself, came with its own risks since others connected to that organisation might, to put it mildly, disagree. The director and producer showed great foresight in standing back and letting the historic, unprecedented meeting play out. The interaction between Winston Irvine and me was entirely spontaneous and unprompted. Stuart and Allie understood the enormity of what we had just achieved and that we might be on the cusp of turning something truly awful into something positive and hopeful. It was all in the can now, but there was still a long way to go. Post-production would determine how everything they had filmed would be presented and that would be done thousands of miles away in Los Angeles. I trusted Stuart and Allie completely, but I have no doubt that there was apprehension in certain quarters in Belfast. When we met in the hotel lobby later that evening to go to dinner, I noticed that Allie had a trolley case with her. I asked if she was leaving for the airport, but she just smiled and said, 'No, I'm not taking any risks with this film. It's coming to dinner with us.'

The following day, Stuart and Allie drove south through a snowstorm to fly out of Dublin. When they arrived at the Dublin airport, bleary-eyed and pushing two carts of camera gear, they were in for one final surprise. Upon arriving at customs, the officer stamped Stuart's passport and sent him along, but she motioned for Allie to wait in a nearby office. Allie's name was on the official carnet paperwork, and the customs officials had questions. Stuart jumped forward to accompany her, but customs wouldn't allow him. Only the person whose name was on the paperwork was allowed to enter the office. Stuart and Allie exchanged worried glances. This had never happened before.

Inside the office, Allie was instructed that she wasn't allowed to speak to anyone or use her mobile phone. She had her passport and paperwork taken from her. She sat alone in a row of plastic chairs, staring at the partition that separated people like her from the staff. The minutes ticked by. She caught glimpses of the man who took her paperwork; behind the partition, he was passing it from person to person. They had already been cutting it close to their flight. She imagined Stuart being forced to fly home without her. She wondered whether this was a coincidence. Surely it was nothing more than a paperwork snafu and the customs officers had to perform due diligence to make sure she wasn't smuggling expensive camera gear in and out of the country without declaring it. But just hours before, she had been across the border in Belfast having tea with three of the highest-ranking members of the UVF. *Was* this a coincidence? Behind the partition, she heard a fellow traveller being questioned about his possession of marijuana and cocaine. She gritted her teeth. This did not bode well.

After what felt like hours, a series of customs officials came out to speak with her. They had isolated the errors on her paperwork. They offered her instructions to correct the errors before any return trips and sent her on her way. She grabbed her things and peeled out of the room as fast as she could. She found Stuart just outside their gate. The doors were about to close, but he sighed with relief. 'I had a bad feeling about that. I wouldn't have left without you.'

Before its release, Netflix sent me a special preview link. I thought it was perfect. I sent a coded message to the UVF via Winston Irvine expressing my view that while the documentary was hard-hitting, it was fair. It was not a film about revenge. I felt it was a major and unprecedented breakthrough in dialogue and I thanked them for their courage and trust.

On 22 March 2019, when Netflix officially released *ReMastered: The Miami Showband Massacre*, I was anxious to see the international reaction. It was like waiting for each country to cast its vote on the Eurovision Song Contest, but with much higher stakes. Netflix had been circumspect about the order in which the eight monthly episodes were released. Ours was the sixth episode to be aired. They had already broadcast the Johnny Cash episode targeting middle America and the hundreds of millions of country music fans around the world. The Jam Master Jay episode attracted the black and younger global audience. The month before our episode aired, they presented the story of Victor Jara, known as the Chilean Bob Dylan, who was murdered after the 1973 coup led by the dictator Augusto Pinochet, which guaranteed the *ReMastered* series a massive South American audience. By the time our episode was released, the series had attracted a huge global audience. From Brazil right through South America, to North America, Asia and all across Europe, people – ordinary people, politicians, diplomats, journalists and victims of injustice around the world – were talking about the Miami Showband massacre. In what felt like a lightning-fast moment after so many years of trying to be heard, we had finally broken through the adamantine dome of political censorship. Our story had burst onto the world.

In 2020 *ReMastered: The Miami Showband Massacre* was nominated for an Emmy Award. Even today, it seems like a dream that our story had its worldwide premiere on Netflix.

25
Sharing the Pain

No side has a monopoly on suffering or loss.

On the evening of 21 November 1974, bombs exploded in two Birmingham pubs. The first bomb went off at 8.17 p.m. in the Mulberry Bush, and ten minutes later a second bomb exploded in the Tavern in the Town. The explosions left twenty-one people dead and 182 people injured. In the days following the explosions, six men were detained by police investigating the attack and subsequently, in 1975, charged and found guilty in Lancashire Crown Court. These convictions were later found to be unsafe and all six were released after serving sixteen years in prison for crimes they did not commit.

In 1994, subsequent to the release of the six innocent men, the police opened investigations but no further suspects were brought before the courts. Later that year, a Public Interest Immunity Certificate was sought and obtained by the UK authorities, which put all documents relating to the Birmingham pub bombings under seal and beyond the reach of the public until 2069. In 2016 the coroner announced that there were to be new inquests into the bombings based on new evidence, which suggested that the West Midlands police received prior telephone warnings about the bombing but failed to act to clear the area. The families and friends of the victims led a high-profile campaign prior to and throughout the inquest process in an effort to discover the truth about that night and how twenty-one people could have lost their lives in such circumstances.

Through their Twitter account, I first engaged with the Campaign for Justice for the Twenty-One Victims of the Birmingham Pub Bombings and their Families in April 2019. The families, friends and I began retweeting each other's posts. I was surprised to see that they were protesting about the lack of UK government support and British media coverage in their fight for truth and justice for their murdered and maimed loved ones. Given that such heinous crimes were committed in one of Britain's largest cities, it seemed bizarre that, according to the group's social media, they had even been denied legal aid by their own government. In May 2019 the campaign spokesperson, Julie Hambleton, whose sister, Maxine, was murdered in the Tavern in the Town, invited me to meet the group to 'share, not only in our fight for truth, but also our grief and loss'. I contacted my friend Pat Hynes, the community and political dialogue programme manager at the Glencree Centre for Peace and Reconciliation in County Wicklow and suggested he accompany me to meet the J4the21 group, and Pat and I flew into Birmingham on 24 April.

We met Julie Hambleton and two of her group at the central station for breakfast and from there we were taken to Julie's home. Paul Bodman, whose father was murdered in the bombings, George Jones, who also lost his father that fateful evening, and Bill Craig, whose brother was the last victim to die of his injuries twelve days later, were already there, along with Julie's brother, Brian, and their sister, Jayne. Pat and I listened attentively as each of them spoke of their lost loved ones. After almost fifty years their grief is still raw. It was astonishing, however, to learn how poorly the J4the21 families had been treated by their own government. They were denied legal aid and were forced to raise funds on the streets to cover their own legal fees. It made no sense.

We took a welcome break for lunch at a nearby restaurant, where we were delighted to learn that a great friendship had been struck up between Julie's mother, Margaret Smith, and Paddy Hill, who, along with Hugh Callaghan, Gerard Hunter, Richard McIlkenny, William Power and John Walker, had been wrongfully imprisoned. In fact, Julie told us that her mother treated Paddy 'like one of her own family'. But it was also clear to us that the suffering of the J4the21 families was not being publicly acknowledged. We were determined to do all we could to help. The Glencree Centre for Peace and Reconciliation is renowned throughout the world for its work with victims, and Pat proposed that, on his return home and with the families' permission, he would explore the possibility of bringing them to Ireland to meet with other victims of the Troubles to share their stories and experiences. True to his word, Pat contacted me a few weeks later to say that Glencree was keen to help the J4the21 families in every way possible and that they had secured funding from the Department of Foreign Affairs to bring them to Ireland for three days. The President of Ireland, Michael D. Higgins, would host a presidential dinner at Áras an Uachtaráin for the group and a mayoral reception at the Mansion House invitation was extended to them by the Lord Mayor of Dublin, Paul McAuliffe.

On 1 October 2019 the J4the21group flew into Dublin Airport and were driven up to the Glencree Centre. The group spokesperson, Julie Hambleton, with her brother, Brian, and sister, Jayne, and their mother, Margaret Smith, were accompanied by Paul Bodman, George Jones, Bill Craig and Beverley Sykes, along with Paul Bridgewater and Michelle Sealey, the brother and sister of Paul Anthony Davis. Only 17 years old at the time of the murders, Paul, along with 16-year-old Neil 'Tommy' Marsh, was killed by flying glass from the Mulberry Bush bomb-blast as they were walking past the pub. We were happy, too, to see Soraya and Paul Rowlands, whose father was murdered in the Mulberry Bush bombing, and Michael Lutwyche, a long-time supporter of J4the21, alight from the coach at Glencree.

We were also delighted to welcome Maurice Malone, CEO of the Birmingham Irish Association, who continues to work with the J4the21families and their supporters to repair the once treasured community bond that was so badly damaged half a century ago. Professor Gavin Schaffer from the University of Birmingham and Maureen Slattery-Marsh, who together work tirelessly to repair and heal ruptured 'Irish-in-Birmingham' community relations that resulted from the bombings and their aftermath, completed our list of guests.

On 23 October 2023 I wrote to Julie Hambleton for her thoughts and recollections of the visit, and I received a warm and dignified reply, emphasising the 'heartrending, stirring, humbling and at times humorous' nature of the trip. Julie ended by writing, 'The memories may fade over time, but the feeling of kindness, support and love could not be denied.'[3]

26
Do You Know Who I Am?

I confront the difficult issue of mental illness.

When I first joined the Miami Showband in 1975, it didn't take long to get used to the attention that came with being in such a popular band. Our pictures were in all the music magazines and on the entertainment pages of the national and regional newspapers. People I'd never met were mentioning me in the gossip columns and on the radio and TV as if they'd known me all my life even though I hardly recognised the person they were talking about. The words of my favourite Eagles song, 'New Kid In Town', summed it up well: 'Even your old friends treat you like you're something new.'

I was suddenly living a whole new life, and it was exciting and bewildering at the same time. The management told me how to look and dress and how to behave in public, even when we weren't working. I went along with the plan because, although I knew they were reconstructing me, I felt it was necessary and for my own good. I was made to feel special when I went into restaurants and shops and other public places. In fact, after a while, I even came to expect it. My career had taken a significant leap forward and I'd moved up another notch on the music totem pole. My world had changed, and I felt that I had to change to fit into it. Strangers wanted to be photographed with me and clamoured for my autograph. Many of my great musical heroes became my friends – we hung out together when we stayed at the same hotels.

At first, the normal, everyday things kept me grounded. I still had to adjust to life in Dublin, but sharing a house with our old friends from Carrick-on-Suir, Billy and Maria Byrne, made that easy as I knew that Anne was safe and in the best of company when I was away. I learned to switch on and off and to jump in and out of my new public persona when required, but after a while it ceased to be an act – I had passed through the looking-glass. Sure, it was fantasy, it was an illusion, but it was an illusion that I, along with thousands of Miami fans, enjoyed believing in. The young people in the North certainly needed the illusion of normality that we created when we played up there. For those precious few hours, sectarianism was left outside the dancehall doors and the sounds of the Troubles were drowned out by the sound we made. The carnage they saw every night on their TV screens was replaced by the spectacle we provided for the short time they watched us perform on stage. I was now one of six super-sound sorcerers who, by combining our musical magic, could conjure up joy and excitement across the length and breadth of the country. We were loved for it and we loved being loved.

Looking back now, however, I can also see that I was selfish and self-centred. I had lost track of who I was and of the things that were most important in my life. Ascent to summit to descent, Shakespearean tragedies such as ours will continue to play out all over the world. I sometimes ask myself if I would have joined the Miami had I known where that blue and white VW minibus would take me. The only sane answer is a resounding 'no!'. What rational musician would want to tour hell for the rest of their life? Almost half a century later the answer is still 'no', but perhaps not quite as emphatic. Maybe that 24-year-old *needed* to be reconstructed, and while the cost has been enormous, I sometimes ask myself if it has been my saving grace.

In preparation for my 2021 civil action against the chief constable of the PSNI and the British MOD I had to undergo a psychiatric examination in October 2012 with a further review in June 2021, but I was ill-prepared for the outcome. In fact, the report shook me to the core. I didn't want to believe its conclusions, and so, right on cue, my imposter syndrome rode to my rescue. I assured myself that I did not experience 'enduring personality change post trauma' and I dismissed the findings of 'chronic post-traumatic stress disorder, hyper-vigilance, intrusive recollections, mood lability and survivor guilt' as psychobabble. In fact, there were times when I was convinced that I did not suffer any physical or psychological trauma whatsoever as a result of the massacre and I felt enormous guilt and embarrassment whenever the matter was raised.

In December 2017 my friend Colm Smyth called to say that *No Stone Unturned*, a hard-hitting documentary produced by Trevor Birney and directed by Oscar-winning director Alex Gibney, was coming to the Triskel Arts Centre in Cork city and asked if I would like to meet him there. *No Stone Unturned* tells the story of the notorious loyalist terrorist attack on the Heights Bar in the little County Down village of Loughinisland on 18 June 1994, when six men were murdered and five others were wounded while watching Ireland's historic World Cup win over Italy. Colm was shot four times and critically injured that evening in what is now commonly referred to as the Loughinisland massacre. *No Stone Unturned* is a powerful film but also one that I knew would be difficult for him to watch. As usual, we enquired about each other's health and, for the first time, I mentioned that editing the recorded testimonies of victims of the TaRP project, 'Speaking For Myself', was proving to be difficult. The heartbreaking testimonies, which often lasted for up to two hours, had to be reduced to forty-five minutes in length for the online series, but to do that seamlessly meant listening to some of the most horrific and distressing stories imaginable, again and again, for hours on end. It was taking its toll on me. I told Colm (whose own testimony was recorded for the series alongside that of Stanley McCombe whose wife, Anne, was murdered on 15 August 1998 in the Omagh bombing) that, typically, after working on the project for hours, I would go to bed with the awful details racing around in my mind. I'd wake up drained and mentally exhausted only to relive them, again and again, throughout the days that followed.

Eventually, the horrendous accounts began to enter into our family conversations, and my wife, Anne, who has her own catastrophic, life-changing trauma to deal with, had to tell me how upsetting they were for her and for our daughter to have to listen to on a daily basis. I hadn't realised that I was normalising the abnormal. What I and so many other victims of that bloody period accept as normal is shocking and abnormal to those who, fortunately, do not harbour such dark memories. Colm asked if I might consider counselling; if so, he would highly recommend a County Cork-based psychologist. I was sceptical. I couldn't imagine a local, southern practitioner understanding Troubles-related trauma, but, on learning that this particular practitioner is one of the most respected and experienced in conflict-related trauma in Europe, I decided that it would be worth trying.

I eventually made an appointment in October 2020, and, since we were in the middle of the COVID-19 pandemic, there was an option to have the counselling online. I didn't know what to expect. In hindsight, I must confess I didn't have much faith in 'shrinks'. I thought psychotherapy was for the weak-minded but I couldn't have been more wrong. I logged on, and I was no sooner in a virtual waiting room when my psychologist appeared and greeted me with a warm, welcoming smile. The woman on my laptop screen was instantly my friend, and, although we had never met before, we chatted about everything and anything. We talked for an hour about our favourite music and art and politics and the state of the world and how we could fix it, and in no time at all the session was over and we agreed to continue talking once a week for the next ten weeks. Afterwards,

I sat back in my office chair and thought, *Well, that was easier than I expected*, but then it dawned on me that I had told her things I'd never told anyone before: not even my own family. As the weeks progressed, I looked forward to talking to her. She was a great listener, who understood and made sense of what, until then, I didn't have words for, and she was interested in everything I had to say, regardless of how bizarre it might have sounded. Without condescension, she explained why I behave and react in the way I do as a result of 31 July 1975. There were some very difficult sessions that left me drained, but I trusted her. The discussions we had about imposter syndrome, in particular, were of enormous benefit and helped me to understand and deal with an issue that had tormented me for decades. My 'enduring personality change post trauma' wasn't reversed and I wasn't 'cured' of chronic post-traumatic stress disorder, hyper-vigilance, intrusive recollections, mood lability or survivor guilt, but, in acknowledging those disorders, I was now better prepared to manage them.

27
Electric Wood and Carbon Graphite

My lifelong obsession with sound and why it makes me proud and keeps me sane.

I have always been both flattered and embarrassed by attention, and while I know it was part and parcel of my chosen profession, I have never learned to handle it. However, I valued any encouragement or compliment about my bass playing because they counteracted the self-doubt and loss of confidence in my own musical ability that had resulted from my new status as a survivor of an atrocity that continues to overshadow everything I do. When, after the massacre, we reformed the Miami Showband in October 1975, I became aware that I could never be seen as just a bass player again.

Yet there were times when I enjoyed blissful anonymity. When Anne and I moved to London in 1982, I kept a low profile. By then, the story had faded from the public discourse and I was confident that it would also fade from my mind too. London is a wonderful melting pot and along with fabulous English, Scottish, Welsh and, of course, Irish musicians, I played with many amazing musicians of other nationalities. Our audiences were cosmopolitan, knew nothing of my background, and I was accepted purely on merit. I was doing well as a live and recording studio musician, and it felt particularly good when my peers complimented me on my playing. Whenever I was asked who I'd played with in the past, I rarely mentioned the Miami because I knew that would eclipse everything else and change the relationship dynamic. I am very grateful for the many fond musical memories I have from the two decades I spent living and working in London.

My main instrument for a number of years was a beautiful red Wal Pro II E bass guitar, which I brought with me from Ireland. It looked and sounded fabulous (there are still live video recordings of me playing my Wal on YouTube). One evening, however, I noticed an intermittent crackle coming through my bass amplifier, and since, nine times out of ten, the culprit is usually the lead that connects the instrument to the amplifier, I changed my guitar lead. But when the problem persisted I deduced that the crackle was due to the cable insert on the guitar. As luck would have it, Electric Wood, the makers of Wal basses, were based in High Wycombe, about twenty minutes' drive away from our house, so I headed off the following day to have a new insert fitted into my precious bass. On arrival, I was thrilled to meet Ian Waller, the inventor and designer of the Wal bass and whose name is on the headstock of every one of the iconic bass guitars. While Ian's business partner, Pete Stevens, took my bass away for inspection, Ian invited me to check out his new Wal Custom range. My eyes widened when I saw three beautiful new Wal Custom bass guitars standing proud in front of a row of brand-new Trace Elliot bass rigs. It also terrified me, since Wal basses are expensive and I could imagine trying to explain to Anne that I went out to buy a small metal component and came home with a very costly new bass guitar, especially as we had just bought the house in Hillingdon and we were about to build on a new extension.

Ian, or Wal as he was better known, wasn't leaving anything to chance. I was a prospective customer, and whether I liked it or not, I was going to hear his latest range, and so he introduced me to a young man who, he said, would 'demonstrate' the quality and versatility of the Wal Custom. I instantly recognised Gary Tibbs, whose work with Roxy Music and Adam and the Ants I admired, but I was getting the big sell and I wasn't used to that approach. Whenever I walked into a music store in Ireland, I would be greeted by my first name and nobody would 'demonstrate' or explain the workings of a bass guitar to me. Of course Ian didn't know me, but nevertheless I was annoyed. When he eventually asked me if I would like to check it out, I took the bass from Gary and played a funky version of an Irish reel called 'The Mason's Apron' at breakneck speed and handed it back to Gary. The laughter that ensued only stopped when Pete Stevens returned to tell us that he had fitted a new jack-plug insert to my own Wal Pro II E bass and that the problem was fixed, but Ian told him to take it back for a full upgrade. Chuckling away to himself, Ian proceeded to roll out the refreshments, after which he, Gary and I spent the afternoon jamming and swapping bass licks and talking about Irish and Scottish and Central European folk music.

When my own bass was returned, looking fabulous, Ian refused to accept any payment whatsoever but asked me if I would consider demonstrating his new Wal Custom basses at Musikmesse Frankfurt, Europe's biggest music industry trade fair. At that stage my diary was full. Between live and studio work, I was fully booked and I couldn't take time off to go. However, our band had a regular Tuesday night residency at a pub called the Pineapple in nearby Amersham and Ian would regularly send one of his basses straight from the factory to the venue for me to check out before sending it on to a customer, many of whom were, and still are, iconic bass players. I got to road-test some of Wal's most fabulous custom bass guitars. The last time I saw Ian was at a trade show at the Olympia Exhibition Centre in West London. Sadly, the great man passed away in 1988, but his legacy lives on and Wal basses continue to be played by top bass players all over the world. An easy-to-fix problem with my bass went a long way to fixing my lack of self confidence in my bass playing.

I've always loved experimenting with timing and rhythm and cross-pollinating musical genres and styles. I have a fascination for world music and the treasure it embodies for those of us nurtured within the confines of Western music. In the early and mid-1980s, our band, the Great Hunger, had Thursday and Sunday night residencies at the Manor House Pub at the junction of Seven Sisters Road and Green Lanes in North London. The Rolling Stones, the Animals, the Who, the Jimi Hendrix Experience, Rod Stewart, Steve Winwood, Jeff Beck, Cream and Fleetwood Mac, along with many others, played there in the 1960s. The venue boasted one of the longest bars in Britain and it was always very busy. On Thursday nights in particular, famous faces mingled freely with the cosmopolitan crowd. I still remember the night David Knopfler from Dire Straits and a group of his musicians, who I had met earlier in a recording studio just up the road on Green Lanes, came down to the Manor House to hear our band. When it was suggested to the venue owner, Chris Browne, that David and his friends might join us on stage, Chris, who didn't recognise the superstar, replied, 'No, they're doing fine on their own.' We teased Chris about that for a long time and I don't think he'll ever live it down. We played a mix of pop, rhythm and blues, country, jazz and classic rock by artists as diverse as Billy Joel, Little Feat, Frank Sinatra, Jimi Hendrix, Kris Kristofferson, Bob Marley and Chuck Berry. Our incredibly versatile guitarist/vocalist, Andy Richardson, and our equally talented multi-rhythmic drummer, Maurice McElroy, would slide seamlessly from one style into another. It was a good-time, fun band that everyone related to.

Andy played mandolin and so we also included Irish jigs and reels and hornpipes in our set. One night, while playing some up-tempo Irish traditional tunes, a young man came up to the front of the stage and, while others were dancing to the music, he just stood there staring at my fretboard. I could see that he was listening with his eyes as well as his ears and I instinctively knew he was a musician. When we finished, he questioned me about the piece we had just played. He told me his name was Aubrey Oaki and that he was the bass player with a band from Botswana called Kalahari. I was dumbstruck. I knew that Kalahari was Hugh Masekela's band at that time. Hugh Masekela began collaborating with Kalahari shortly after he arrived in Gaborone after touring in the US, and they continued to work together throughout the 1980s. Hugh Masekela was a world-renowned flugelhorn-playing jazz superstar. He is also the singer and composer often referred to as 'the father of South African jazz'. I couldn't believe that the bass player with the man who wrote anti-apartheid songs such as 'Soweto Blues' and 'Bring Him Back Home', and who had scored a number one hit in America in 1968 with his version of 'Grazing in the Grass' was asking me how I played Irish jigs and reels on my bass guitar. Aubrey was particularly interested in how I 'continued to play in Irish' when I improvised over the traditional tune. When I told him that I just play variations of the melody and seldom think about the chord sequence, his eyes lit up and he said that was his approach too.

Aubrey didn't beat about the bush; he insisted on coming to my house the following day after he finished his recording session with the former Genesis legend, Peter Gabriel, so we struck a bargain. I would teach Aubrey Oaki to play and improvise over 'Carolan's Concerto', 'The Dingle Regatta', 'The Mason's Apron', 'The Irish Washerwoman' and anything else he wanted to play 'in Irish', if he would teach me a particular African style of bass playing that had fascinated me for a long time. The brilliant young bass player from Botswana and I spent many wonderful days playing and jamming at my home in Hillingdon, and as a result my musical horizons were significantly broadened.

Andy and Maurice and I got to know Hugh Masekela and Kalahari very well during their time in London. They came to hear us on many occasions at the Manor House, where their fabulous guitarist, John Selolwane, regularly joined us on stage. Needless to say, I wasn't at all surprised when I learned that Hugh recommended John to

Paul Simon for his Graceland touring band and John went on to play with Paul Simon from 1987 until 1994.

It is always an honour to be invited to play or record with musicians that I respect and admire, and there was no one I respected and admired more than the iconic Horslips guitarist, Johnny Fean. Johnny and I played together for over two decades and we always pushed each other to our musical limits. Nothing daunted us. Musically, we were 'game for anything' and our irreverent approach resonated with some of the finest musicians in the country, who would regularly join us on stage and in the recording studios. When our inspirational drummer, Blendi Krasnichi, counted us in, neither Johnny, nor I, nor even Blendi himself, knew where a number that we might have played a thousand times before would take us. It was that 'dangerous uncertainty' which excited us most and it was that same unpredictability that carried our devoted followers along with us on countless thrilling, magical mystery rollercoaster rides too. I miss Johnny very much, and it's difficult to accept that we won't play together again in this life. I have many wonderful memories of him and I will be forever grateful for the confidence he gave me in myself as a bass player, but there is one particularly fond memory that will stay with me forever.

In 1985 I traded-in my beautiful Wal Pro II E bass guitar for a Steinberger XL-2 carbon graphite bass at Monkey Business in Romford in Essex, and I have loved that amazing headless bass ever since the first moment I held it in my hands. When I first got it, it was a four-string, but I soon converted it to a five-string by changing the bridge and the nut, and I used it on every live gig and on every recording session for many years. Sound engineers and producers loved it too. However, during a spate of musical equipment thefts, I worried that it might be stolen, so in August 2000 I bought another Steinberger XL-2A/5 at the Bass Centre on Wapping High Street in London. Even though I then had two Steinbergers, I decided to buy another 'road' bass and only use my original Steinberger in the studios or on special occasions, so Johnny suggested that I check out the extensive range of Warwick bass guitars at the Steamboat music store in Limerick City. The management and staff were most accommodating, and I got to try out their full range of Warwick and other top brands through a variety of bass amplifiers after which Johnny and I went out for a coffee and a chat. I asked him which bass he preferred and his reply will remain with me forever: 'Steve, I would know you anywhere no matter what bass you play or what amp you use. The sound is in your hands.'

I have no doubt that my desire to be acknowledged primarily as a musician is wishful thinking since my unprecedented history overshadows everything else that I've done in my life, and so I treasure such kind reassurances from my peers because, in my darkest moments, it is a comfort to know that the incident I am best known for does not entirely define me.

In 2019 I was thrilled to receive the following email from Ned Steinberger, the genius who invented the Steinberger bass guitar, in reference to our Emmy-nominated Netflix documentary.

> Hi Stephen,
> It was great to see you pick up your Steinberger Bass near the end of the film, in this context a symbol of hope and rebirth. Thank you for choosing to include the bass in your ongoing musical life. I am honored, and hope we might find a reason to stay in touch.
> With best regards,
> Ned

28
'America, America'

Opening up to a whole new world encourages me to keep on speaking truth to power.

Cliff Carlson, the publisher of *Irish American News* contacted me in July 2019 to say that I had been chosen as the iBAM Chicago Person of the Year. Previous winners included the Nobel Peace Prize winner John Hume and my friend Richard Moore, the founder of Children in Crossfire. In October of that year, I travelled to Chicago to receive the award in person at the iBAM festival gala dinner.

I had also been approached by Yvonne Watterson, a prominent expat in Arizona originally from Antrim, and her colleague Mary Moriarty, who invited me to give a talk in Phoenix while I was in the States for the award ceremony. I happily agreed, and after a good night's sleep following my arrival in Phoenix, I was rested and ready for my first speaking engagement in the US, but I had no idea how my talk would be received. Would my message of 'dialogue and resolution over intransigence and disagreement' be accepted or would it be rejected out of hand by Irish America? I expected that the majority of those in attendance would be Irish or of Irish descent, but Yvonne and Mary had cast a wide net and, coupled with the global success of our Netflix documentary, the event had also attracted others who were curious about the compatibility of truth, justice and reconciliation. Whenever possible, I include a Q&A at the end of each presentation, and I was impressed by how familiar the audience was with my story and the quality of the questions I was asked, many of them challenging.

I was relieved that my first talk in America had been so well received and I looked forward to enjoying the music that Yvonne, her partner, Scott, and their Irish-Americana band, Old Souls, had organised for the rest of the evening. I had been warned in advance that I'd be called upon to join them on bass guitar for a song or two, so Aric Avina, bassist with the popular Phoenix-based heavy-metal band Benedictum, loaned me his Warwick five-string bass.

I ended up playing with Old Souls for forty-five minutes and I thoroughly enjoyed myself, but about halfway through the set the band performed an up-tempo song in which each of the musicians took a solo on their own instrument. Lead guitarist Dave Jones was the first to solo and was quickly followed by Scott, but just as Tim Sadow finished his fabulous fiddle solo and I expected the band to go back into the vocal, Scott indicated that I was to take a solo too. However, I had barely kicked the Warwick five-string up a gear and started soloing when the audience stood up and cheered. Once again, as so often happens in my life, I was reminded that the public generally sees me as something other than a bass player, but they are always pleasantly surprised (and perhaps relieved) when they realise that I can actually play too.

After a weekend being shown around some of the sights of Arizona, I took an early morning flight back to Chicago on Monday, in advance of what was to be a very full schedule of visits and speaking engagements organised by iBAM and social worker Susan Hickey.

My first speaking engagement was scheduled for Wednesday 16 October at the Gage Restaurant, owned by Billy and Anne Lawless. Billy Lawless was Ireland's first overseas senator, having been appointed by then Taoiseach Enda Kenny in 2016. The Galway city native, who had served as president of the Vintners' Association of Ireland in the 1980s, had a long-held ambition to open a business in the US. So when their daughter received a rowing scholarship to Boston University in 1998, Billy and Anne upped sticks and moved to Chicago. He had gone on to make a name for himself in political circles in both America and Ireland, as well as expanding his restaurants business with Anne.

When Billy suggested hosting a luncheon for me at his restaurant, I imagined speaking to a small group of his friends and associates. However, when I learned that, due to an overwhelming response to the invitations, they had to cap the number of attendees at a hundred, I knew I was off to a flying start in the Windy City. The welcome I got on arrival was astonishing. The first person I was introduced to was a former mayor of Chicago and that set the tone for the event. The Irish consul general to Chicago and the Midwest USA, Brian O'Brien, introduced me to the great and the good, and before I could catch my breath, it was time to give my talk. The restaurant was packed to capacity and every place at every table was taken. I began with my own story. You could hear a pin drop when I told my audience why I was compelled to tell them about the reality and the consequences of violence and why I fervently believe that violence serves only to divide rather than to unite our shared island. When I finished speaking, I received a long standing ovation. Sadly, Billy Lawless passed away on 8 November 2024, aged 73. *Ar dheis Dé go raibh a anam uasal.*

Two days later I attended the 2019 iBAM gala dinner, held at the Irish American Heritage Center in Chicago. The formality of black-tie events can camouflage individuality and personality and make it difficult to read the room. However, the playing of the American and Irish national anthems and the flying of their respective flags on a huge screen before dinner, along with the opening address by the president of the centre, Michael Shevlin, left me in no doubt that this was the ritualistic, ceremonial Irish America that I had only heard about from others.

As I walked onto the stage to receive my 'Person of the Year' award, the names and faces of countless victims of the Troubles scrolled past my mind's eye and obscured my view of the gathering in front of me. So instead of my intended polite acceptance speech, I spoke about the futility and consequences of violence and how it would put back our shared hope of a united Ireland by at least another fifty years. I was pleased at how well my message was received and I said a silent prayer of thanks to John Hume and Seamus Mallon for their foresight, wisdom, courage and inspiration.

I flew home a couple of days later. I was tired, but my mind was racing, trying to digest the many different views and opinions and debates on recent Irish history, current affairs and predictions about Irish unity that were presented to me during my visit to America. Sailing through the Watergrasshill toll plaza barrier, like the relieved romantic in James Stephens' wistful poem, 'The Shell', I was startled back into reality: 'And then I loosed my ear … / O, it was sweet, / To hear a cart go jolting down the street.' But it wasn't a cart that jolted me, it was the sharp ping of a message from my Belfast solicitor, Michael Flanigan, telling me that he had something important to show me.

29
'You were right all along'

Discovery points to the identity of the British officer in charge of the massacre.

Shortly after I arrived back in Ireland I met up with Michael Flanigan in a small café close to Belfast's Lanyon Place railway station. I was curious to see what he wasn't prepared to talk about on the phone. He waited until the waitress had delivered the coffees and left us before reaching into his leather briefcase for a slim file. Without saying a word, he placed it on the table and slowly pushed it towards me. I read it carefully and looked up at him in astonishment. I read it again, double-checking every word, and then I read it again, scrutinising every single letter, dot and comma.

What I saw made me both happy and angry. I was happy and relieved to see that, after four and a half decades of insisting that a British army officer was in command of the Miami Showband Massacre, my evidence had been validated and confirmed in a written statement by a serving member of the British security forces in an official British government document. Nevertheless, I was angry that it took ten long years to force the British MOD to hand over that incriminating file, which is only one of many hundreds of thousands of incriminating files that they keep hidden and locked away from the public.

I have never been able to positively identify the British officer that I saw take charge and heard giving orders at the murder scene that morning. I had been shown a picture of a smiling Robert Nairac with curly black hair, which didn't tally with my description of the British officer with the straight hair falling below the back of his fawn-coloured beret. However, his official ceremonial photograph, along with many other photos, shows him with straight hair. I had also suggested that the officer with the 'posh' English accent in charge of the murder squad might have had fair hair but I had to admit that, under the moonlight and with only the interior light of our minibus to go by, I could have been mistaken about the colour of his hair.

I do not remember faces very well, as evidenced by the fact that I could not identify the two murderers, Thomas Raymond Crozier and James Roderick Shane McDowell, even when they stood before me in the dock at their trial and subsequent conviction for their part in the massacre. I have been told that, as a self-preservation mechanism, my mind still blocks out much of what I saw that night, especially faces given the condition of my friends who I tried to comfort after the shootings.

However, to my astonishment, just as Michael was dropping me off at the railway station, he turned to me and said, 'It appears you were right all along.' Until that moment, it hadn't dawned on me that he, or anyone else that I knew and trusted, might have had any doubt whatsoever about the presence of a British army officer at the murders.

I was angry and, on 24 January 2020, posted the following on Twitter:

When it awarded him The George Cross, was Buckingham Palace aware that Captain Robert Nairac was named, in an official Ministry of Defence document, as having been 'involved in the planning and execution of The Miami Showband murders' or was the palace misled by the government?

30
Learning Curve

What I have learned through my work and association with Truth and Reconciliation Platform (TaRP) since 2016.

In April 2023 I was invited to revisit Cavan County Museum (where I had previously spoken at a TaRP event with Eugene Reavey and Kate Carroll) to deliver that year's Arthur Griffith Lecture.

The previous seven years with TaRP proved to be a steep learning curve. I was engaging with and learning from victims – the collective embodiment of the trauma of the Troubles – and while their experiences are diverse and their perspectives manifold, they are real and terrible and their suffering and loss is real and terrible. When I began working with TaRP I felt embarrassed that, until then, my sole focus had been on my own experience – but the more I engaged with victims, the more I felt unworthy of being their 'fellow victim' and, as a consequence, I suffered greatly with imposter syndrome.

Over time, I began to question the accuracy and viability of many terms such as 'reconciliation' and 'forgiveness', which we employed as a matter of course without fully understanding them. I began to consider the collective, depersonalising or even dehumanising names applied to victims of atrocities such as 'Bloody Sunday', 'Bloody Friday', 'Dublin and Monaghan', 'Omagh', 'Ballymurphy' or 'Enniskillen', as remote and impersonal clichés. I still find it tragic that the individual names of the victims of such atrocities are seldom, if ever, used.

COVID changed the world. The elderly, in particular, were wary of attending public events. During that period, all of our TaRP public events were conducted online, and while that gave us a worldwide audience and an opportunity to connect with and to feature a global panel of witnesses, we did miss the material interaction with fellow victims and with our audiences. Although by 2023 social distancing restrictions no longer applied, people were still cautious about gatherings and so I wondered how well the first 'live' Arthur Griffith Lecture in three years would be attended. Happily, despite my initial misgivings, I delivered my address, 'Long Day's Journey into Light: the Bomb and Bullet Legacy', to a capacity audience, which included local and national dignitaries and politicians:

I've called today's talk 'Long Day's Journey into Light'. It's a play on words on the title of the American playwright Eugene O'Neill's magnum opus, *Long Day's Journey into Night.*

But this is about my own, personal journey and I believe, or perhaps I want to believe, that it is a journey of continuing enlightenment. So far, it has taken almost forty-eight years, and who wants to believe that they've been walking in the wrong direction for that long? I know it's not finished yet. Today is just a stocktake, and to paraphrase a certain economist, 'If my information changes, I will alter my conclusions.'

It's particularly good to be here at Cavan County Museum, a permanent reminder of who we were and why we are who we are today. But it's the World War I trench experience on these very grounds, a cenotaph to the mass slaughter of just over a century ago that, for me, brings the current, catastrophic war in Europe into sharp relief. We are shown the edited highlights on our TV screens, morning, noon and night, with the tactics and manoeuvres enthusiastically pored over like *Match of the Day* by 'experts'. War is not a video game or a reality TV show! I know how it feels to be bombed and shot and to crawl across a blood-soaked field among the mutilated, lifeless bodies of my friends. I know the smell of burning human flesh and the awful sounds a human makes when it is being slaughtered. No video game or virtual reality innovation can recreate or construct such an experience. No news report or well-scripted commentary can even come close to articulating the abject horror, visited upon more than 43,600 people, just a short distance north of where we are today, with the authority of those who personally experienced it. I am convinced, now more than ever, that there is not a more efficient deterrent to such violence or a more effective or valuable antidote to radicalisation than the personal, truthful testimony of the victim. Sadly, the truth doesn't always fit the narrative of those with most to gain from conflict, and, consequently, all too often, the victim is silenced and sidelined, and history is all the poorer for it.

In 2016, along with three other victims of the Troubles, I spoke at a unique event in central London. My fellow speakers were Eugene Reavey whose three brothers were murdered at their family home in Whitecross, County Armagh, in 1976, Joe Campbell, a son of the RUC Sergeant, Joseph Campbell, who was murdered at Cushendall, County Antrim, in 1977, and Alan McBride, the husband of Sharon McBride who was murdered in the Shankill Road 'Fish Bar Bombing' of 1993.

While that event afforded victims from diverse backgrounds a platform from which to share difficult, personal, intimate testimonies of their experience, it also presented the audience with a rare opportunity to appreciate the appalling consequences of politically motivated violence. And while it was, at once, shocking and inspiring, it was the highly charged emotional reaction of all in attendance that evening which left us in no doubt that such a powerful experience had to be shared with a wider audience.

On that day, Truth and Reconciliation Platform was born to give every victim of the conflict, regardless of social standing, political affiliation or religious persuasion, an opportunity to tell his or her own personal story, to put the truth on record and to try to prevent the rewriting, reworking, distorting or redacting of history. Truth is in the DNA of civilisation. Unfortunately, those with most to fear from the truth are currently progressing a bill through the British Houses of Parliament, a law deliberately designed to deny victims of the so-called Troubles access to the courts of justice. Ironically, this so-called 'Northern Ireland Troubles Legacy and Reconciliation Bill'[4] is the ultimate accessory to murder. Not only does it pervert the course of justice, but it also puts the final nail into the coffin of truth which, as we know, is always 'the first casualty of war'.

In the seven years since the founding of Truth and Reconciliation Platform, or TaRP as it's generally called, I have at times experienced the most disheartening emotions – shock and disbelief and scepticism and suspicion – to such an extent that, time and time again, I bury my head in my hands in frustration and bemoan the fact that I don't know who the good guys are anymore. But then, I take my late father's advice: Occam's razor argues that the best explanation of any phenomenon is the simplest; that the one which makes the fewest assumptions is the most reliable. In doing so, I invariably reach the same unambiguous conclusion that destroying the lives of the innocent is wrong and that anyone with hand, act or part in such actions, or who covers them up, must be held accountable in law. Contrary to what the British government claims, it is naive in the extreme, if not criminally insane, to think that the most outrageous and obscene legislation proposed by any British government since the Penal Laws, 'the denial of the right to justice', will 'draw a line under the Troubles'. Britain's Legacy Bill will not 'draw a line under the past'. Contrary to what it claims, it will not 'facilitate reconciliation'. Britain's Legacy Bill will, in fact, play into the hands of those who advocate violence as the only response to injustice. In the words of President John F. Kennedy: 'Those who make peaceful revolution impossible will make violent revolution inevitable.'

In those seven years working with TaRP, I have come to look at victims and perpetrators, and indeed my own experience, in a different light than I had over the previous four decades. Although I was a typical southerner, oblivious and indifferent to the suffering in the North until it impacted me, I eventually came to realise that my experience is, and always will be, inextricably linked to every other Troubles-related atrocity. Like every victim, and indeed every foot soldier, I was, and remain, just an expendable pawn in an age-old game of thrones. I'm embarrassed at the naivety with which I first approached the project. I now question the meaning, context and multi-purpose, one-size-fits-all use of the word 'reconciliation', which, for so long, was regarded essential for peace. I know now that 'reconciliation', in the general sense, is not about convincing two diametrically opposed factions to meet in the middle of some expensive, newly built Peace Bridge and hug each other. It is the establishment of mutual respect and trust founded upon truth. Olive branches are grown, not manufactured.

Words matter, and if by 'reconciliation' we mean 'reunion', then it's hardly appropriate to apply that term to the 'bringing-together' of nationalists and unionists. While many were indeed good neighbours, they hardly sang from the same hymn sheet, nor could it be said that they were ever united. In that context, I now prefer the word 'resolution'. Differences and distrust that, for generations, have remained undeclared, need to be aired and the underlying problems identified and resolved. The concerns and fears of both communities must be listened to with respect and every effort made to appreciate and assuage them. For example, in the event of a united Ireland, the legitimate fears of the unionist people that pogroms such as the Dunmanway massacre of April 1922 might be repeated cannot be dismissed or glossed over. By the same token, in the event of irreconcilable differences between the UK and the EU, the nationalist community's fear of a hard border on the island of Ireland, and the ensuing consequences, is perfectly rational.

In fact, that reasonable and wholly logical concern is shared by authorities around the world.

The word 'reconciliation', however, is by no means redundant. For those who hope for, and believe in, an agreed, peaceful united Ireland, it is essential that the anguish and suffering of those who were left behind and cast adrift by the partition of Ireland a hundred years ago is recognised and acknowledged. Debating the Anglo-Irish Treaty of 1921 is best left to the academics now, but what is not up for debate is that, for decades, the south turned its back on its own kin and abandoned them to a sectarian state that treated them as second-class citizens. An unspoken but vital reconciliation necessary for a harmonious united Ireland is the reconciliation of northern and southern nationalists.

Speaking at a TaRP event a few years ago, Seamus Mallon said, 'The Catholic people are not going anywhere, this is their home, and the Protestant people are not going anywhere, this is their home, so we are left with a stark choice: live with each other or get on with killing each other.' Tragically, there are some who opt for the latter.

None of us, no living community, has a monopoly on suffering or loss, but, for the sake of this and future generations, we must all contribute to the healing which will inevitably involve sacrifice and compromise but must begin with respect for each other's culture, traditions and political aspirations and will require rigid adherence to the peaceful, democratic will of the people. We must also accept that the ongoing righteous struggle for truth and justice, for all, is not incompatible with healing for there cannot be healing or lasting peace without truth or justice which, with courage, empathy and compassion, can be achieved.

During the 1980s, I was producing a young rock band in an exclusive West End recording studio in London. It was part of their prize for reaching the finals of a nationwide 'battle of the bands' competition. During a break in the recording, there was some lively banter between the guitarist and the drummer about the influence of their respective heroes on popular music. What began as friendly repartee was developing into a disruptive argument, but, confident that he could deliver a quick knockout line, the drummer, whose father is Irish, exclaimed that 'Rory Gallagher conquered the world with his guitar, but the Brits could only manage it with guns'. However, it was the young English guitarist who delivered the indisputable knockout blow when he replied, 'Well, I didn't shoot anyone.' They both laughed and got on with recording their music. As their producer and mentor, I was there to guide and help them, but it was they who guided and helped me and left me with an abiding optimism: those who are hell-bent on passing a law to deny victims access to the courts are not responsible for the outrages of the past and so, for the moment at least, they can justifiably say, 'Well, I didn't shoot anyone.' But, if they cover up atrocities by denying victims the right to justice with their already infamous 'Legacy Bill', they will be complicit.

We can make great music together if we are all willing to acknowledge and learn from past mistakes instead of burying them like toxic nuclear waste that will inevitably seep out and contaminate our fragile shared space again.

The majority of victims demand justice through the court system, and that is their inalienable right. There are also some who feel unable or do not want to go through years or decades of torturous litigation and who would settle for truth in exchange for a conditional, victim-led amnesty that they can control, but that should be a matter of choice rather than compulsion.

The ten long years that I fought the British Ministry of Defence and the chief constable of the PSNI in the High Court were among the most difficult years of my life, but I would do it all again if necessary. I will continue to oppose the British Government's unjust and immoral Legacy Bill which was used as a threat and as leverage to force me to settle my case, especially in the final year, and which continues to threaten, intimidate, retraumatise and terrorise the very victims they claim it will help.

My 'long day's journey into light' began in the early hours of Thursday, 31 July 1975. Little did I know then that it would take me across the great seas and oceans of the world, over rainforests, within touching distance of Africa's highest mountain peaks and down among the most deprived, poverty-stricken communities on the planet. Little could I have imagined then that I would witness the scourge of racism and segregation in the world's richest and most powerful nation. My 'long day's journey into light' would take me deep into the murky underworld of political intrigue, to be subjected to an unexpected betrayal by those I least suspected, only to return many years later and stand face-to-face with those who set me upon my journey that bloody summer morning. Dark days when I longed for even the smallest chink of light. Terrifying days when I was running on empty and fear of failure was my only driver. Hopeless days when I gave up living for myself and the only light I saw was in the eyes of my wife and our daughter. Helpless days when I knew that a greater power was carrying me, and my only hope was that it would use me as a battering ram against the gates of the hell that kept me prisoner for almost half a century. But just when I thought I had nothing left, those infernal gates burst open and light flooded in. The darkest hour was just before dawn.

But, while it is a journey that I am grateful for, I will continue to do everything in my power to ensure that no one else will have to travel that road.

31
Every Dirty Trick in the Book

Blackmail, bullying, coercion and threats lead to a forced settlement.

On 24 September 2014 Michael Flanigan emailed me to say that the defendants had served their defence in my case in mid-August and that he had sent it to counsel to draft the reply. He went on to say that there were two other main issues outstanding: discovery of documents from the defendants and a forensic accountants' report on my loss of earnings plus interest. He emphasised that discovery was a very important part of my civil action but, first, it was a matter for the defendants to serve a list of documents they intended to share. He suggested it was likely that we would consider their list to be incomplete, in which case we would need to apply to the court for an order for 'specific discovery', which might well result in the defendants applying for a 'public interest immunity certificate' (PII) to prevent us gaining access to the additional documents.

An article in the *Belfast Telegraph* on 25 January 2020 by Alan Erwin says:

> A failure by police to fully disclose documents in a major legal action over alleged collusion with loyalist terrorists behind the Miami Showband massacre is 'appalling', a High Court judge has said. Expressing anger at the ongoing delay in providing all material to lawyers representing survivors and relatives of murdered group

members, Mr Justice Maguire yesterday warned he may consider striking out the PSNI's defence to the claim.

He said: 'This is an appalling situation where this case has been going on since 2012, and we are at a stage in 2020 where the obligation of discovery on the police service has not been complied with. The court seems to be getting the runaround. It makes me angry (and) shows so much disrespect to the court.'

Victims of the atrocity are suing the Ministry of Defence and PSNI over the suspected level of collaboration between serving soldiers and the paramilitary killers. Three members of the popular band were taken from their tour bus and shot dead on a country road after a gig in Banbridge, Co Down in July 1975. They were travelling home to Dublin when a fake army patrol made up of UDR soldiers and UVF members stopped them at a bogus checkpoint outside Newry. Band members were made to line up at the side of the road while attempts were made to hide a bomb on the bus. The device exploded prematurely, killing some of the would-be bombers. Gunmen then opened fire on the band, murdering lead singer Fran O'Toole, guitarist Tony Geraghty and trumpeter Brian McCoy. Two other band members, Des McAlea and Stephen Travers, were also injured but survived the atrocity.

In 2011 a report by the Historical Enquiries Team raised collusion concerns around the involvement of an RUC Special Branch agent. It found that UVF chief Robin Jackson, a one-time UDR member who died in 1998, had been linked to one of the murder weapons by fingerprints. Jackson claimed in police interviews he had been tipped off by a senior RUC officer to lie low after the killings. He went on trial charged with possession of a silencer attached to a pistol used in the murders but was subsequently acquitted. Two serving members of the UDR were eventually convicted for their part in the attack.

Based on documents uncovered by campaign groups, writs have been issued against both the MoD and chief constable. Damages are being sought for assault, trespass, conspiracy to injure, negligence and misfeasance in public office.

A barrister representing the Chief Constable cited 'administrative problems' and asked for two weeks to sort out any application for Public Interest Immunity.

Mr Justice Maguire granted a two-week adjournment but stressed the court's 'patience is (running out)'.

On 18 March 2021 Michael Flanigan called to tell me that the defendants in our civil action against the chief constable of the PSNI and the British Ministry of Defence had offered to settle the case. Considering that I had multiple claims against the defendants and that my forensic accountants had calculated my loss of earnings, alone, to be £1,500,000, I was shocked at their derisory settlement figure. Furthermore, to add insult to injury, he said that their offer would not include an apology or an admission of liability. I refused the offer.

In the days and weeks that followed, I had a number of online meetings with my solicitor and barristers who did their utmost to convince me to accept the settlement, but I held firm. I was astonished to hear that, despite the fact that there were four separate cases, the offer was contingent upon all four parties – Fran's widow, Valerie Andersen, Brian's widow, Helen McCoy, Des McAlea and I – accepting it. It was crystal clear to me that the chief constable of the PSNI and the MOD wanted all claims against them in relation to the Miami Showband massacre to go away and that the compelling evidence against them should never be aired in the High Court. On 25 February 2021, during an online meeting that my barrister Eilis McDermott attended, I was told that Des, Valerie and Helen wanted to settle and, furthermore, if I were determined to fight the case on my own, I was reminded in no uncertain way that I did not have legal aid.

Curiously, at a very early stage in the civil action, I had been told by my solicitor that the defendants had argued that our case was 'statute barred', i.e. subject to a statute of limitations, but they failed and the case proceeded, so I asked why counsel was warning me that this might be raised again. I queried why the defendants hadn't argued it when, for example, they were trying to block specific discovery of files which they had fought tooth and nail to prevent from being disclosed. It made no sense to me, but on 14 July 2021, less than five months later, the British government published a command paper to deal with legacy issues in Northern Ireland. This departed from the mechanisms agreed under the Stormont House Agreement and, instead, set out proposals for: a statute of limitations applicable to all Troubles-related offences; a statutory bar on the Police Service and Police Ombudsman prohibiting them from investigating Troubles-related incidents; the cessation of judicial activity across all criminal cases, civil cases and inquests in relation to Troubles-related incidents; and the establishment of an independent body to enable families to seek and receive information regarding deaths and injuries.

I felt guilty that my refusal to accept the settlement offer was prohibiting the others from settling their cases, and while I was still determined to fight my own case in the High Court, I asked Michael Flanigan if there was a way to allow the others to accept their offers without me accepting mine, but he told me that the defendants had since withdrawn their original offers to all four parties. The British government was confident that the Northern Ireland Troubles (Legacy and Reconciliation) Bill would be passed into law within months, after which all Troubles-related cases, and possibly ours, would be shut down before they got to court. However, it became clear that the British government's plan to deny justice to victims was facing opposition in the House of Lords, and in the meantime Valerie Anderson's case was listed for 13 December 2021 at the High Court in Belfast. It was too close for comfort for the defendants, and so the chief constable and MOD renewed and increased their offer.

Once again, I refused it, but I knew that, even if I went to trial, they could appeal any decision that went against them and, before any appeal would be heard, their cowardly Northern Ireland Troubles (Legacy and Reconciliation) Bill could become law and automatically shut down my case. I couldn't risk being responsible for denying the others the closure that I was told they wanted. However, as a matter of principle, I refused to allow them to set the figure so I added a token amount to their offer to which they readily agreed and so I accepted the settlement under duress. We were also awarded our full legal costs.

Counsel for the MOD and the PSNI told the court, 'The claims had raised complex, novel and unusual issues of both fact and law.' 'The major issues which arose in this case concern questions of vicarious liability and limitation,' said Paul McLaughlin QC. 'The settlements which have been reached represent compromises. They are compromises in the interests of all parties in the case, and therefore avoided the necessity of reaching a final adjudication, one way or the other, on these difficult issues.' I am in no doubt whatsoever that they managed to keep their dirty secrets hidden – at least for the time being. Nevertheless, I was greatly heartened by the outpouring of congratulations and good wishes from all over the world and especially from other victims of the so-called Glenanne Gang who were also fighting for justice. Nobody was fooled by their refusal to admit liability; the fact that the defendants paid £1.5m (€1.75m) plus all legal costs to settle our cases was, in the court of public opinion, a clear admission of guilt.

32
Victim Impact Statement

Some days are diamonds, some days are stone.

In an unusual move in a civil action Mr Justice McAlinden allowed us to deliver victim impact statements and I made the following statement to the court on 13 December 2021:

It was a big deal for everyone in the beautiful market town of Carrick-on-Suir, under the shade of Sliabh na mBan, when 'one of their own' joined the Miami, and it was a thrill for me to be so warmly welcomed by the lads when I became their bass guitarist.

On the way to the gigs, I'd sit in the middle seat of our blue and white Volkswagen minibus, between Fran O'Toole and Tony Geraghty, talking about guitars and cars and keyboards and telling jokes and winding each other up and, on the way home, while the others slept, I would sit up front with Brian McCoy to keep him company and keep him awake while he drove the VW back home to Dublin. It was my great adventure.

I got to know all three of them very well; we became close friends, we confided in each other and trusted and relied on each other's musical ability to make the band the best it could possibly be during the warm summer of '75.

I loved playing with them; it was a brilliant, exciting band.

I can still hear the clear, rich tone of Brian's trumpet soaring above our musical arrangements and the superb quality of his voice when he delivered a 'big ballad' to his thousands of adoring fans.

Fran was an extraordinarily gifted musician and vocalist who oozed fun and charisma.

Tony, our brilliant guitarist, was undoubtedly a genius and a master of many playing styles whose influence resonates among great Irish guitarists to this day; I miss him very much.

Sadly, my abiding memories of these three talented young men, that I had just been on stage with playing 'Clap Your Hands, Stamp Your Feet', are forever fused with the most horrific, ever-present images imaginable.

I went on to quote from the popular John Denver song 'Some Days Are Diamonds', reflecting the impact of that terrible event, which defined my life from the age of 24 and the life of my beautiful 21-year-old wife, Anne. I have always felt that the face I see in the mirror is a stranger to the person I was before.

I finished up by thanking my legal team, Michael Flanigan, Éilís McDermott, Donal Sayers and Brian Fee for their dogged determination to overcome every obstacle to get me there that day, but most especially my wife Anne and daughter Sean for their unconditional love and support. I lived for them.

Mr Justice McAlinden then stated, 'I have heard my difficult cases, but the comments expressed to me today will remain with me throughout the rest of my career and indeed throughout the rest of my life.'

33
Setting the Record Straight

The legacy of the showbands is finally acknowledged.

In the summer of 2023 a former commissioning editor for RTÉ, Billy McGrath, told me he intended making a documentary about the rise and fall of the showbands in Ireland.[5]

In 2024, when RTÉ commissioned a two-part TV series entitled *Ballroom Blitz*, with U2's Adam Clayton presenting, Billy asked me if he could film a 'bass player to bass player' conversation between Adam and me for the series and I agreed. I met Adam back in 1982 when U2 were recording 'New Year's Day' at Windmill Lane Studios in Dublin. I was recording some bass tracks for another artist and we were both sharing the house Ampeg bass rig. When I'd finish, I would often stay on to listen to the producer, Steve Lillywhite, working on the U2 track.

Billy McGrath's decision to have Adam Clayton present the new series raised a few eyebrows. As Adam says in the film, 'Each new generation tends to diss [disrespect] that which precedes it,' and the showbands were not spared the ire of some of the new wave that followed them. (Many showband musicians, however, were perfectly content with their lifestyle and had no desire to leave home to pursue fame and fortune.) One of the later Irish rock stars, in particular, castigated showbands for not concentrating on original material. Ironically, that same star regularly came to hear Johnny Fean, Dave Lennox, Danny 'Bongos' Smith and me when the

Psycho Pats played our weekly residency at Bad Bob's nightclub in London's Covent Garden.

Adam proved to be an inspired choice, and the series finally set the record straight about the quality of musicianship in showbands and the vital role they played in the international success of rock bands, such as U2, that followed them.

34
Finale

'Something terrible there in the first place.'

Tommy and Catherine Sands' house in Rostrevor resonated with music and folklore and history and tradition, and through the slow-dropping twilight on Carlingford Lough the Cooley mountains unrolled an enchanting backdrop to their home that evening and the spirit fingers of every musician that ever coaxed a note from the instruments perched upon the walls and the hand-hewn oak shelves beckoned us to join them in a tune. It was impossible for me not to gently stroke the strings of each seasoned fiddle, mandolin, mandola, guitar, banjo, bouzouki and autoharp and eavesdrop on the decades if not centuries-old tales they told by humble firesides or called out at the crossroads of history. Lilting sweet in the mother tongue of every ear, they led the well-heeled and the shoeless in the dance, and as I gazed upon them I wondered quietly if they rejoiced at the touch of genius or despaired at the hands of the inept, but those deep-grained secrets stayed unsaid for their secrets are who they are.

I asked Tommy to sing 'There Were Roses', one of his best-known and well-loved songs, and those who know Tommy know you don't have to ask twice. When he finished, I told him how it brought back my own misfortune and how it was a sorrowful reminder that terrible things were done on all sides at the time of the Troubles, and without hesitating he replied, 'Terrible things indeed, but there was something terrible there in the first place.'

All atrocities must be condemned, but there cannot be a genuine, lasting peace without justice nor can there be a reconciliation without truth and the acknowledgement of wrongdoing. Let us hope that truth, justice, equality, tolerance and respect for all will prevail to prevent such a terrible thing being there again.

'There Were Roses'
Written by Tommy Sands © Elm Grove Music

So my song for you this evening,
it's not to make you sad
Nor for adding to the sorrows
of this troubled northern land
But lately I've been thinking
and it just won't leave my mind
To tell you of two friends one time
They were both good friends of mine

Alan Bell from Benagh,
he lived just across the fields
A great man for the music,
and the dancing and the reels
O'Malley came from South Armagh
to court young Alice fair
And we'd often meet on the Ryan Road
and laughter filled the air

Chorus

There were roses, roses
There were roses
And the tears of the people ran together

THE BASS PLAYER

Though Alan he was Protestant
and Sean was Catholic born
It never made a difference,
for the friendship it was strong
And sometimes in the evening
when we heard the sound of drums
We said it won't divide us,
we will always be the one

For the ground our fathers ploughed in,
the soil it is the same
And the places where we say our prayers
have just got different names
We talked about the friends who'd died
and we hoped there'd be no more
It's little then we realised the tragedy in store

Chorus

It was on a Sunday morning
when the awful news came round
Another killing has been done
just outside Newry Town
We knew that Alan danced up there,
we knew he liked the band
But when we heard that he was dead
we just could not understand

We gathered at the graveside
on that cold and rainy day
And the minister he closed his eyes
and he prayed for no revenge
And all the ones who knew him

from along the Ryan Road
We bowed our heads and we said a prayer
for the resting of his soul

Chorus

Well fear it filled the countryside
there was fear in every home
When the car of death came
prowling round the lonely Ryan Road
A Catholic would be killed tonight
to even up the score
Oh Christ it's young O'Malley
that they've taken from the door

Alan was my friend! he cried,
he begged them with his fear
But centuries of hatred
have ears that can not hear
An eye for an eye, was all that filled their minds
And another eye for another eye
till everyone is blind

Chorus

So my song for you this evening,
it's not to make you sad
Nor for adding to the sorrows
of this troubled northern land
But lately I've been thinking
and it just won't leave my mind
To tell you of two friends one time
They were both good friends of mine

THE BASS PLAYER

I don't know where the moral is
or where this song should end
But I wonder just how many wars
are fought between good friends
And those who give the orders
are not the ones to die
It's Bell and O'Malley
and the likes of you and I

There were roses, roses
There were roses
And the tears of the people ran together
There were roses, roses
There were roses ...

Epilogue

Where is our place in history?

As we got closer to the fiftieth anniversary of the massacre and I found myself speaking to a generation that had never experienced a live showband performance, I asked myself, what is the true, lasting legacy of the Miami Showband?

I believe that every musician that ever stood on a stage north of the border during the so-called 'Troubles' was a hero and, although they didn't realise it then, showbands from all over the island of Ireland were the primary source of harmony and respite during those troubled times. Night after night, they brought communities – regardless of their political or religious differences – together to meet and dance with each other in the ballrooms and the marquees. While no generation has a monopoly on talent, in the 1960s and 1970s it was widely accepted that to join a top showband, a musician was required to play every musical style. Such was the respect for and the popularity of the showbands that their era saw more musicians in full-time employment than ever before or since.

At that time, there was danger in travelling the highways and byways in the dead of night, but, mistakenly convinced that musicians were exempt from the violence, the brilliant, young, apolitical Dublin-based Miami Showband paid the ultimate price for bringing joy and happiness to their massive, mixed fan base.

Let that be our epitaph.

Afterword

When I read the draft of *The Bass Player*, I was transported back to the first time I saw Michael Cimino's devastating masterpiece *The Deer Hunter*. In it, Cimino portrays a group of friends in Pennsylvania going about their lives with very little knowledge or understanding of what's happening in the wider world. We are carried along with them as they happily prepare for a wedding and we enjoy all the music and dancing that accompanies it, but suddenly, abruptly, without any warning, the viewer is plunged into the unspeakable horror of the Vietnam War.

Stephen Travers enjoyed a good life. It was a lot more fun than that experienced by the characters in *The Deer Hunter*. He was the bass player with the Miami Showband, an incredibly popular group, fondly remembered by many as 'Ireland's Beatles'. He joined the Miami after playing with a string of bands, all delightfully captured between the covers of this book. However, I must admit that I read those pages with trepidation since, unlike my first viewing of Cimino's film, I was aware of the horror that lingered beyond the horizon.

In 1975, the popular young musicians had no inkling of what was planned for them.

Unfortunately for the evil architects, however, they met more than their match in the person of Stephen Travers. Little did he – or they – know what he would discover when he first embarked upon his quest for the truth, but, as a result, the story of the Miami Showband has become, globally, the most notorious example of Britain's 'Dirty War' in Ireland. Stephen Travers and his new band of truth-seekers have clearly shown the court of public opinion – the most important tribunal of all – what really happened on that awful night and who was ultimately responsible.

As Stephen progressed along his path, he has conducted himself in an intelligent, courteous and measured manner. Researchers, broadcasters, journalists and authors all attest to his integrity and decency. *The Bass Player* is the latest stop on his journey for truth and reconciliation, neither of which can exist in isolation.

For me, the most enduring message in this book is that the criminal actions of the counterinsurgency underworld gurus must be exposed in order to stop them. Authors like me can write about such things from a distance, but there is no substitute for the first-hand testimony of someone who has personally experienced them. *The Bass Player* achieves this in spades.

David Burke
(author of a number of books about British intelligence activities in Ireland, including *Kitson's Irish War*)

Endnotes

1. On 5 January 1976 ten Protestant men were murdered on their way home from work and another, Alan Black, was seriously injured near the village of Whitecross in south Armagh in Northern Ireland. The only Catholic among them was spared by the gunmen and told to flee.

2. *Keith McCoy*: We, the families of Tony, Brian and Fran, as well as survivors, Stephen and Des, have waited a very long time, over thirty-six years in fact, to learn the circumstances surrounding the deaths of our loved ones who were shot down so brutally and so callously in the early hours of a summer morning.

    The Historical Enquiries Team finds that Tony, Brian and Fran were murdered at a bogus British army checkpoint on the A1 Belfast to Dublin Road near the junction with Buskhill Road, County Down at 2 a.m. on Thursday 31 July 1975. The murder was a planned attack, carried out by a UVF gang, which included a number of serving UDR soldiers. Most of them were wearing British army uniforms. The presence of two men, acting suspiciously at the Castle Ballroom, Banbridge, suggests that the Miami Showband was being observed. The interception point on the A1 beside a UDR shooting range was pre-selected and a 'spotter' was positioned in a vehicle to drive ahead of the minibus and warn the gang of the band's imminent arrival. The original intention of the perpetrators seems to have been, under the guise of a legitimate military road check, to hide a bomb on the minibus. If the original plan had been successful, the band would have continued on their journey south and at some point the device would have exploded, killing them all. The band could then have been portrayed as being killed by a bomb they were transporting while involved in moving explosives for the IRA. However, the bomb detonated prematurely while being covertly placed in the minibus by Wesley Somerville and Harris Boyle, killing both of them. All the band members survived the blast, although shocked and injured. The loyalist gang then opened fire on the defenceless men, at close range and with automatic weapons. The intention was to kill them all and leave no witnesses. As a consequence, Tony, Brian and Fran were killed, Stephen Travers was seriously wounded and Des McAlea injured. The UVF admitted responsibility for the attack.

Desmond McAlea: The original RUC investigation led to the arrests of UVF members, including members of the Ulster Defence Regiment. Thomas Raymond Crozier was soon implicated in the murders, while other suspects admitted to different sectarian murders and bombings. Spectacles found at the scene led to the arrest and charging of James Roderick Shane McDowell. Both McDowell and Crozier were serving members of the UDR at the time of the murders and had used their military uniforms and expertise to facilitate the attack. John James Somerville, brother of Wesley, was subsequently arrested in 1980 for other matters. He admitted his involvement in the Miami murders while in custody, as well as the murder of Patrick Falls. Crozier, McDowell and Somerville were all convicted of the murders of Tony, Brian and Fran and other serious offences. They were all sentenced to life imprisonment. Somerville was also convicted of the attempted murder of Stephen Travers. None of the three was convicted of my attempted murder.

David O'Toole: Since it is believed that at least ten attackers were involved, this means that five perpetrators were never brought to justice. Ballistic reports link six firearms to the attack. These weapons were used in other murders, attempted murders and robberies. (This linkage will be explained more fully shortly.) The Miami Showband was a hugely popular group, young men who lived for their music and their families. They became the victims of a sectarian murder gang, amongst whose members were former and serving military personnel. Stephen Travers and Des McAlea recall one of the attackers as being more authoritative than the others and that he spoke with a 'posh English accent'. The issue of whether an Englishman was present cannot be resolved to everyone's satisfaction. The HET believes that the man with the smart bearing and 'posh' accent was McDowell. Stephen Travers and Des McAlea are both adamant that the man with the 'posh' accent was English.

Stephen Travers: The most alarming HET finding concerns the involvement of Robin Jackson, aka The Jackal, a notorious UVF member. Jackson was arrested at an early stage in the inquiry but was released without charge. The HET review found disturbing evidence that Jackson was tipped off in May 1976 that his fingerprints had been found on a silencer attached to the Luger pistol used in the Miami murders. Jackson claimed that two RUC officers, one a detective superintendent, had advised him, in Jackson's words: 'to clear as there was a wee job up the country that he would be done for'. We are about to provide you with further detail on this HET finding. The HET conclusion is: 'To the objective, impartial observer, disturbing questions about collusive and corrupt behaviour are raised. The HET review has found no means to assuage or rebut these concerns and that is a deeply troubling matter.' We believe the only conclusion possible arising from the HET report is that one of the most prolific loyalist murderers of the conflict was an RUC Special Branch agent and was involved in the Miami Showband attack.

David O'Toole: These dreadful murders absolutely tore apart our lives and those of our families. They left two young women without their husbands and four very young children fatherless. We hope that this report can bring some closure to us and help us to come to terms with our terrible loss. It has been particularly devastating for us to learn that, in all likelihood, one of those involved in the murders of our loved ones was an agent of RUC Special Branch. We intend to pursue this issue with the authorities in the North.

3 *The letter reads*: After receiving such a warm welcome that the Irish are renowned for, the families were invited to attend their first meeting with cross community family members who also had suffered loss, grief and trauma from the loss of a loved one during the Troubles. This was intense for all concerned. The frustration and anger that permeated from many, particularly those from England was tangible. Hearing different stories, but all with the same ending of harrowing loss was immense for all participants. Each person in the room knew and understood the anguish of the person speaking. Listening was at times very distressing, where one or two were either visibly upset or felt the need to leave the room. So many lives taken, leaving those still living with the broken pieces. All still fighting for what is right; truth, justice and accountability.

On the second day, there were more meetings with other families and participants from a range of groups who work towards reconciliation. These, too, were as moving and in parts distressing for many of those attending. Margaret (mother of Maxine Hambleton) was struck with an infection. Eugene Reavey generously offered his time to transport her to a hotel so she could rest. Pat Hynes had planned such a full itinerary that on the third day, the group were taken to Dublin for a meeting with The Minister for Foreign Affairs, Simon Coveney TD. He was most gracious with his time and interested in what people had to say. Mr Coveney was astonished to hear how poorly the families had been treated by the British government and offered any support that may be within his remit.

Later that day, the visitors had the pleasure of meeting Dublin's Lord Mayor at his official residence. Another incredible Irish welcome greeted the visitors from England. There were politicians from a range of parties who made time to speak and listen. With such a tight schedule the group, in particular the ladies, were given the privacy to change into their evening dress as they were all being taken for a very important dinner with the Irish President at his official residence that evening. Once there, the group, alongside Stephen, Pat and others to meet the President and his wife, where entertainment and delicious food, drink and company was flowing. The President allowed Brian and Julie Hambleton to ring the special bell 21 times, in memory of those killed in Birmingham. A precedent was set by the very diplomatic President. The evening was a huge success and one that will be remembered for the kindness and generosity of spirit shown to the families of Birmingham, the Birmingham Irish Association, too, and Kevin Winters of KRW LAW LLP who represent the families present.

Pat Hynes and Stephen Travers had planned a full and extensive itinerary for the visitors from England that was fulfilled professionally and effectively. The trip was heartrending, stirring, humbling and at times humorous. The emotional turmoil had taken its toll on many who attended this poignant 'pilgrimage'. Every person had been touched by the warm embrace received by everyone they met, to the point where many felt 'at home'. The memories may fade over time, but the feeling of kindness, support and love could not be denied.

4   As of July 2025, the subsequent Act was found to breach human rights by ECHR and the new British Labour government had committed in December 2024 to repeal and replace the Act.

5   Billy quit working at RTÉ in 2002 to pursue a number of projects and eventually set up his own production company Sideline Productions. Having promoted their London debut as part of the London Irish festival in 1980, Billy managed U2's PR campaign for their homecoming open air show in Dublin's Phoenix park in 1983.

Index

Al Jazeera TV network 73, 150
All Souls Church in Belfast 73, 150
Anderson, Valerie (Fran's widow) 127, 207–08
The Animals 11, 112, 185
Anne 31, 61, 145, 163, 211
   African excursion, concerns about 56
   'America calling' for Stephen! 163
   Dublin, adjusting to life in 180
   evidence of British officer 117
   holiday with 29–30
   horrendous testimonies 182
   London, blissful anonymity in 184–5
   marriage, Stephen to Anne (July, 1974) 26
   Miami Showband Massacre, book launch and 45–6
   move to West London (1986) 108
   reconstruction of new lives 114
   Stephen's audition, move and 27
   wedding plans 22
Áras an Uachtaráin 177
Arcadia ballroom in Cahir 15, 18–19, 20
'Around and Around' (Rolling Stones) 112, 114
Arthur Griffith Lecture 197, 198
Ashford, Paul 52, 53
Athenry 102
atrocities during the Troubles
   Ballymurphy massacre 81, 82, 197
   Bloody Friday in Belfast 197
   Bloody Sunday in Derry 51, 58, 71, 79, 81, 197
   Dublin bombings 51, 162, 197
   Enniskillen, Remembrance Day in 51, 84, 197
   Kingsmill massacre 69–70, 86, 146–7, 149
   Monaghan bombing 51, 162, 197
   Omagh bombing 51, 182, 197
attack on Miami Showband 34–5, 37–43, 82
   architects of 39, 42
   blood-soaked aftermath 42–3
   bomb on minibus 39
   branding as terrorists, aim of 39, 43
   calls from Des in ditch 41
   English accent of officer in charge 38–9
   explosion, force of 39–40
   instruments, protectiveness towards 37
   knocked back in line 38
   lined up, hands on heads 37
   Luger pistol used in 120, 121
   Newry, statement at 41
   opening fire on band 39–40
   questioning about bags and cases 37–8
   red light stop on Buskill Road 34–5, 37–43
   relaxed atmosphere 37
   silence descending 40–41
   survival, but not for all 40–3
   uniforms of attackers 38–9

Ball, Jonathan 1–2
Ballroom Blitz (RTÉ TV) 212
Ballymoney 103

INDEX

Banbridge 33, 123, 153
  security system around 34
Bay City Rollers 16–17, 55, 106–07
B.B. King 11, 102
BBC 51–2, 59, 67, 71–2, 73
Beach Boys 11, 13, 16
Beatles (and Beatlemania) 11, 17, 103, 108, 112
Belfast
  City Hall 146, 149
  East Belfast 48
  Falls Road 48
  Frizzell's on Shankill Road 72
  High Court in 127–42, 146, 203–4, 208
  Sandy Row 48
  Shankill Road 48
Belfast Telegraph 205–07
Belfast-Newry road 34–5
Bell, Eric 26, 105, 111, 114
Berry, Bren 52, 53
Berry, Chuck 102, 111, 112, 187
Bessbrook 146–7, 149
Birmingham pub bombings 175–6
  Campaign for Justice for Victims of 176, 177–9
Black, Alan 146–9
  Eugene Reavey, friendship with 148
Bloody Sunday March Committee 79
Bomb and Bullet Legacy' event in Lisburn (2018) 159
Boutcher, Jon 68, 153
Bowyer, Brendan 17, 20, 22, 55
Boyle, Harris 124, 144–5
Breaking Star Codes (Barry Devlin) 107, 108
Brendan Bowyer and Big 8 Showband 15, 17–19, 20, 21, 34
'Bring Him Back Home' (Hugh Masekela) 188
British government 73, 195
  Hermon's plea on behalf of UDA to 154–5
  'Internment without Trial' legislation (1971) 82
  Irish requests for UVF files 162
  Legacy Bill proposal 200
  Northern Ireland Troubles (Legacy and Reconciliation) Act (2023) 71, 209
  paper on legacy issues (July, 2021) 208
  protective responsibility of 59
Bunmahon 10, 14
Burke, David 221–2
Buskhill Road, attack on 34–5, 37–43, 47, 119, 131, 144
Byrne, Billy 6, 31, 180
Byrne, T.J. 17, 18–19, 20

Caldwell, Detective John, attack on (2023) 93
Campbell, Joe 71, 73
Campbell, Mandy 97, 98, 100
Campbell, Rosemary 94–100
Campbell, RUC Sergeant Joseph P. 71, 94–100
Campbell Jr., Joe 94, 96, 98
Can I Give Him My Eyes? (Moore, R.) 58–9
Canal Court Hotel in Newry 153, 164
Caproni's ballroom in Bangor 31–2
Carrick-on-Suir 6–7, 10, 13–14, 22, 23, 180
  move to new house in (September 1974) 27
  Urban District Council 26
Carroll, Constable Steve, PSNI ('Micky Brit') 87–94
Carroll, Kate 87–92, 159, 197
  TaRP testimony (2018) 87–94
Carroll, Shane 87, 93
Carville, Audrey 159–61
Cash, Johnny 163, 173–4
Castle Ballroom in Banbridge 152
Cavan County Museum 93–4, 197, 198
CBS Records 12, 108
Prince Charles, later King Charles III 81–3

INDEX

Children in Crossfire 55, 56, 57, 60, 79, 191
Clancy Brothers and Tommy Makem 23
'Clap Your Hands, Stamp Your Feet (Bonnie St Claire/Unit Gloria, 1972) 34, 211
Clayton, Adam 212–13
Clenahan, Andrew 56, 62
Clonan, Senator Tom 71
Clonmel 6, 7, 21, 22
  shooting contest in 7
Cocker, Joe 102, 112, 113
Comeragh Lounge in Carrick-on-Suir 23
Commons, UK House of 69–70, 86
conflict of interest 153–62
Continuity IRA 92
Cork City 9, 14, 65, 68, 101, 107, 181
Cottage Restaurant in Carrick-on-Suir 23
Council of Europe 155, 156
Country Club in Portmarnock 12, 106
County Cork, 'goodwill visit to' 78–9
COVID-19 pandemic 80, 182, 198
The Crack 12, 108
Craughwell 101, 109–10
Cream 108, 187
Creggan estate in Derry 55, 57–9
Crofton Airport Hotel 30, 33
Crozier, Thomas Raymond 123, 124, 168, 196
Crumb, Morris 56, 62
The Crystals 10–11, 13, 14
Cushendall 94, 98
  Police Station at 96

Daisy Hill Hospital in Newry 69–70, 85
  morgue at 148
'Dana' 47, 48, 55
D'Arcy, Fr Brian 46, 72
Dean, Gary 102, 110–12
Dean, Gavin 101, 102, 105, 110–12

Thee Deans (Athenry rock band) 101, 102, 103, 104–05, 109
Defence Ministry (MOD, UK) 36, 130, 151–2, 160, 196, 206
  apology to O'Hares (2011) 71
  collusion, hidden files and 162, 195–6
  fight against, difficulties of 203–4
  psychiatric exam for civil action against 180–1
  settlement offer (and refusal of) 207–09
  writs against, issue of 127–8
DMC documents, 'dumping' of 165–6
Dolan, Joe 25, 106
Donaldson, Sir Jeffrey 73
Dover, Jo 1, 2, 3–4
Drew, Detective Superintendent Ernest, RUC 119–22
Dublin, bombings in (May 1974) 51, 162, 197
Dunphy, Tom 17, 18–20, 33–4
DUP (Democratic Unionist Party) 73, 92
Dwyer, Liam 23–6, 28, 114–15
  passing of (2022) 115

The Eagles 105, 179
ECHR (European Convention of Human Rights) 155, 156
Enfield revolver, serial ZJ3691 124–5
Enniskillen, Remembrance Day bombing at (1984) 51, 84, 197

FCO (Foreign and Commonwealth Office, UK) 36, 162
Fean, Johnny ('King of Celtic Rock') 114, 212–13
  Deans' idolisation of 105
  Horslips and 105
  legendary guitarist and vocalist 54
  personification of cool 111–12
  Stephen and, paths crossing 107, 108–09, 189–90
Fender Stratocaster guitar 10, 12, 112

INDEX

Fetherstonhaugh, Neil 44–5, 46, 83, 168
Flanigan, Michael 68, 146, 153, 194, 211
   British officer at Miami massacre, validation of 195–6
   dirty tricks, dealing with 205
   settlement with MOD and PSNI (and refusal of) 207–08
   writs issued on MOD and PSNI 127–8
Foreign Affairs, Ireland Department of 73, 177
Fort Seagoe, UDR depot at 124, 125

Gallagher, Rory 17, 102, 105, 106, 114
   contribution to Deans' debut album 109, 110–11
   Stephen and, 'guitar talk' 107
An Garda Síochána 94, 121, 153, 161–2
   International Liaison Protection section in HQ 154
Geraghty, Tony 3, 4, 12, 28, 29, 32, 52–3, 64
   attack on Miami Showband and death of 37–8, 40–43
   Banbridge gig, before and after 33–5
   murder of, HET report on (and reaction to) 118–26
   Victim Impact Statement on 210–11
Gibson 335 guitar (cherry-red) 31, 37, 112
Gibson Les Paul Goldtop guitar 12, 112–13
Gillespie, Judith 157, 158
Glencree Centre for Peace & Reconciliation 169–70, 176, 177–8
Glennane murders (and Glenanne Gang) 68, 155, 161, 209
Good Friday Agreement 78, 79, 87, 90, 92
Grand Opera House in Belfast 16–17, 54
Green, John Francis, murder of (1975) 121, 122
Gustafson, John 103–04

Haass, Dr Richard 157–8
Hackett, Sergeant (Irish Army) 6–7
Hambleton family 176
Hanrahan, Mike 52, 53
Harris, Andrew ('Drew') 153
   criticism by families and survivors of 157
   Garda Commissioner, objections as 159–62
   independent investigation, subversion of 155
   LSU (Legacy Support Unit) control by 158–9
   resignation from PSNI 159
   RUC 'shoot to kill' deaths and 158–9
   UVF-RUC collusion, refusal to investigate 156
Harrison, Chief Superintendent William, RUC 121–2
Heaney, Seamus 15, 72
Hendrix, Jimi 11, 105, 112, 187
Hermon, Sir John 154
HET (Historical Enquiries Team) 127
   attack on Miami, team report on (and reaction to) 118–26
   evidence from, claim on MOD/PSNI based on 129–35
   JFF (Justice for the Forgotten) and 116–17
   Kingsmill massacre, report on 86
   loyalists and state forces, inquiry into collusion of 155–6
   watch labelled 'Miami Showband,' investigation of 66–7
   White Team at 118
Higgins, President Michael D. 177
High Court in Belfast 127–42, 146, 203–4, 208
High Court in Belfast, proceedings in matters litigated 127–9
   defendants' immediate response 129
   'statement of claim' 129–42
   parties 129–30

INDEX

background 130
Miami Showband, attack on 130-2
UDR, subversion in 132-3
HET investigation 133-5
first defendant, particulars for 136-8
second defendant, particulars for 138-9, 139-40
personal injuries, particulars of 140-1
loss and damage, particulars of 141-2
damages against defendants, particulars for award of 142
Holroyd, Fred 165, 166-7
Home Office (UK) 36, 162
Horslips rock band 54, 105, 106, 107, 108, 189
Hughes, Charlie 147-8
Hume, John 191, 194
Hynes, Pat 169-70, 176

IBAM (Irish Book Arts and Media) 191, 192
gala dinner in Chicago 193-4
Person of the Year 79, 191-4
IRA (Irish Republican Army) 39, 58, 72, 84, 99, 148
murder at Mullaghmore (1979) 82-3
see also Provisional IRA
Irvine, Winston ('Winkie') 171-2, 173

Jackson, Robin ('Jackal')
Luger pistol model PO8, serial no. 655 and 120, 121
RUC tip-off to, allegations of (and cover-up) 121-2
Jamerson, James 9, 11
Jara, Victor ('Chilean Bob Dylan') 163, 174
JFF (Justice for the Forgotten) 66, 116-17, 127
Johnson, Robert 11, 112, 163
Johnston, Denise 87, 159

Kelly, Noel (childhood neighbour) 5, 7, 9
Kenny, Taoiseach Enda 192
Kingsmill (or Whitecross) massacre (January, 1976)
Alan Black and truth about 146-7, 149
Paisley's false accusations in Commons about 69-70, 86
The Kinks 9, 103
Knatchbull, Doreen and Nicholas 82-3

Lambeth Palace 76, 78
Lawless, Billy and Anne 192-3
Lee, Des (Des McAlea) 28, 64, 130, 206
attack on, HET team report on (and reaction to) 118-26
attack on Miami and survival of 37-8, 41-3
Banbridge gig, before and after 33-5
HET interviews with 116-17
justice, beginnings of fight for 127
on 'last official photograph' of Showband 29
meeting with Mayor in Belfast City Hall 146
revived Miami Showband, series of concerts with 54-5
saxophonist, vocalist and band leader 29-31
settlement with MOD and PSNI (acceptance of) 207
Leinster House 49-50
Lemass, Taoiseach Seán 15
Lennox, Dave 108, 212
Luger pistol model PO8, serial no. 655 120, 121
Lundy, Tommy 12, 108
Lutwyche, Michael 178

Madden, Ciarán 74
Magee, Henry and Lottie 148
Magee, Kevin 67

INDEX

Maguire, Brian 30, 34, 37, 127
'Make Britain Keep Promise of Legacy Justice' webinar (2021) 74–5
Mallie, Eamonn 71, 150
Mallon, Seamus 87, 153, 159, 194
The Marian Finucane Show (RTÉ) 45
Masekela, Hugh 188–9
'The Mason's Apron' (Dubliners, 1965) 186, 188
Maxwell, Paul (Eliskillen victim of Mullaghmore tragedy) 82–3
McAlea, Des see Lee, Des (McAlea)
McAleese, Dr Mary 71
McAlinden, Justice Gerry (Belfast High Court) 210, 211
McAuley, Jackie 103–05, 111
McAuliffe, Lord Mayor Paul 177
McBride, Alan 71–2, 87, 159
McBride, Sharon 71, 72
McCartney, Paul 9, 102, 108, 112–13
McCoy, Brian 28, 117, 127, 130, 131
   attack on Miami and death of 37–8, 40–2
   Banbridge gig, before and after 33–5
   'doing it for,' Stephen and 52–3
   on 'last official photograph' of Showband 29
   murder of, HET report on (and reaction to) 118–26
   Victim Impact Statement on murder of 210–11
   watch labelled 'Miami Showband,' mystery of 63, 64, 66
McCoy, Helen (Brian's widow) 63, 127, 207
McCoy family 116
McCullough, Henry 17, 102–3, 104–05, 112–13
   fascinating stories and magical moments from 112–14
McDermott, Éilís 127, 146, 207, 211
McDowell, James Roderick Shane 116–17, 124, 168, 196
McGuinness, Martin 47–8, 49, 73
McKeown, Les 16–17, 55

McLaughlin QC, Paul 209
McQuillan, Alan 118
McVeigh, Martin, murder of (April 1975) 124, 125
MI5 (British Military Intelligence)
   Harris's daily dealings with 161–2
   removal of Stalker from 'shoot-to-kill' inquiry 154
   security and intelligence ops, responsibility for 36–7
   undercover forces as indigenous, policy for 36–7
Miami Showband 3, 72
   Albert Reynolds' praise for 46
   Anniversary Concert in Dublin (2005) 52–3
   attack on 34–5, 37–43, 82, 122, 123, 124, 154, 163, 185
   Belfast concert (2008) 54–5, 56, 62
   Britain's 'Dirty War' in Ireland and 221–2
   concert series in 2008, plans for 54
   dropping 'Showband' (1974) 27
   Dublin concert (2008) 54, 62
   hitting ground running 31–2
   job with, ability to play anything for 16–17
   joining (1975), new life and 179
   joy and happiness to fanbase, ultimate price paid for 219
   ladder to the stars, step on 27, 28, 29–30, 31–2
   lasting legacy for? 219
   New Spotlight Award ceremony (1976) 106
   Newell's work on case of 63
   'O'Willie's Welcomes' in Dar es Salaam 61–2
   Pavilion Ballroom, gig at 30–1
   reformation of (October 1975) 184
   set list (for 1975) 54
   St Anne's Park photoshoot 29
   UVF antipathy towards attack on 168
   see also attack on Miami Showband

INDEX

New Miami Showband 114
  New Spotlight Award for (1976) 106
  reformation of (October, 1975) 184
The Miami Showband Massacre: Survivor's Search for Truth (Travers, and Fetherstonhaugh) 44, 83, 168
Miami Showband Peace Centre *Online* 80
Miller, Ray 28
  Banbridge gig, driving to Antrim after 34
  Bay City Rollers, Portmarnock cooping up of 106-07
  Belfast concert, charity dimension for 55
  fight-back lawsuit participation 127
  on 'last official photograph' of Showband 29
  powerhouse drumming of 29
  return to the Showband 54
  watch labelled 'Miami Showband,' mystery of 64
Monaghan, bomb atrocity in (May 1974) 51, 162, 197
Monks, Dave 27-8, 33
Moore, Richard 55-61, 79, 191
Morning Ireland (RTÉ Radio 1) 159-61
Mountbatten, Lord Louis 82-3
Mulberry Bush pub in Birmingham 175
  bomb blast in 177-8
Murray, Ken 45, 48, 49, 79

Nairac, Robert 196
National Archives (UK), Kew 165-6
  Miami Showband, records connecting to 166
Neill, Samuel Fulton 123, 124
Netflix 163-74
Newell, Ian 63-4, 66-7

Newry 34
  police station at 41
  RUC base, Provisional IRA attack on 88
  TaRP plan for 'peace centre' at 79-80
NIO (Northern Ireland Office) 36, 73, 162
NIRPOA (Northern Ireland Retired Police Officers Association) 157-8
Northern Ireland Troubles (Legacy and Reconciliation)
  Act (2023) 71, 78
  Bill 208, 209

Ó Muilleoir, Lord Mayor Máirtín of Belfast 146
O'Brien, Shamie 10, 13
Ocean Road Cancer Institute, Dar es Salaam 57, 60-1
O'Hare, Michael 69-71, 150
  'Troubles, Tragedy and Trauma' 71, 72-3
Omagh, bombing in (August, 1998) 51, 182, 197
O'Neill's Irish-themed UK pub circuit 104, 109
OPONI (Office of Police Ombudsman for Northern Ireland)
  formal complaint sent to, details of 118-26
  summary of complaint to 122-6
'Orangeman' (witness) 151-2
Ormond Ballroom in Carrick-on-Suir 102, 112
Orton, Alexandra ('Allie') 164-73
O'Toole, Fran 127, 130, 206
  attack on Miami Showband and death of 37-43
  Banbridge gig, before and after 33-5
  charismatic nature of 29, 30-31
  'doing it for,' Stephen and 52-3
  dynamic vocalist and keyboard player 27

first gig with Miami, high after hug from 31
on 'last official photograph' of Showband 29
murder of, HET team report on (and reaction to) 118–26
tantalising offer from 31–2
tape of band's songs from 29–30
thumbs up at audition from 28
Victim Impact Statement on murder of 210–11
watch labelled 'Miami Showband,' mystery of 64
see also Anderson, Valerie (Fran's widow)

Paisley MP, Rev Ian 47–9
Kingsmill massacre, false accusations about 69–70, 86
parachute regiment (British army) 70–71, 81, 82
Parry, Tim 1–2
Peace Centre in Warrington 1–2, 4
'Person of the Year' (IBAM, 2019) 79
pigeon, revelation in shooting of 7–8
PII (Public Interest Immunity Certificate) 175, 205
post-trauma personality change, dismissal of findings of 180–81
Presley, Elvis 17, 20
Provisional IRA 1, 87–8
ceasefire (1997) 90
PSNI (Police Service of Northern Ireland) 68, 92
Carroll, murder of Steve (2009) and aftermath 87–94
Crime Operations Branch, information gathering and 156, 161–2
difficulties endured in challenges against 203–04

disclosure failures, endemic nature in 157, 205–07
HET (Historical Enquiries Team) of 116, 155–6
independence of HET, assurances of 156
loyalist-RUC collusion, closing down of analysis of 156–62
MI5 links with 161–2
'out-of-bounds' order from, possibility of 151–2
public interest immunity, block to evidence against 160, 175, 205, 207
Relatives for Justice, accusations against Harris and 157
RUC 'shoot to kill' deaths, Harris and 158–9
settlement offer from (and refusal of) 207–9
traffic diversion by (2012), 'if only' thoughts after 143–4
writs issued against MOD and 127
Psycho Pats 108–09, 213

Radio Caroline 12–13, 16
Radio Éireann 16
Radio Luxembourg 12–13, 16, 106
Raitt, Bonnie 47, 48
Ralph, Ken 102, 110–12
Reavey, Anthony 84, 153
Reavey, Brian 70, 84, 85, 148
Reavey, Eugene 77, 87, 146, 197
abusive behaviour from British army 85
Alan Black, friendship with 148
'Bomb and Bullet Legacy' 159, 199
false accusations about Kingsmill massacre and 69–70, 86
joyful and intelligent strength of 83–4
King Charles and, 'craic' with 83
Kingsmill massacre, witness to aftermath of 148

murder of brothers at Whitecross (1976) 71, 84, 148
Orangeman witness and 152
retaliation for death of brothers, rejection of 84–5
TaRP co-founder 67
victims, TaRP and insight on suffering 73–4
victims of British forces, shock of messages to 153–4
Reavey, Jimmy 84–5
Reavey, John Martin 84, 85, 148
Reavey, Sadie 84, 85, 148
ReMastered: The Miami Showband Massacre (Netflix) 46, 173–4, 191
Reynolds, Taoiseach Albert 44, 45, 46, 49
RFJ (Relatives for Justice) 156, 157
Rolling Stones 9, 11, 103, 187
Rory Gallagher Festival in Bundoran 109
Rowlands, Soraya and Paul 177–8
Roxy Music 103–04, 185–6
Royal Albert Hall 17, 114
Royal Showband 17, 34
RTÉ 45, 46, 212
'rubber bullets' for riot control 55, 58–9
RUC (Royal Ulster Constabulary) 37, 63, 71, 88, 119
  arson attack on Belfast HQ of 155
  Campbell, Sergeant J.P., murder of (1977) and aftermath 94–100
  Catholics in, dangers for 89
  Complaints and Discipline Department 122
  Corry Square, Newry, Provisional IRA attack on 88–9
  Headquarters 121–2
  HET (Historical Enquiries Team) and, imbalance in relationship between 155–7, 160
  LSU (Legacy Support Unit) 158–9
  proxy assassins, use of 154
  removal of Stalker from 'shoot-to-kill' inquiry 158
  Special Branch 36–7, 95, 122, 123, 125, 154–5, 159
  tip-off to Robin Jackson, allegations of (and cover-up of) 121–2
  UDA–RUC collusion 157, 158–9

Sands, Tommy 214–18
Scallon, Dana Rosemary ('Dana') 47, 48, 55
Scanlan, Dr Trish 57, 60–61
Schaffer, Professor Gavin 178
Sender, Stuart 164, 167, 169, 170–73
Shankhill Butchers 168
Sheanon, Martin 102, 110–12
Sherlock, Liam 10, 11, 12–14
Sinclair, Edward Tate 119–20
Sinn Féin 73, 92
The Sinners 26, 28
Smith, Danny ('Bongos') 108, 212
Smith & Wesson revolver, serial C5381 124, 125
Smithwick Tribunal on Garda-IRA collusion 162
Somerville, John J. 125, 168
Somerville, Wesley 124, 144–5
Stalker, John 154, 158
Stardust Hotel in Las Vegas 15, 17, 34
Steinberger, Ned 190
Steinberger XL-2 carbon graphite bass 189–90
Stormont Castle 47–9
Sun Street Recording Studios in Tuam 102, 109, 111

Tanzania, whistle-stop tour of 56–7
TaRP (Truth and Reconciliation Platform) 67, 83, 153, 163, 164
  Prince Charles on 'tremendous' work of 83

INDEX

COVID and events online 198
first event (April, 2016) in Mullaghbawn, Co. Armagh 150
Kate Carroll, TaRP testimony of (2018) 87–94
learning from 197–204
life changing influence of 80
Newry, plan for 'peace centre' at 79–80
Rosemary Campbell, testimony of (2018) 94–100
'Speaking for Myself' online series 80, 181–2
trauma of victims, force for good of 69–80
victim experience, shared testimonies and birth of (2016) 199–200
victims and perpetrators, struggle for peace between 201–4
victims of the Troubles, TaRP and insight into suffering of 73–4
website 80
Tavern in the Town pub in Birmingham 175, 176
Thatcher, Prime Minister Margaret 165
Thin Lizzie 105, 108, 111
Thompson, John ('Robert') 124–5
Thompson, Superintendent William, RUC 122
Topline Promotions in Dublin 27, 28
Travers family 45, 119, 151, 207, 211
Treacy, Sir Seamus, Lord Justice of Appeal 156
The Troubles in Northern Ireland 2, 48, 177, 180, 199, 201
   Albert Reynolds' interest in machinations of 45
   atrocities, collective naming of victims 51
   atrocities, need for condemnation of 214–15
   Ballymurphy massacre (August, 1971) 81, 82, 197
   Bloody Friday in Belfast (July, 1972) 197
   Bloody Sunday (Bogside in Derry, January 1972) 51, 58, 71, 79, 81, 197
   clichéd characterisation of 167
   dancehalls during, forgetting woes in 61
   Dublin, bombings in (May 1974) 51, 162, 197
   Enniskillen, Remembrance Day bombing in (1984) 51, 84, 197
   'found us,' Richard Moore on family and 58–9
   HET (Historical Enquiries Team), review of Troubles-related deaths 116, 155–6
   investigation of Troubles-related incidents, prohibition of 208
   justice after, no lasting peace without 215
   Kingsmill (or Whitecross) massacre (January, 1976) 69–70, 86, 146–7, 149
   lives changed forever by 71–2
   Monaghan, bomb atrocity in (May, 1974) 51, 162, 197
   musicians in north during, heroism of 219
   nighttime travelling during, dangers of 219
   Omagh, bombing in (August, 1998) 51, 182, 197
   outcry by victims of 76
   parachute regiment during 81, 82
   raging conflict (1975) 36
   'rubber bullets' for riot control in 55, 58–9
   Shankhill Road bombing 79
   'something terrible there in first place' 214–15
   stereotypical characterisation of 167

INDEX

victims of, collective embodiment of trauma of 197
victims of, denial of access to justice for 200
victims of, importance of acknowledgment as 'real human beings' for 51
victims of, TaRP and insight into suffering of 73-4

U2 212-13
UDA (Ulster Defence Association) 154
UDR (Ulster Defence Regiment) 35, 37, 119, 124
Urwin, Margaret 66, 127
UTV (Ulster TV) 73
UVF (Ulster Volunteer Force) 37, 119, 125, 128, 131-2, 134, 135
  collusion between RUC and 156-7, 159-60, 206
  'Craftsman,' conversation with 168-71
  files about, British refusal for release of 162
  senior representative of ('Craftsman'), conversation with 168-9
  victims of political violence, engagement with 169-70, 171-3

victims
  betrayal of, monumental conflict of interest and 153-62
  of Birmingham bombings, campaign for 175-6
  collective embodiment of trauma of the Troubles 197
  commemoration of 2, 79
  denial of access to justice for victims of the Troubles 200
  denial of right to justice for, fight against 203-4, 206-9
  engagement with 78-80
  forgiveness, victimhood and 100
  Glencree Centre for Peace and Reconciliation, work with 177
  hierarchy of (and inequality of acknowledgement) 81-6
  impact on 1
  of injustice around the world, breakthrough for 174
  learning from, engagement with 197
  names and faces of, reflection on 194
  outcry by 76
  of political violence, UVF engagement with 169-70, 171-3
  'real human beings,' importance of acknowledgment as 51
  rejection as label of 1
  state collusion, victims of 154-7, 160-61
  suffering of, insight into 73-4
  TaRP and insight into suffering of 73-4
  TaRP and trauma of, force for good of 69-80
  testimonies of, antidote to radicalisation 74, 199
  testimonies of, TaRP and platform for 150, 181-2, 199-201
  unique experiences of, sharing and learning about 1
  Victim Impact Statement, contents of 210-11
  VoTTA, collective voice for 75-7
VoTTA (Victims of the Troubles Assembly) 75-8
  cross-community membership 76

Wal Pro II E bass guitar 108, 185, 189
Walsh, Clem 101-2, 109-10
Walsh, Joe 105
Walsh, Mary 109-10
Warrington Peace Centre 1-2, 4
watch labelled 'Miami Showband,' mystery of 63, 64, 65, 66-7, 68

Watterson, Yvonne 191–2
The Webb (beat group in Carrick) 9–10, 11
Wheeler, Bill 163–4
'Whiskey in the Jar' (Dubliners, 1967) 26, 105
Whitecross 70, 71, 84, 147–8
The Who 103, 187
Wilson, Brian 11–12

Windmill Lane Studios, Dublin 108, 212
Wings 102, 108, 112, 113
Woodstock music festival (1969) 11, 102, 112, 113

The Yardbirds 11, 102

Zen Alligators 107, 108